FOXTALES
behind the scenes at Fox Software

FoxTales: Behind the Scenes at Fox Software
Copyright © 2003, 2013 by Kerry Nietz

Cover Designer: Joshua Van Wynen
www.evergreencreativeservices.com

Interior Design: Kerry Nietz
www.kerrynietz.com

Library of Congress Cataloging-in-Publication Data An application to register this book for cataloging has been filed with the Library of Congress.

International Standard Book Number: 978-0-9839655-4-1

For the Fox Developers

You're all virtuoso stunt-men (and women) to me.

Acknowledgements

To Marlene Troxel, now deceased, for taking a high school sophomore to work with her. Thanks for living beyond yourself.

To David Chilson, for a job recommendation that opened a can of wombats.

To my parents, Rex and Helen, for allowing my path to find me. You're the best.

To my wife, Leah, for her love, prayers, and perpetual support. I guess I *will* be published before I die, Sweetie!

To Whil Hentzen, my first publisher, for taking a serious chance on a random piece of email. This book would've been really boring without you.

To Nicole McNeish, for her copyediting skills and support on the first version.

To Mike Feltman and Toni Feltman, both for proofreading and keeping a secret.

To Dave Fulton. Though the narrative may make it seem like I don't appreciate the things you did in those long ago days, I still do. Aside from taking a chance on me, you took hundreds of risks and made thousands of "right" decisions to create a "lyrical" product and build a company into something that Microsoft paid some serious dough for. Few people can say that. I see some things differently now than I did out of college.

And finally, to the Lord, who constantly works in the circumstances.

Additional acknowledgements for this edition

To David Gage Heindel, for your encouragement and support

then, and your awesome foreword now. May God continue to bless you.

To Randy Brandt, for your editorial suggestions, and for being a legend.

To Jeff Gerke and Jill Williamson, for answering all my publishing questions. Thanks!

Foreword

Where does greatness come from? As an idealistic college kid, I assumed the answer is simple: it comes from excellence. As a developer at Fox Software during its meteoric rise over the period of time *FoxTales* chronicles, I learned there is nothing simple about it. In our case, greatness came from pressure applied by strong, decisive, visionary leadership and an ever-changing marketplace that demanded constant reaction and little rest.

Some of us risked our stable jobs with huge corporations to ride the start-up wave. Others, like Nietz, landed this opportunity right out of college, and this was the great adventure they studied for. (To an extent.)

Even so, I doubt any of us expected to become rock-stars in the software industry. I never did, but I often felt like one as a developer for this wildly successful family business. I was surrounded by incredibly talented people. Our products were like hit records. The critics loved us, and their laudatory reviews poured in week after week to prove it. Our fans zealously defended us even as they continually demanded more from us.

We made it look easy, but it wasn't. All we did was create a series of products that allowed us to eat the crumbs that fell from Ashton-Tate's table. Then they noticed us and began to target us, as did competing start-ups with similar objectives. Almost overnight, it seemed our adventure had become an industry-wide war.

Quickly, awe over our fame gave way to the stark reality that we were one mediocre release away from becoming has-beens. I'll bet every rock-star has felt this. But in our case there were young support technicians, sales people, marketers, and so many others who were counting on us. I remember looking out from my office at their cubicles and thinking, "We better do this right, or this could end as quickly as it started, and it won't end well."

Did we do it right? Did it end well? You'll have to draw those conclusions yourself.

I have to admit, Kerry's memories of these events are more vivid than mine. I remember a lot of laughter, a lot of yelling, and a tremendous sense of accomplishment. During those years, even while we muttered among ourselves about our demanding leaders, I gained respect for them. They pushed me to accomplish things I couldn't have otherwise, and to become someone I never would have been.

Not only is the tale of Fox Software amusing, it's idiomatic. Somewhere amidst its twists and turns, its successes and excesses, the situations and personalities mirror those found in every successful business venture. If you're a future rock-star looking for a roadmap, you'll find one here.

David Heindel
Microsoft Software Engineer
(and former Fox developer)
September, 2011

Morning

There's been no phone call yet, but that doesn't mean anything. It's still early

The overhead lights came on only a few minutes ago, signaling that Howard, the head of Tech Support, has made it in. He's a real business-as-usual guy. Always wears a button-down shirt.

But, I'm not. I never turn the lights on when I come in. The florescence is too bright, especially in the morning. In fact, most of us in the outer circle removed bulbs from our overheads. Too much glare on the computer screen.

I like it when it's still a little dark in here. It's usually quiet and you can get some good coding done without fear of interruption. After nine, you never know what might happen.

My machine is compiling my latest change, so I glance around my office, my fortress of privacy. Within its off-white walls are glimpses of what my life has become.

On one wall hangs a picture of a space shuttle taking off. It's an early morning launch, so the scene is really an explosion of light and activity from a place of solitude and darkness. Sort of like this place after nine.

I look behind me. I have a white table with a small collection of CDs and a semi-usable Sony Discman. It doesn't work very well since the Marketing guy unknowingly checked it at the airport. Sometimes it makes a loud humming sound.

Next to that is my window. It's a perk of my position—I can view the outside world. All I can *really* see, though, is the roof of the adjoining building and the dumpsters in the back. But, it's something that only a handful of us have, so I'm not complaining.

Beyond the dumpsters and the few buildings that mark the edge of town, is the beginning of Ohio's farm country. I grew up on one of those farms. It's comforting to know it's still out there. I reach forward and adjust the blinds slightly. Of course, I'm allergic to everything that grows, which is part of the reason I'm here.

I glance back at the screen. Still compiling. I look at the top of the monitor where Snippet-Man tremors slightly. He's just a little metal spring guy who holds a tennis racquet, a knickknack someone gave me. I dressed him in his first bit of clothing recently—a wrapper from some candy named "Snippets." They taste a lot like Tootsie Rolls, but the name has significance to me now. The wrapper draped around the little guy makes him Snippet-Man. Visitors who understand the joke think he's funny. And he is, and that's good. Things have been really tense here lately, and we all need a little more laughter.

On the front wall of my office, just below the Plexiglas portion, is a metal bookshelf with a small selection of computer books and manuals in it. Just next to that is a poster of two bikini-clad women Heindel and Eric (or his alter ego Skippy) hung up for me. It's their way of harassing the single guy. Everyone else on the staff, except my next-door neighbor Sally, is married. I'm the proverbial nice guy who never has a date. But hey, I'm only twenty-three!

I don't know why I'm not hitched (or even have a girlfriend). I don't think it's all my fault, though. Things just never work out. Besides, management fired my last girlfriend.

And, here's a thought, maybe if I had my weekends back...

I frown. Still no phone call. Maybe I'm home free today. It would be great not to have to take *The Walk*. I have a lot of things to do. A bug list *filled* with chores.

I look at the top of my bookshelf. The previous version of our product rests there. It's a white box with the outline of a fox's head. The head appears to be looking to its right and behind it is a purplish-red rainbow of color. The fox gives the product a friendly feel, as if it's something for the kids. But it isn't, and I know. The fox is nimble and the fox is driven, but often *the head* is downright mean.

I hear a sound, a distant booming footfall. Uh, oh. There won't be any phone calls today. He's coming on his own. Things are bad.

Still, he may not be coming for me.

He's moving steadily, but quickly. Boom, boom, boom. The floor reverberates. He's past Bill and Eric's office already. Still coming…but maybe he'll stop to see Heindel or Chris. They get to take The Walk often. Please let it be READ, I pray, just let it be READ.

No such luck. Sally is next in line, but she isn't working on anything that's a hot button. A pain starts in my gut.

There are offices past mine, of course. He could be on his way to see Janet. That happens sometimes. Snippet-Man is jiggling now. I focus on my computer screen. It finished compiling. I click a few keys to open my editor and look busy. Things will be fine. I'm a good worker!

The footfalls stop. I try to concentrate on my code, but I can't. I know what's going to happen next. I hear tapping on the Plexiglas and look up. Just to the left of the door I see his face glowering in at me. He doesn't look pleased. His finger appears and curls itself toward him. He wants me. It's me again.

I frown, stand up, and circle around the desk.

I have a walk to take, and I bet it's *not* going to make me happy.

3

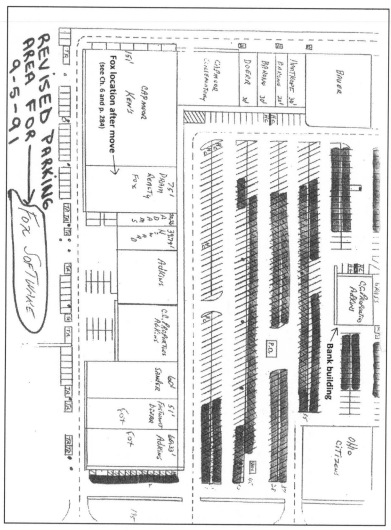

Map of the Country Charm shopping center
(Bank building is middle right)

4

Chapter 1
Fox Den

I was in my room at my parents' house, when the phone rang.

"Kerry!" my mother yelled up the stairs, a little softer than she normally would. "It's for you!"

I dropped my textbook on the bed and made for the door. Finals week was approaching and I still had a lot to ingest. To get an A in a Computer Science class at Bowling Green you needed at least a 93. If I got all A's that semester I would graduate with honors and that would mean a lot. I may not have a job, but at least I'd make a good show of it.

I walked to the phone in our white paneled hall. My short, spectacled mother was still at the foot of the varnished stairs. She looked up at me and smiled.

"Who is it?" I asked.

"It's for you," she said, still smiling.

I frowned and picked up the receiver. As much as I liked talking to my friends (and I had the same three my whole life) this would have to be short. I had work to do.

"Hello…"

"Ah, Kerry," the jovial-sounding voice on the phone said. "I think I'm going to make you happy."

I recognized the voice. Someone I met only a few days before.

"I'm going to offer you a position with us," he continued, "—with Fox Software."

I smiled and glanced down at my Mom. Finally. Just when I'd nearly given up. An offer.

Finally.

• • •

I like to think of it as God working in the circumstances, a string of seemingly unrelated events that sent my life down a path. But, whatever you call it; it was a diversion from the norm.

I grew up on a farm in Ohio. My father was a farmer, his father was a farmer, and—if you get right to it—the first Nietz that stepped off the boat, was probably, a farmer. So, when I was born, it was assumed that I would be a farmer too; the corn doesn't fall far from the stalk in Wood County.

It came as a surprise to all involved when, at an early age, I was diagnosed with an incurable condition—one that would jeopardize my future career. I was allergic to farms. Well, maybe not farms themselves, but nearly everything growing on or around them. Especially ragweed.

So the question became, what should I be? When asked, I usually said "fireman" or "astronaut" but I really had no idea. The only thing I *liked* to do, aside from hanging out with my three friends, was read.

However, if you check the phone book, there aren't too many "professional readers" listed. In general, people won't pay you to do something they wish they could be doing themselves.

My only other interest, creative doodling, wasn't an acceptable occupation either. My parents frequently threatened me with military school.

I needed direction.

• • •

A turning point came when a family friend, Marlene, took my friend Rusty and I to her workplace. It was 1981 and I was a sophomore in high school. The computer industry was well established by then, but most useful computers still filled a room.

Marlene worked at the top of a ten story bank building in downtown Toledo. Her office was spacious, tidy, and provided more than one terminal to the company's mainframe computer. Just beyond her door lived that room-filling computer. Rows and rows of spinning tape machines. Lots of wires. A general hum of activity.

That night she let Rusty and I try our best at the text based adventure games that were loaded on the machine. We weren't so good.

"I died again," I said, shaking my head. "The troll caught the knife and threw it back at me."

Marlene laughed. "Hey Kerry," she said, "Look at this."

I turned her direction. Marlene was a tall woman with dark hair and a pleasant smile. The mound of green striped paper in her arms made her look much shorter, though.

"What's that?"

She nodded toward my terminal. "It's the code to that game you guys are playing."

"What?" I squinted at the mass of green. "All that?"

She laughed again, then looked at the paper and nodded. "Well...yeah...isn't that something?"

I glanced at Rusty. His eyebrows were high, hidden beneath blonde locks. "Dang," he said. "That's a lot of typing."

It was, but it was something else too. It planted a seed. To me, playing the game was almost like reading a book. Maybe, aside from enjoying the game, I could help write it, or something like it.

Maybe.

• • •

The first personal computers came out in the years that followed. My parents—realizing I needed something to do during allergy season aside from reading and doodling—bought one for the family.

It was a silver Texas Instruments TI-99/4A. It had only 16K of memory and read programs from a tape recorder, but I thought it was great. Aside from the games I played, I learned a little about programming. It was another piece of the puzzle.

Plus, I needed something to make me special. As a 6 foot, 145-pound teenage boy, I didn't fit into much of my high school's scene. I was too lanky (and uncommitted) for sports. I played in band, but only because my Dad said, "You have to do *something!*" And girls...well, girls were like deer sprinting across a field. Something my friends and I talked about, but watched from a distance.

At my school, if you weren't a jock, a doper, or a member of the FFA (Future Farmers of America) you didn't have a group. I was none of the above. Couple that with the fact my mom taught there, my slight physique, and it isn't hard to see why I was an easy target for bullies.

For me, high school was four years waiting for graduation.

• • •

Senior year was when I met my first career challenge.

I'd already decided I was going to try this thing called "Computer Programming" and fortunately within twenty minutes of my parents' home was a university with courses in that very thing—Bowling Green State University (BGSU, for short). In a few months, I could send in an application.

To help prepare us for graduation, my class took a field trip to BGSU. As part of our campus tour, we stopped at the college's Placement Office. Housed in a building shaped like a slide projector, it was the office that—if we attended the school—would one day help us find a job. One of the resident "Placement Officers" took time away from her busy schedule to answer our career inquiries. Immaculately-dressed with short blond hair, she had us huddle in one of the building's open areas.

"I have a question," one of my classmates said, waving a hand in the air.

"Yes?" the Placement Officer said.

This classmate excelled at sports in high school, but was offered few scholarships. I knew he was searching for direction. "Yeah," he said, smiling broadly. "I was wondering what you think about a career in computers?"

The Officer frowned and placed both hands on her hips. "In my honest opinion, I don't see much hope for a long term career in programming."

My classmate looked as stunned as I felt. "Why?" he asked.

She shrugged, scanned our questioning faces. "I just think we will get to the point where computers will program themselves. Human programmers won't be needed."

My classmate's face wilted. His direction changed entirely.

I frowned and shook my head. From my experience with Marlene and my home machine, I knew programming didn't happen by magic. Someone's going to have to write the program that makes those computers program themselves, right?

If nothing else, I'd write that.

• • •

So I enrolled at BGSU in Computer Science, not knowing if the computers themselves would be competing with me for a job someday, and really not knowing whether I'd *like* to program. I'd written a few programs at home, but they were trivial. Simple lists of commands to print text or move an object around the screen.

At college, it would be for real. Pages of green striped paper just like Marlene showed me. Understanding the problems, and solving them. Composing those solutions into the languages that the computer understands, and typing them in. Testing them. Revising them. Long hours in the lab. Deadlines. Tension to get it all done. To make it work right.

After only one class, though, I knew I liked it. Programming tapped into the imaginative aspects of my personality, just like reading and doodling, and it was something I could actually do for a living. Actually get paid for.

Computer Science was a challenging major, though. A winnowing fork of studies. As the semesters went by, more and more of my colleagues left to pursue other things. But I managed to stay with it. Put in the time. And despite leaving little time for a social life (or perhaps providing a convenient excuse), my academic career went remarkably well. I learned how to program.

Being good in school is one thing, though. Finding a job that uses those skills is something else entirely.

• • •

The closing weeks of my senior year found me waiting for some company, *any* company, to make me an offer. I had no clue where I would work following graduation and it was beginning to seem like I might not be working at all. But, not for lack of trying.

Through the same Placement Office that once tried to harpoon my career choice, my peers and I were able to interview with many reputable companies, all with positions to fill. We dressed our best and took our shot. We smiled, we answered, we asked informed question, and we sent out letters of appreciation afterwards.

For whatever reason, though, it was always one of my peers that got the offer. Never me. And the time until graduation was short.

Then one day the head of the CS department, Anne Marie Lancaster, invited me to her office. She was a pleasant person with dark curly hair who taught my senior level Operating Systems course. Her office was immaculate, with a desk situated along one wall, giving the room an open and accepting feel.

She smiled softly. "Your grades are certainly high enough to garner an offer or two," she said. "Tell me about your interviews."

Translation: What are you doing wrong?

Next came an interviewing skills review. Was I smiling enough? Was I answering thoroughly? Was I dressing appropriately? Were my questions well researched?

But I had few answers. I was following the checklist perfectly…at least I thought I was. I interviewed a lot. I wrote letters of appreciation to those who interviewed me. If I was breaking any of the "rules of interviewing," it wasn't obvious.

"Students who have the sort of grades you have do not fail to find a job," she said. "Not Bowling Green grads, anyway." A smile. "So, what's the problem?"

There were follow-up meetings. Eventually, I began to suspect that they were as much about the department's reputation as they were about my success. Failure was not an option. What was I doing wrong?

There were doubtless *many* reasons for my failure to find a job, but deep down I knew of at least one reason. All the positions I interviewed for, attractive as they were, were mainframe work—work that would find me locked within a huge lab with only the drone of disk drives to keep me company. It was the land of bean counters, propeller heads, and dark suits worn all day. I'd be a mere resource in a business whose primary concern was oil, or department stores, or tires.

I hadn't fully realized it myself, but I wanted to work on small machines, on personal computers. I wanted to program the same sort of machines and write the same sort of (software) code I'd used ever since I sat at my TI 99/4A at home. I wanted a job where you could physically carry your work home if you had to. I wanted to be a name, not just the number on an ID badge. I wanted to make a discernible difference.

The time came, though, when I was completely out of options. The interview schedule was nearly at its end. I had no offers, and my only idea was to stay with my grandparents in Florida after graduation and try to find a job there.

I distinctly remember lying on my bed one night, eyes toward the sky and praying "God, I've got nothing here. Whatever happens next is up to you. Programming seemed right. Seemed to fit. But if you want something else from me, want me to do something else, then let me know. Because, seriously, I've got nothing."

• • •

Throughout my junior and senior years I had a part time job for BGSU's Office of Admissions. Along with another student programmer, I provided statistical lists for the Admissions Counselors. This meant that if one of them wanted to know how many honor students the University admitted the year before, I would construct a small program to glean that information from the school's mainframe. It was a job that fit easily into my school schedule and helped pay my tuition.

Our office, if you could call it that, was essentially a curved white table in the back portion of the first floor of the Admissions Office. Behind us were the copying machine, rows of desks, and a non-stop hubbub of Admissions employees in action. Lots of phone talk, lots of scurrying around, lots of paper being moved.

One afternoon, while I was seated at the curved table with a green striped printout in front of me, the phone rang.

"This is Doctor Chilson," the voice in my ear said.

It was an unexpected call. Doctor Chilson was a favorite instructor in the Computer Science Department, and probably the most methodical of any. When he lectured, he would tell you what he was going to tell you, then he would tell you "it" (whatever it was,) and then he would tell you what he just told you. There were never any tricks on his tests. If you attended the lectures and studied the notes, you would do fine.

Consequently, I did well in his class. I knew what to expect from him. He was also partially responsible for my part time job.

Still, he never called me at work.

"Do you like the C programming language?" he asked.

I had only one class that touched on C, but it was enough to know that I liked it. It was more human readable than many of the other programming options, yet it could do very intricate and low level things. One of the operating systems I studied, UNIX, was written entirely in C. "Yes..." I said.

"Good. Do you like database work?" he asked. "My database course last semester, did you like that?"

I smiled. Any class that I got an A in, I liked. "Sure," I said. "Of course."

"Okay," he said. "Have you taken the 408 course?"

CS 408 was the Operating Systems course taught by Ann Marie, the head of the department. "Yep, I took it."

"Good. How would you like to interview with a small company in Perrysburg. It's called Fox Software."

"Fox?"

He went on to explain that the owner of Fox Software, Dave Fulton, used to instruct at Bowling Green. Dave asked Doctor Chilson to recommend good students as interview candidates. He thought of me. "They write database software for PCs," he said. "Would you be interested in that type of work?"

They make software that runs on PCs? "I'd be interested in that," I said, trying not to sound too excited.

"You want me to set up an interview then?"

They work in C, and produce a product that I could go to the local software store and find on the shelf. Is he kidding? "Can you?" I asked. "That'd be great."

"Will do."

Maybe I won't have to go to Florida after all.

• • •

With a scheduled interview in hand, I thought it wise to do a little research. I had to know if Fox Software was everything I hoped it was. I visited my college library. It was housed in a nine-story building shaped like a series of books on end, complete with a mural where the cover art might be.

The articles I found said that Fox Software, which employed around thirty people, was started by four programmers like me. They created and sold a database product called FoxBASE+ that ran on personal computers. FoxBASE+ had gained a respectable amount of success, largely because it was a "workalike" of the industry's leading database product, *dBase*.

I knew little about dBase, but in the eighties, workalike

products were prevalent. A workalike was a program built to look, act, and feel exactly like another company's (often highly successful) product. The three most successful products—WordPerfect (a word processor), Lotus 1-2-3 (a spreadsheet) and dBase—all had workalikes. In fact, some had more than one. dBase had two reasonably successful workalikes—FoxBASE+ and another called Clipper by Nantucket—along with others that were marginally successful.

These workalikes (later called "clones") survived because the software market was large enough to allow them. They made their niche by being a cheaper version of their cloned rivals. They also tended to have fewer bugs, be more responsive to user requests, and sometimes—as was reported to be the case with FoxBASE+—they performed better. Produced the intended results quicker.

Their legality, however, was still a point of contention. Even though the clones looked nothing like the products they were duplicating on the inside (at the level a programmer would see them), on the outside (at the level a user would see them) they were designed to look and act *exactly* like the product they were cloning. At the time I was leaving college, the legitimacy of this "look and feel" similarity had yet to be decided.

I dug deeper, hoping to find more specific information about the origins of Fox Software and its products. I found some, but some I didn't learn until later. It was a story that revolved around one person: Dave Fulton.

Sometime prior to the formation of Fox, Dave co-owned (with his first wife) another company named DACOR. During his ownership of DACOR he managed to hire three of his former BGSU students—Bill Ferguson, Eric Christensen, and Amy Chapman (who later became Amy Fulton) as programmers.

DACOR was in the business of writing custom software,

and in 1983 they were hired to write a manufacturing application. While investigating the right tools to use, they happened upon dBase by Ashton-Tate. The feature set of dBase suited their needs, but in trying to develop their application they kept running into problems or inconsistencies in dBase that made completing the project next to impossible.

This eventually led them to write their own product, one with the same functionality as dBase, but without all the problems. When the "clone" product was complete, they then used it to finish their original manufacturing application, only to find that the market for it had dried up.

It was a near-tragic turn, one that threatened the future of DACOR.

At that point, a handful of factors came into play. First, Dave was having relationship difficulties with his wife (DACOR's co-owner). Second, the company was now having financial difficulties and would have to downsize severely to stay viable. And finally, Dave's small development team had constructed a working dBase clone—a product that *might* be marketable.

The ultimate outcome was Dave divorced his wife—selling his share of DACOR to her—and along with his three favorite programmers, started a new venture. So was born Fox Software, and FoxBASE, its first product.

The story hinted at another important aspect of dBase (and its clones). dBase was unique from other software programs because it was really two products in one. In one respect it was a database program a user could interact with through its interface and use to manipulate their personal data, much like someone might use a word processor to manipulate their words.

dBase also had a built in language, known as the dBase (and later xBASE) language, which users could create and run programs against, much like I as a programmer was hoping to do with a language called C. So, dBase was both an interactive user program *and* a language program.

And because it was a language program, dBase could be used as a developer tool. This gave rise to a group of highly sophisticated users known as "dBase developers." These developers made their livelihood by creating customized applications using the dBase language. In general, their applications could run on dBase or any of its clones.

What those developers found, and what contributed to Fox's early success, was that when they ran their applications on FoxBASE+, they ran more efficiently. Their databases could be accessed quicker and sorted faster. Their interface was more responsive. In command-by-command comparisons, FoxBASE+ performed better than Ashton-Tate's product, with few exceptions. Usually the difference between the two products was remarkable. Fox essentially created a better dBase than dBase, with only a small support staff and a Cracker Jack team of C developers.

And what still-unemployed college grads would want to miss that? It was a chance for significance and an opportunity to work on personal computers for a living. It was the sort of job I wanted. The answer to my prayers.

Now all that remained was to convince the Fox people of it.

• • •

When the day of my interview arrived, I put on my blue suit and set off for the town of Perrysburg.

Perrysburg is a quiet suburb of Toledo located just down Highway 25 from Bowling Green. The city's most notable feature is Fort Meigs, a large wooden fort on the west side of town. It was constructed by General (and later President) William Henry Harrison. Situated on the Maumee River, Fort Meigs played a vital defensive role in the War of 1812.

Similarly, Perrysburg played a vital role in the history of Fox Software. It served as Fox's home since the company's inception, first as a single hotel room where the product was written, boxed and shrink-wrapped, and later in rented office space. By 1988, their dwelling was a retooled bank building set near one of Perrysburg's main thoroughfares, West South Boundary.

I was thrown off initially by the fact that the two-story brick structure also housed the office of a pediatrician. I searched the exterior for a bit before finally locating a glass door with a red Fox logo on it. I walked in and was greeted by a dark-haired receptionist who promptly directed me up the stairs to my left. At the top of the stairs were two wood doors—an unmarked one and one that clearly read "Dave Fulton."

I knocked on the latter and was soon greeted by a round, nearly bald man who I guessed to be over forty. He was wearing a white Polo shirt and Khaki pants.

"Ah," he said, smiling, "you must be Kerry. I'm Dave Fulton. Come in, come in." He gave my hand a firm shake and directed me into his sizable corner office. To my right was an L-shaped wooden desk and bookshelves. To my left was a small, circular table, a wall mounted white board with little written on it, and an interior door leading to what looked to be another office.

Dave indicated the table. "Have a seat here. I'll gather the rest." He then exited through the interior door.

While I waited, I examined Dave's desk more thoroughly. There were two computers on it. Near the center of the L was a color Macintosh II, a recently released and *expensive* machine.

To the right of that was a DOS-based machine, of unknown make. Racked near the bookshelf behind the L was a sizable collection of music CDs. I knew of only one other person with a CD player, and he had like two CDs. I was jealous.

Dave returned with three people. A lot more than I expected.

The first was a petite woman with short, dark hair. "This is my wife, Amy," Dave said. Amy smiled politely, shook my hand, and sat down to my right.

Next was a stocky man with salted black hair and a thick mustache. "Bill Ferguson," Dave said. Following a quick handshake, Bill drew out the seat across from me.

"And this is Eric Christensen," Dave said. A taller, thinner man with sandy-colored hair stuck out a hand, and then slid into the seat between Bill and Amy.

I was about to be gang-interviewed by the founding quartet of developers. I expected a one on one interview like those at the Placement Center. Not a four on one. I began to feel nervous.

Adding to my anxiety was the fact that in all those other interviews, I was never quite sure what I did wrong. I thought I acted appropriately, but I always came up empty.

The department head's words echoed in my mind: be confident and enthusiastic.

"So tell us about your programming classes..."

From there the interview progressed along typical lines. They asked about my coursework and what programming classes I enjoyed. I did my best to emphasis my achievements, and the database course I elected to take. The fact that I was top of that class, grade wise.

They also asked about the individual projects—the code I created. Typically each Computer Science course had about four or five programming projects per semester, ranging in difficulty. With eight semesters of one or two courses per semester, I had a large portfolio to pull from. I highlighted those projects I thought relevant.

"What about home programming projects?" Bill asked. "What have you done there?"

That question was odd, because though a sizable part of America had at least some sort of home computer, certainly not everyone did. Most of my classmates—myself included—relied on the college lab machines to do their coursework.

I *did* have a home machine, of course. That now-archaic TI 99/4A. The one program I'd written on it since starting college was a program to store my individual class grades and calculate my overall GPA. I was proud of it because it saved and restored data from a disk drive, a technology I hadn't really understood until college. That's the project I talked about.

Bill responded with a slow nod and a stroke of his mustache.

"Have you coded in C before?" Eric asked.

"I have. I had a class that exposed us to four different programming languages. APL, Lisp, C and Snobol. I really liked C."

"And why's that?"

"Because it is human readable like Pascal, and structured, but also allows low-level operations." I shrugged. "I don't know, I just like it." Pascal was a widely used instructional language. Everyone who learned to program started in Pascal. C was like Pascal's adult older brother.

That answer brought more head nods. From there we talked about what I wanted in a job. I tried to be enthusiastic in my answers. Painting a situation that was fairly close to what I imagined Fox Software to be.

I thought I was doing well. The founding four seemed like nice, normal people who enjoyed their work. They exuded a passion for their product, but in more than one instance Dave emphasized, "We all have lives outside of work."

In addition, their appearance made it clear that the dress code at Fox was something on the order of jeans and a clean t-shirt—a detail that appealed to me strongly. I only had one suit.

The thing I wondered about was the little smile Amy wore throughout. I suspected she knew how nervous I was.

"We have a top notch team here," Dave said.

Bill Ferguson cradled his chin is his hand, yet managed to nod once slowly. "Yes," he said. "We all work to the edge of our abilities."

Eric covered a smile with his hand and Dave frowned slightly. "I don't know about that," he said. "But we do work some extra hours close to release." He studied me intently. "Do you think you can do that?"

All eyes rested on me.

It was another question I'd never been asked before. Every other interviewer seemed to rely on their own tests and intuition to determine whether I could do the job or not. They never just asked me. Can you do this?

Confidence and enthusiasm. "Yes," I said, nodding my head firmly.

The room remained serious. Only Amy seemed relaxed. Still smiling.

"That means an occasional Saturday," Dave continued. "Not regularly, but sometimes. Just whatever it takes to get the product out. Can you handle that?"

I kept my resolve. "Yes," I said again.

There were slow nods from around the table, and then the mood relaxed. The benefit of free pop in the refrigerator was mentioned, along with the flexible hours and casual dress style. We finished with handshakes and I left, hoping I made a good impression.

Otherwise, it was off to Florida.

. . .

Dave called the following week. "So, do you want to join us?" he asked, speaking rapidly. I wondered if he needed to use the restroom.

"When would you want me to start?" I still had a couple weeks of school left. Though relieved to finally have an offer, I was hoping for a little time to catch my breath.

"As soon as you can," he said. "So, are you with us?"

I wanted to work for Fox. The work was close to home, it seemed like an exciting challenge, they had free pop in the refrigerator, and I wouldn't even have to wear a suit. There seemed to be no downside.

Still, the Placement Office advised us seniors to take some time in making our decision. You shouldn't look too anxious, they said. Any reputable company would *gladly* give us time to think through such a major decision. "I'd like some time to think about it," I said.

Dave seemed startled. "Think about it?" he said. "Well, for how long?"

Placement suggested two weeks. I halved that. "A week?"

"A week! Well, that's a long time…"

Okay, I thought, I'm not going to lose this chance because of the Placement Office. The computers may have the jobs soon, after all. "How about two days?" I said.

"All right, two days," Dave said. "We'll hear from you then."

"In two days," I repeated.

I smiled and hung up the phone. I had a couple days, but I didn't know why. I didn't even need two minutes. It wasn't like there were other offers on the table. My path had led to this, and it seemed right.

After my two days of *thinking about it*, I called back to accept. I would walk through graduation on May 7th, and walk into Fox Software on May 9th.

No sense wasting time, I had work to do.

```
208   BRADEN, MELLISA
201   BRILLHART, DAWN
207   BROWN, SANDY
215   BUSCH, PAT
205   CARLTON, CHRISTINE
202   CELLURA, MIA
213   CHAPMAN, NORM
212   CHRISTENSEN, ERIC
211   FERGUSON, BILL
255   FULTON, AMY
209   FULTON, DAVE
219   GRAFTON, BEV
221   HANLINE, BART
230   HEINDEL, DAVE
208   HENRY, CHRIS
220   HINTZ, BILL
232   HOLTH, JEFF
218   JAYNES, JACKIE
206   LAUBENGAYER, KIM
228   LEWANDOWSKI, ELAINE
203   LYNCH, TOM
214   MOHR, MICHELLE
226   MORRIS, DEWAYNE
231   NEY, RICHARD
216   NIETZ, KERRY
216   OJJEH, BASSEL
227   PLOTNER, KEVIN
206   ROSE, MIKE
257   SEDLUK, MARTY
222   SELHORST, RANDY
259   SKARHA, LEE
217   SPEARS, PAM
204   SPERLING, JEANETTE
258   TALLMAN, BRIAN
225   TANKOOS, DIANNE
256   TANNER, HYMAN
224   VENZKE, DAVID
223   WALKER, JANET
229   WALKER, JOHN
224   WEINER, JAMES


PRODUCTION
HOLIDAY LANE

WOMACK, LORI
MAREK, JOHN
HENRY, KIM
KANIA, GREGORY
RADCLIFFE, DAVID
CANNON, RENEE
DOLBEE, SCOTT
```

Early company directory

24

Chapter 2
Introductions

It was my first day of work. Dave told me that everyone got in around eight o'clock in the morning. I wanted to make a good impression, so I arrived at the bank building at a quarter 'til.

The front door was locked. All I could see inside was a darkened room with a few large boxes on the floor.

Now what?

I stayed at the door, uncertain. Even tried the door again. Still locked.

As I turned for my car, I saw motion on the stairway within. A few seconds later a young man with dark, curly hair came down and picked up one of the boxes. He then noticed me, and with a puzzled expression on his face, stepped forward to open the door.

"You look like you need something," he said.

I glanced at the box he held—a new computer. "Well...this is my first day," I said. "And I don't have a key."

He smiled. "Come on." He nodded at another, larger, box on the floor. "Could you give me a hand?"

"Ah...sure..." I stooped to pick up the box—a monitor—and turned left to follow him up the stairs.

"My name's Kevin," he said as we climbed.

"And what do you do here?" Given he had a computer in his hand; I thought he might be a programmer too. Someone like me.

"I'm in sales." He reached the second store landing, and waited for me to catch up. "And when I'm not doing that, I'm busy setting up employee machines and solving network problems."

Busy guy.

"So what did you get hired for?" he asked.

I checked my feet on the stairs. "Programming," I said. "Working on the product."

Kevin's eyes widened. "You're a developer? Wow! How did you get hired as a developer?"

I shrugged. I was a little unclear on the reasons for my hiring too. "One of my instructors set up an interview."

Kevin gave me another long look. He was young, but I was a few years younger. Finally, he tipped his head. "Well, most of 'dev' doesn't get in until closer to nine. I think Eric is here, though. I'll show you around." He leaned back to leverage his box against his body, and opened the door.

As I entered the upper floor, the most obvious feature was the corral of yellow-walled cubicles—offices for over a dozen people—that filled the central portion of the room. The rectangle of the corral began just beyond the door, and created an inner bounding hall that ran around the whole interior of the building. On the opposite side of that hall—the right side as you moved counterclockwise through the building—were the floor's walled and windowed offices.

Kevin followed the path that ran straight ahead of us from the door, the southern hall. As I followed, I noticed the names on the exterior offices. They were all familiar—Amy Fulton, Bill Ferguson, Eric Christiansen—the developers who interviewed me.

Kevin led me to the room at the easternmost point of the hall. It was empty aside from a few boxes. He placed his box on the floor, and so did I. I glanced at the door. It read "Dick LaValley."

"Who's that?" I asked.

Kevin checked the name on the door too. "Dick LaValley? Oh, he's one of the company owners."

It was the first time I heard of another owner aside from

Dave Fulton. "What does he do here?" I asked.

Kevin shrugged. "He has a legal firm downtown," he said. "He's not really here that much. I think he's officially the company's CFO or something." He indicated the boxes on the floor. "They let me use his room for putting machines together." He moved back to the door. "Come on, I'll show you around."

He gave me a brisk tour of the building. While we walked, he alternated between prying me for details on my background and experience, and lauding Fox and its products. "Fox is the best database product ever," he said. "No one is as fast as Fox. We're hundreds of times faster than the rest." I understood why Kevin was a salesman. He would've been my pick for company cheerleader, were the position available.

His tour revealed that the top floor housed offices for development, technical support, sales people, and other support personnel. The bottom floor had a small receptionist desk in front, and behind was…

"…the production facility," Kevin said as we walked into the largest room in the building. The room had a number of machines in it. One had Saran-wrap material running through it. "The shrink-wrap machine," Kevin said. The facility was where the product was put into a box and shrink-wrapped for sale.

"How many work here?" I asked.

"In production? Maybe seven."

"And the whole company?"

"Thirty to forty. Something like that."

It wasn't quite a software company in a garage, but Fox was still a small, family-run business. I could make an impact here, I thought. I'm getting in while the company is still young.

Kevin's tour also confirmed that few made it in before nine. "Pretty empty here yet," I said.

"Yep," he said, smiling. "Come on. I'll take you to Eric."

• • •

We arrived at Eric's office to find him seated in a black office chair near the center of the room. In front of him was a white rolling computer stand, and on it was another Mac II computer. To our right, along one wall of the room, was a long white desk with a DOS machine. There were a number of moving boxes in the office as well, both open and closed. Eric looked deep in thought, with a hand to his chin.

He greeted us with a smile, though. Kevin asked if I could stay with Eric until everyone arrived. Kevin had no idea where my office would be.

"Sure…" Eric said.

Kevin left and Eric's eyes returned to the screen.

"What're you working on?" I asked.

Eric frowned. "Oh…speeding up the Mac product," he said. "Trying to, anyway." He spoke softly and his manner was relaxed, but there was a hint of something—impishness, maybe—in his eyes.

"How do you do that?" I asked. "Speed up the product." In college, we didn't much care how fast our programs ran. As long as they worked.

I saw the impishness again. "Well," he said, crossing his legs, "you find the slow parts, and you take them out."

I nodded slowly. "I see." I wasn't sure if he was picking on me or not.

I didn't know it yet, but Eric was a bona-fide computer genius. He could almost breathe code—and not just any code, but code that would run twice as fast as anyone else's. His primary job was making Fox products faster, and he was exceptionally good at it. He was master of "taking out the slow parts."

I was hoping to be master of something too. Someday. "Do you know what I'll be working on?" I asked.

He stretched out both hands, raised his shoulders. "I don't know."

"Well, do you know where my office will be?"

Eric raised his shoulders again. "Sorry. They don't tell me anything." He nodded at another black chair. "You can just sit here if you want."

I took the seat and Eric returned to his computer screen. He went on to tell me that, although *he* usually got in at seven-thirty, most of the rest of "dev" didn't get in until closer to nine.

I stayed in Eric's office, watching, until someone came in who knew what to do with me. Which was nearly an hour later.

From that morning forward, though, I took Eric's seven-thirty starting time as my own. Learn from the best.

• • •

The office they finally gave me was in the central corral, adjacent to another of Fox's young programmers—a guy named Marty Sedluk.

Marty's cube was empty that first morning, but after lunch I heard someone shuffle in and then the chiming sound of a Mac being turned on. A short time later there was a friendly "Huh-low" from behind me.

Marty was a head shorter than me with bushy, brown hair. In appearance and temperament he most closely resembled Sean Astin, the actor who played the hobbit Sam Gamgee in *The Lord of the Rings* movies. Marty also had the large feet relative to height typical of hobbits. Marty's defense of that condition was, "Well, I was supposed to be tall."

After introductions, I asked him what he was working on. He motioned me toward his cubicle, so I stood and looked over the side.

On Marty's screen was a window that resembled a typical Macintosh drawing program. It had a column of small pictures along the left side (a "palette") and a design surface with a pattern of dotted "grid lines" on it.

"It's the Screen Painter for our Mac product." Marty then gave me a demonstration of his work. It was the coolest thing I'd ever seen. It allowed users to fashion interactive input screens by placing and positioning different objects—such as pictures, lines, and text—on a design surface. This "What You See Is What You Get" interface could then be incorporated into their FoxBASE application. It would save a user from typing in hundreds of lines of code.

"How long have you been working here, Marty?" I asked.

He shrugged. "About six months."

"Six months?" I couldn't imagine creating something like a Screen Painter in that time. I wouldn't know where to begin. My projects in college hadn't even scratched that level of complexity.

"Yeah, but I'm only part-time," Marty said. "I'm still finishing school at UT (University of Toledo)."

I couldn't believe he was still in college and working on such a crucial component. Part-time. "Wow," I said. "How did *you* get hired?"

"They demoed FoxBASE+/Mac at my Mac-users group in Toledo." Marty smiled and puffed out his chest. "Yeah, they decided they needed my help." He chuckled a little.

It wasn't far from the truth. During a demonstration of an early version of FoxBASE+/Mac, Marty so besieged the Fox people with statements to the effect of "we don't do it like that on the Mac" they finally realized they needed someone with his firm ideals and tenacity to make their product truly "Mac-like." Consequently, they offered Marty a job. He was the company's resident Macintosh-whiz.

I was part of a talented group. The company was called *Fox* Software, but I was going to be running with wolves.

• • •

What followed was about a month of reading manuals, looking at code, and learning about Fox products. Even though the Fox staff found me an office, there still weren't any spare computers available. Those Kevin and I carried in were already spoken for, apparently.

So, while they spent weeks trying to find me one, I was told to use the computers in the office of someone named Dave Heindel. Mr. Heindel was another developer, but he was out on vacation. They said he wouldn't mind.

Like the original four developers, Heindel had an exterior office with a window. He also had two computers and a long solid white desk. The desks Marty and I had were metal and fiberboard constructs. A bit noisy, but I wasn't complaining. I *had* a desk, at least.

One morning found me sitting at Heindel's desk with my back to the door. I had a portion of the source code to the Mac product, the very innards of the project, laid out before me on the screen. Trying to understand just how it all worked.

"Go away for a few days," a voice said from behind me, "and they give away your office."

Startled, I turned to see a brown-haired man with a markedly boyish face. He was grinning broadly. "See if I take a vacation again."

"Um…sorry…"

He gave a little wave. "That's okay. You must be the new

guy. I'm another one of the Daves." He extended a hand.

"The Daves?"

"Yeah, there are three of us. Me, the good doctor, and a guy named Dave Venske. He's a writer."

I wasn't sure what to say next. I was still occupying his desk, and using his machine.

"So, you're a BG grad, huh?" Heindel asked, still smiling.

I nodded my head.

"Me too."

"Really?" I stood up to give Heindel his chair back.

"Yeah, a few years ago. Is your degree in Computer Science?"

I smiled. "Yep."

Heindel took his seat. "Did you know your boss *started* the CS department at Bowling Green?" He leaned back in his chair some.

"*Dave* did?"

Heindel nodded. "Yeah, he started it. His degree was in Statistics or something. Before him, there was no Computer Science at BG."

"Hmm..." Now I knew why Doctor Chilson recruited for Fox. Dave's connection with the CS department was huge. "Is your degree in CS too?" I asked.

Heindel nodded again. "With a minor in Journalism."

"Journalism?" It was an unusual minor for a CS student. Most of us had little time for a minor so disparate. A minor of just *science* was the easiest path. I filled mine with Astronomy courses.

"Yeah, they hired me to code *and* write," Heindel said, smiling. "But they've kept me in development ever since they found out how much I suck at writing." He laughed.

I smiled and shook my head. Someone else with a double title. Fox employees were flexible.

The next twenty minutes were filled with countless "me toos." Heindel and I both grew up in Ohio, graduated from the same university, loved sports (while *none* of the other developers could tell a goal line from a foul line), and we shared a lot of views—socially, politically and spiritually. It was the beginning of a long friendship.

Heindel's current task was to complete an upgrade to FoxBASE+, Fox Software's DOS product. Designated "version 2.10," this upgrade would supply users of the 2.0 product with new standalone applications.

One of them was a code generation program called CodeGen that Fox purchased from an outside developer named Luis Castro. Another was called FoxCentral and it was a front-end program for FoxBASE+ that would make some of the more tedious operations easier to accomplish.

Soon after we met, Dr. Fulton made the decision to put me under Heindel's supervision. So, along with my continued studies, testing FoxCentral became one of my assignments.

Already, I'd been given two jobs.

• • •

My first real coding assignment didn't come until a few weeks later, around the middle of June.

I was in my cubicle one morning, studying the manual from the Mac product. My office space was now stocked with the standard equipment for a cube-dweller at Fox. Positioned along the wall opposite the cubicle opening—my "door"—I had that beige metal desk with a brown, faux-wood surface.

On the desk, I had my own Mac II computer, oriented to the left. I also had a small, hanging bookshelf that gripped the wall just above the Mac. In it was the box from my complimentary copy of Fox's Mac product and a few of my programming books from school.

Over my desk to the right, was a picture of the space shuttle taking off. That wasn't standard issue—I just liked the way it looked. The other object unique to my cube was the large rectangular building support that ran just in front of the right edge of my desk. It took a good chunk of my space, but it was something I could prop my feet on when I needed to "kick back."

I liked to stay positive.

I was kicked back with the manual on my lap when I heard a deep baritone voice to my right.

"So…," the voice said, and then nothing else.

I swiveled in my chair. Bill Ferguson stood at the entrance to my cube. "Bill…"

Bill was dressed in a short-sleeve button-down and shorts. His hands were balled and he swung them as he spoke. "So…," he said again.

I already knew Bill chewed his words before spitting them out. He was the definition of *deliberate*. "Yeah?" I said, smiling.

Another pause while the hands swung. "Are you ready to do a little C programming?" he asked. Finally.

After weeks of studying, trying out Fox products, and testing I was more than ready to code. I threw the Mac manual on my desk. "You bet!"

Bill nodded again. "Ohh…kay."

I shrugged. "Well, what am I going to do?" I asked.

"Well…we need the strings taken out of the Mac product," he said. "That's what we thought we'd have you work on next."

Every C programmer knows what a string is. In fact, the first program I wrote in my college C course had a string in it. That program looked like this:

```
#include <stdio.h>

main ()
{
    printf ("Hello World!");
}
```

Its purpose was to print the words "Hello World!" on a computer screen. The first line ("#include <stdio.h>") just made the C language's standard output routines available. The second line ("main()") signaled the start of a C program and the braces—both the one at the beginning and the end—just set the program's boundaries.

The third line was where the magic happened. That line printed the *string* "Hello World!" to the screen by calling the routine printf().

So, the definition of a string in the C language was essentially anything contained within quotation marks. "Hello World" was the only string in that college example, but in a product like FoxBASE+/Mac there were thousands. Every error message, every bit of text in the menus, every prompt in every dialog—all of them, were strings.

My job was to replace each string I found in the code, with a call to a routine that would load that string from a separate file. There were a number of reasons to make such a change, but the primary advantage was that it got all the strings in one place so that our groups working in other countries (called "localizers") could replace the English text with strings from whatever language they were translating. With that separate string file available, they wouldn't have to touch our C code at all—just the file the strings were in. When they got through, there would be a German, or French, or Spanish version of FoxBASE+/Mac.

There wasn't much C coding in that portion of the project,

though.

"You'll need to write a string compiler too," Bill said, nodding as if the meaning of "string compiler" was obvious.

"A string what?" In programming, most things with the word "compiler" in their name were very, very difficult to write. For instance, the program that took C code and turned it into the numbers necessary for the computer to understand it was called a "compiler."

Bill smiled briefly. "Follow me back to my place. I'll explain."

I followed, and Bill explained.

The string compiler was to be a small application that would take strings from the separate string file and place them in the portion of the Mac product called "the resource fork." I never heard of a "resource fork" before, but apparently every Macintosh application had one. Each Mac application file was composed of two parts—a "code fork" and a "resource fork"—and different portions of the application resided in each part. DOS applications—like the stuff I worked on with Heindel—typically had only one file for everything. On the Mac, though, the resource fork was where things like pictures and strings were supposed to live.

"And the compiler needs to be relatively fast," Bill said. "This is something that will be getting used a lot."

A trial by fire. I nodded. I get it.

What wasn't clear, though, was why I was given a new supervisor. I liked working with Heindel, and I learned a lot.

I got the answer a few days later.

"Heindel's a good programmer," Dave Fulton said to me in passing, "but he's sort of a nine-to-fiver."

A nine-to-fiver? What's wrong with that? I thought developers "all have lives outside of work."

"Yeah?" I said.

Dave nodded. "We thought it'd be best for Bill to watch over you for a while."

• • •

My time with Bill did nothing to exercise any "nine-to-fiver" leanings I picked up from Heindel. I *did* learn a few things about my new mentor, though.

Bill was a problem solver. To the uninformed it might *seem* like he didn't have a solution because he was slow in expressing himself. But more often than not he *had* a solution. The lag between the time Bill knew, and the time he let you know, was just because he was churning it in his head a little more.

As a fortunate side effect of his deliberate nature, Bill was patient to a fault. He had no problem explaining something more than once, nor did he expect a quick answer to a question. He was a fitting coach for someone still trying to learn the ropes.

Under his guidance, I made swift progress. In only a few short weeks I had the strings all in a separate file, which meant I touched nearly every one of the hundreds of files in the product and changed thousands of lines of code. (…though trivially…) I also was putting the finishing touches on my string compiler.

Finally, I went to Bill's office with a floppy disk that contained—what I thought—was the finished compiler. Bill was one of the few developers that arranged his desk so that he faced the door. Never liked to be surprised, I guess. In addition, his office always had the feel of *something* going on. There were technical documents to be studied, boxes of arbitrary software, and possibly a Starlog magazine somewhere in the mix.

"I think I've got it," I said, raising the disk where he could see it.

Bill's eyes widened. "Okay…" he said. "Let me have it." He took the disk, slipped it into his machine, waited for the drive to grind its way to opening the disk. He then double-clicked the icon for my compiler. "I *really* want to check the speed," he said.

Speed was the Fox thing, after all.

As the program began, it prompted Bill for the names of two files: the separate string file, and the application to put the strings into. Bill filled in those two names, and the application immediately began to run. It ran for only a few seconds before it finished. He then checked the results: the strings were all in their proper place.

Bill crossed his arms, and slowly reached up to smooth his mustache. He looked at me then and gave a quick little nod. "That'll do."

I smiled. My first success. I proved that I could write code near Fox Software standards and I did it in a relatively short amount of time. I felt confident, useful.

"One more thing," I said, still smiling. I leaned forward and went through the steps to run my program again. When it reached the point where it was doing its work, I pointed at the screen. "What do you think?" I asked.

Bill squinted and leaned close. "You mean the cursor?"

"Yeah!" On the Mac it was common for the cursor to appear as a wristwatch when an application was performing a task that would make you wait. I did something a little more creative, though.

"Is that a running fox?" Bill said.

"Yeah! A little running fox."

Bill frowned, shook his head slowly. "Kids…"

• • •

A few days later, Heindel and I were gathered outside Eric's office. Early on I became a member of the 11:30 lunch crew, a small grouping of developers who would venture out at the same time every day in search of food. Typically it was composed of Eric, Heindel, Bill—and now—me.

"When is Brian starting?" Heindel asked Eric.

"Who's Brian?" I hadn't met any Brians yet. Plenty of Daves, but no Brians.

Heindel had a hand on the door-jam while he absently watched Eric. Having moved off the Mac product, Eric was now busy on the next version of FoxBASE+, codenamed *FireFox*. *FireFox* was to be our answer to Ashton-Tate's soon-to-be released update to dBase, dBase IV. It would include more optimizations of our product, and whatever additional language commands dBase IV introduced. So far, Eric was the only developer on *FireFox*. He was busy finding slow parts...and taking them out.

Eric checked his screen one last time, and with a firm slap on his knees, stood to join us. "Where're we going?" he asked. When he got to the door, the three of us turned and started down the floor's southern bounding hall.

"Who's Brian?" I asked again.

"A new developer Dave hired," Heindel said.

Another new developer? Someone to be compared against *already*? I saw flashbacks of the swimming lessons my mother took me and a friend to growing up. The lessons were great until the year *he* was promoted to the next class and I wasn't.

Of course, if this Brian was as inexperienced as I was, then I wouldn't be low man anymore. That could be a good thing, right?

We reached Bill's office and Bill quickly stood to join us.

"Where's he from?" I asked.

I lagged Heindel a few paces, so he turned slightly to speak to me. "From Florida now, I think."

"Yeah, that's right," Eric said. "I think he starts this week."

"From Florida?" I said. "How'd he get hired?" If Brian was from *that* far away, he was probably as unknown a quantity as I was.

"He used to work with Eric and I back at Marathon," Heindel said.

Or not.

Marathon was an oil company with its headquarters in Findlay, a town fifty miles south of Perrysburg. Their software group was a land of suits and day-long coffee breaks. Heindel and Eric worked there prior to Fox, though Eric also worked for Dave on the side. Heindel and Eric's Marathon association was part of the reason Heindel was hired.

Which meant I was still the only developer without a prior connection, aside from Marty, and Marty was a proven specialist. I was the odd man out—the programming newbie.

I didn't like it.

• • •

I met Brian a few days later. He was hard to avoid because his cubicle was just outside the entrance to mine. He was about thirty years old, well-manicured, and always dressed a little better than the company standard.

I wanted not to like him. I wanted him to be hard to get along with, or aloof, or have some annoying quality; something to make me feel like I had a uniquely positive trait going for me—the only other new guy.

Brian had few negatives, though. He was bright, friendly, and about as easygoing as they come. I couldn't even hope for programming incompetence. Brian's first project, which was similar in difficulty to mine, was finished in about half the time. I couldn't compete with him, and after a few weeks, I didn't want to. Brian was solid in so many ways I couldn't help but respect him.

If I was going to become a valued member of the team, I'd have to do it on my own initiative, and with my own abilities. I made that a motivating factor.

FOX SOFTWARE TIME SHEET

EMP#   NAME: SS#

TWO WEEK PERIOD STARTING SATURDAY,   ENDING FRIDAY,

| WEEK ONE | | WEEK TWO |

SATURDAY	IN : OUT: IN : OUT:	TOTAL
SUNDAY	IN : OUT: IN : OUT:	TOTAL
MONDAY	IN : OUT: IN : OUT:	TOTAL
TUESDAY	IN : OUT: IN : OUT:	TOTAL
WEDNESDAY	IN : OUT: IN : OUT:	TOTAL
THURSDAY	IN : OUT: IN : OUT:	TOTAL
FRIDAY	IN : OUT: IN : OUT:	TOTAL

SATURDAY	IN : OUT: IN: OUT:	TOTAL
SUNDAY	IN : OUT: IN : OUT:	TOTAL
MONDAY	IN : OUT: IN : OUT:	TOTAL
TUESDAY	IN : OUT: IN : OUT:	TOTAL
WEDNESDAY	IN : OUT: IN: OUT:	TOTAL
THURSDAY	IN : OUT: IN : OUT:	TOTAL
FRIDAY	IN : OUT: IN : OUT:	TOTAL

_____
EMPLOYEE SIGNATURE

_____
SUPERVISOR SIGNATURE

TOTAL REG. HOURS

TOTAL OVR. HOURS

GRAND TOTAL

Time sheet I used while on "probation"

Chapter 3
Evaluations

In August I was given a review form to fill out. My first review with Fox would be the following month and this was my chance to speak my mind. The form itself was straightforward. It was a one-page list of multiple-choice questions covering different aspects of my job. To answer each question I just picked a value from a range of satisfaction. Probably everyone has taken such a test

Finding the appropriate answers was easy. I couldn't have been more satisfied with my job. I was doing the kind of work I wanted to do, the work I trained for. My colleagues were smart and our products were great. It was an exciting place to be, and I said as much on my form.

Then there was one final question. It asked, "Is there anything else that bothers you about your workplace?"

I stared at that one for a while. As I did so, I heard the salesman whose cubicle shared a wall with mine say, "This is John Walker...," for the hundredth time that day. Marty was to my right, but to my left I could hear the clamor of Tech Support. "This is Bart Hanline...this is Jackie Jaynes...this is Randy..." It was an unceasing din. It persisted all day, every day. It warred against my concentration, making it difficult to code. For work, I liked silence.

I hesitated to mention the noise though. The exterior offices were filled already, and even if they weren't, I wouldn't ask for one. I was the new guy. I didn't want to be a whiner.

I listened as the clamor continued. "This is John, this is Jackie, this is Bart..." Salutations repeated endlessly.

Alright, I'll mention it, I thought, but I'll be as subtle as possible.

I put pen to paper. "Sometimes, it's a little noisy in here," I wrote, and left it at that. I signed my name and turned in my form.

Two days later I heard Dave call my name. I turned to see him partially blocking the entrance to my cube. "Yeah?" He had a serious look, but as I turned, he gave a quick smile before getting serious again. "Ah yeah, Kerry, we're going to move Marty and you into the conference room."

That's incredible. "Okay," was all I said.

Marty was standing near the entrance to his cubicle, listening intently. He nodded his head slowly a few times.

Dave bounced backward a few paces. "We realize it's probably noisy out here so we're going to do what we can. Brian is moving in with Eric and we'll put you two in the conference room." He raised his eyebrows slightly, looked at us both. "Is that okay?"

"Fine with me," I said.

Marty shook his head slowly. "Yeah, that's fine."

By the end of that week the two of us were sharing the corner conference room—the building's *only* conference room. It had two large windows, one that overlooked the parking lot and one that overlooked West South Boundary and the small brick houses that lined it. Marty set his desk facing the back window. Mine faced the room's lone swinging door. Between us there was only a single cubicle divider.

The room was light, and big, and completely noiseless.

It was heaven.

• • •

Toward the end of the summer of 1988, Fox Software was gearing up to release an updated Mac product—version 1.10. By then, nearly all of the forty-some employees were using the product on their machines while they went about their normal day of selling, supporting, or writing.

This impromptu testing was the only in-house testing Fox products got. Unlike larger software companies, where dedicated testing departments were the norm, at Fox—just prior to the release of a product—*everyone* became a tester. Aside from a few external users who volunteered to test the product, called "Beta" testers, the employees alone were responsible for finding any bugs that remained before FoxBASE+/Mac was shrink-wrapped and sent out the door.

The release date was in early October.

• • •

Sometime in September the developer force was divided. Most of the team moved on to work on *FireFox* and from then on had little involvement with the Mac effort, aside from occasional consultation. Those that remained—Marty, Heindel, and I—were involved with a specific aspect of the product, called code generation, and were still busy with new development work. We were essentially "under the gun" and became regulars at Fox on the weekends.

Aside from fixing whatever bugs our *in-house testing* turned up, Marty was putting the finishing touches on his Screen Painter. It was the first step in the code generation process.

Heindel—after just finishing the 2.10 release of the DOS product—now had the task of moving the C code for the CodeGen application generator to the Mac product. In the DOS product this entity was a standalone product, meaning it ran separately from FoxBASE+, but on the Mac it would be completely integrated. It would be available via a menu item in the product. CodeGen's purpose was to give users (or more likely a dBase developer) the ability to compose a specialized program called a "template."

There were three separate programming languages involved in this project. Marty and Heindel were programming (i.e. "coding") in the language called C. It had been around for decades, and was considered the standard for software development.

The next language was commonly known as the "dBase language." It was the language users of our product could write in, if they chose to. It was specifically geared toward database manipulation. A simple example might look like this:

```
USE mydata.dbf INDEX myindex.idx
SET RELATION TO name INTO moredata
```

That two line program would open a database file named "mydata.dbf" with an index file named "myindex.idx," and then set a relationship between "mydata.dbf" and another database file named "moredata."

The third language—the one Heindel was adding support for in the Mac product—was a "template language." The template language was in some respects an extension of the dBase language but our product handled it differently. It allowed users to write a generic dBase application where some parts of it could be filled in later by CodeGen with values produced by Marty's Screen Painter. This generic application was called a "template." An example might look like this:

```
USE dbfnam INDEX ndxnam
SET RELATION TO relexp INTO relals
```

When used in conjunction with CodeGen and a screen designed in the Screen Painter, that program could produce a dBase program that looked like this...

```
USE books.dbf INDEX books.idx
SET RELATION TO title INTO borrowed
```

Or like this…

```
USE employees.dbf INDEX employees.idx
SET RELATION TO lastname INTO to_fire
```

It was entirely dependent on the created screen and the user's preference. A template program was a powerful tool. It wasn't exactly "the program that made the computer program itself" that Placement Officer warned about, but it *did* give novice users the ability to write dBase code without having to actually write code. Consequently, it was a huge timesaver.

Creating sample templates was my part of the effort. It came with a good share of frustration, because I was trying to work with a product that was still under construction. Everything I did was dependent on Marty and Heindel's work. I was essentially using features *as* they were being added. It was like trying to live in a house while it's being built, except the doors might move on you while you slept.

My template work progressed steadily through the summer months, though, and as the release date approached, it was nearly complete. I had constructed two separate templates. The first, named Simple.GEN (a name Marty loved to broadcast at random points throughout the day), would produce dBase code that presented the user's screen, just as they designed it. The second, Advanced.GEN, would generate a full-blown database application with the user's screen as its primary interface. This generated application allowed them to view their database, navigate through it, and even add and delete information.

It was a fair amount of work in a language I'd never used

before, but I was confident I'd finish on time—as long as Marty and Heindel did.

There was one extra complication in our push toward shipping, though.

For some unexplained reason, before Fox could actually release FoxBASE+/Mac to the public, Apple required us to ship a few thousand copies to them. This meant the three of us, through no fault of our own, really had another deadline before the release deadline we were initially striving toward.

• • •

At the end of the day, on the Friday before production was to start duplicating product for Apple, Dave phoned my office. "I want a look at your templates before they go out," he said. "Could you bring them down?"

I'd worked on the templates for months with little input so I was glad Dave was finally showing some interest. My only other major project—the string compiler—he didn't see at all. "Sure!" I said.

I was also happy with what I'd accomplished. As far as I knew, the templates were ready to go. They were doing everything they were supposed to do.

Still, as I made my way to the corner office, I couldn't help but feel a little nervous. It was my first time to show Dave my work, and really, the first time I'd been in his office alone. He was the president and co-owner of the company. He had given me a shot at doing what I wanted to do when no one else would, and recently, he even gave me a quiet place to work. I respected him. I wanted to make a good impression.

Dave's office had two entrances. The one at the top of the stairs I used the day of my interview and another accessible from the top floor's southern bounding hall. As an insider, I could use the latter now, and I did.

Dave was staring at the color screen of his Macintosh. Color Mac monitors were a lusted after commodity at Fox. There were maybe a half dozen in the whole building and developers used most of them. I had one loaned to me so I could test my templates in color, but even that turned into a minor scandal. Someone in management—a non-developer—got jealous and made a fuss. Wondered how the new guy rated a color monitor.

"Here you go, Dave," I said, holding up the disk I brought with me.

Dave took the disk. "Ah yes," he said. "Let's see, let's see."

After copying the templates to his machine, Dave started up the Mac product. The most noticeable indication of this was the rainbow-colored "splash" screen, a window of about 3" high by 5" wide, that opened. Superimposed on the rainbow was a white fox head that appeared to be looking to its right—the Fox trademark.

Dave walked his way through the code generation steps. He first navigated the menu system to open up the Screen Painter and create a simple screen that included a number of fields from his database. In this case, the database he used contained an inventory of a home movie collection, so the fields were things like "Title," "Description," and "Running Time."

Following this, he selected a menu item that said "Generate From…." This item engaged Heindel's new Code Generator. The first thing the Generator did was present a dialog that prompted Dave for a template to use. The templates I created were available in the dialog's list, so he chose one—Advanced.GEN. He then clicked the button labeled "Generate."

A new window opened up. Within the window, lines of

text began to flow up the screen. This window was mostly for show; it presented the new dBase code as it was generated. It wasn't something you could actually read though. The code was streaming by way too fast. It was just to illustrate that *something* was happening. It was flashier than a wristwatch cursor...or a running fox.

Earlier, Dave specified his generated application be called "Video.prg," so after the window of flowing text went away, there was a program on his machine with that name. Dave selected the menu item to run that program.

From start to finish his walkthrough worked flawlessly. The application generated fine. The generated code ran fine. Dave could see his data, he could add records, and he could delete records. It was a work of art.

I was quite proud.

Dave reopened his screen and moved a couple of buttons around—a simple, innocuous change—and regenerated "Video.prg" again. Once again, everything appeared to work as expected. And why wouldn't it?

He then ran the generated application.

A string of error messages began to assault his monitor. "NO DATABASE IN USE! INDEX NOT FOUND! RELATION NOT SET!" The windowed chaos seemed to last for many seconds.

Not good.

I looked to the ceiling and tried to figure out where the error messages were coming from. I'd never seen that behavior. When I tested, everything worked flawlessly. Yet nothing about what Dave did was unusual.

I glanced at the door. I wish I could go back to my office and check...

Dave remained still, quietly studying his computer screen.

I took a step toward the door. I might still be able to get

away.

Dave noticed the motion and looked up, stopping me. "You know what the problem is?" he asked.

I felt lost. I searched the nearest wall, where Dave's framed diploma's hung. "Um...no..."

Dave's eyebrows lifted. "What!" he said. "It's your program and you don't know what the problem is?"

The answer was still no. I just shook my head and said nothing.

"Well, I'll tell you what the problem is." He motioned with his hand. "Go get Heindel and Marty."

I made for the door and jogged my way to the opposite side of the building. I gathered the others and together we returned.

After we seated ourselves, Dave ran through the entire offending scenario again. Every step produced the same results—and at the end—the same unknowing looks from both Marty and Heindel.

"It's a flaw in the Screen Painter!" Dave said finally.

Marty slid back a little. "How, Dave?" he asked, sounding defensive.

Dave pushed his head forward. "Because, my friend...Kerry's generated application is closing the databases I used when it finishes."

There was silence for a time. "So, it shouldn't be doing that?" Heindel offered.

Dave shook his head. "No. That's what a properly written application *should* do. It's the Screen Painter that's wrong."

Marty remained still. "The Screen Painter is performing as it was designed, Dave."

Dave shot Marty a stern look. "These errors are *as designed?*"

Marty leaned forward, made soothing motions with his

hands. "Well, the Screen Painter was designed as sort of a standalone tool—"

Dave straightened in his chair. "What?" he said. "It's a part of our product!"

"Yes," Marty said, nodding his head slowly. "But it could be used for other things."

Dave wasn't buying it. In fact, he seemed to ignore the comment completely. "You know how to fix this?" he said, pointed a finger in the air. "The Screen Painter should save a *view* file."

I had no idea what a view file was, but apparently Heindel did. His face got a few shades whiter.

"A view file?" Heindel shook his head. "I don't know, Dave. That's a mighty big hammer."

He went on to describe the contents of a view file. Apparently, there was a command in the language that saved a snapshot of the product's condition: what databases were open, what indexes were in effect (an "index" controlled how the database's information was presented), and a mass of other important data. It *was* a big hammer.

Marty face was expressionless and his voice still calm. "Now Dave, the Screen Painter was designed as a standalone tool…"

"It is not! It is a part of our product!"

What followed lasted nearly an hour. Much of it was like watching a Ping-Pong match, with Dave stated that it was a "flaw in the Screen Painter" and Marty reiterating that the Screen Painter was performing the way it was designed, and should stay that way.

The "match" ended with the three of us schlepping off to make substantial changes to a product that was supposed to ship to Apple the following day. The only in-house testing the product would get *this* time was whatever Marty, Heindel, and I did on our own machines.

Somehow we managed to get it done, though. The product went out to Apple, and then finally to the rest of the world.

And my templates were a part of the Mac product for many years to come.

• • •

A few weeks later I was in Dave's office again, but this time it was only he, Amy, and I. They were on the side of the round table nearest the windows, and I was on the other, nearest the door. The blinds on the windows were closed, so the room seemed a little dim to me.

"We just wanted to let you know that we've decided to keep you on," Dave said. "That you made it through our probationary period."

I nodded my head slowly. Probationary period? No one told me there was a probationary period. "Um...thanks." I forced a smile.

"Yes," Amy said, "and we wanted to say that we really appreciate your work. And your flexibility with the things you work on."

Now my smile was genuine. It was the first feedback I'd received, positive or negative. As for the work, I'd never given the tasks much thought. I was used to doing whatever needed to be done. I grew up on a farm.

Dave nodded. "A company this size, we need people to have some elasticity in the things they work on." He scratched his elbow. "The template stuff...well, that isn't really the sort of work developers normally do." Dave reached out to take his coffee cup from the table, balanced it on one knee. "But you took to it and did a laudable job...a better than adequate job, really."

"Thanks again," I said, still smiling.

"Yes, so, we decided to keep you on with us at Fox, and um…" He looked at Amy as if he'd forgotten something. Amy only smiled sweetly. "Oh yes…" Dave looked at me again. "And we're giving you a raise."

I was getting a raise after only four months. "Wow," I said. "Thanks!"

Dave gave a quick little smile. "Yes, well, thank you."

The review ended a few moments later.

Interesting work, a semi-private office, and a raise in four months. It doesn't get any better than this. I left the room fired up for a new challenge.

I was officially part of the team.

• • •

By the time the russet leaves beyond our windows began to fall, development work on *FireFox* was in full swing. Aside from being our dBase IV workalike, the fact that it was designed for the DOS operating system—a much larger market than the Mac—meant it had the potential to be a big seller. We needed as many coders on it as possible.

So, Marty was left as the sole developer on the Mac product, and Heindel and I moved over. Marty's current project was to add another tool called a "Report Writer." It would be included as part of the next release, planned for some time in '89.

My first task in *FireFox* was to duplicate the language syntax Ashton-Tate added to their product.

There were essentially two parts to adding a new command to *FireFox*. The first portion was the syntax portion. It involved taking the text typed in by the user—"USE employees.dbf INDEX employees.idx", for instance—and checking to see if it was valid syntactically (i.e. the command was spelled correctly and generally made sense), and then translating that text into a more concise (symbolic) form.

This was my part of the process. When my work was complete, any program written for dBase IV could be run on *FireFox* without giving a syntax error. It still wouldn't *do* anything, but it wouldn't give an error.

The second portion, what we called the runtime portion, was semantic in nature. It involved taking the symbols my work generated, figuring out what they all meant, and performing the actions required—opening the database, creating the window, or clearing the screen…whatever it took to make the command do what it was supposed to do.

Although my part was necessary, the runtime portion was where the *real* work came in. To be fully compatible with dBase IV, there was a lot of this type of work to do.

Ashton-Tate's upcoming product was touted to be the end-all of database products. Rumor had it that nearly seventy programmers worked for years in creating it. They added *hundreds* of new commands to give users the ability to create interface elements like windows and menus. It also included a brand new Report Writer, a Screen Painter, and a vastly improved "user-friendly" interface. Ashton-Tate was calling dBase IV their "clone killer."

Our mission, as Dave outlined it, was to get the SBT application running on *FireFox* before Comdex. SBT was a California-based company, and their application was an exhaustive accounting package specifically designed to run on dBase IV. It showcased many of the newly added features.

Comdex, as I only recently found out, was the largest computer show in the world. It was held every November in Las Vegas and was the place where every computer-related company came to show their latest wares. If we got the SBT application working on *FireFox* we'd prove our product was still compatible with dBase IV. And if we did it by Comdex, we'd have plenty of witnesses. We could demo it at the show.

So, with the "SBT by Comdex" goal firmly in our minds, we immersed ourselves in our tasks. Heindel worked on the new commands to create menus. Bill did the first cut of the windowing commands (which was later given to Brian Tallman). Amy and Eric identified and implemented the other miscellaneous commands used in SBT's code, and I put in the syntax for everyone as they needed it.

I was content with my new chore. I spent my first few months of employment working on ancillary things and felt a little ancillary myself. Now I was working *inside* the product. It was relatively safe work, but it was needed, necessary. I was no longer a stranger on the other side of the fence; I was holding the top rail and had a leg over.

And we made swift progress toward our goal, further underscoring for me just how bright the Fox team really was. Though we may not be "working to the edge of our abilities," we were working well together and there was a lot of natural ability on display. Everyone was creative and extremely motivated. We wanted to surprise people.

Consequently, we reached the goal by the beginning of November, only a few weeks before the start of Comdex, and less than a month after dBase IV released. *FireFox* was complete enough to run the SBT application and those who were attending Comdex were busy preparing demos on it. Many of those demos showed *FireFox* running code written for dBase IV *much faster* than dBase IV did—in some cases hundreds of times faster.

So, when the week of Comdex arrived, Dave, Amy, Eric, Bill plus a handful of sales and support staff flew out for Vegas.

They promised to send news as the week progressed.

• • •

Over the course of Comdex week we heard that the show was going extremely well. Most of our loyal customers had no idea we were so far along toward having a fully functioning dBase IV clone and couldn't wait to get their hands on it. Our booth had constant visitors. One of our attendants even thought they saw the CEO of Ashton-Tate, Ed Esber, stop in to marvel at the product.

Back in Perrysburg that rumor got more talk than any. To see the leader of our biggest competitor at our booth was considered an honor. We made our living by eating the scraps that fell from Ashton-Tate's plate; it was a niche we lived comfortably in. We knew we weren't enough competition to make them nervous, nor would we ever be. They were considered one of the "Big Three" software makers, along with Microsoft and Lotus. Ashton-Tate *owned* the PC database market, with over 60% market share. We didn't have a tenth of that.

Ashton-Tate seemed content to let us have our niche. They viewed us and our fellow clones as add-on products— software you buy *after* purchasing dBase.

Still, there had been rumblings of change from their CEO. In October of '87, when a committee of software publishers met to begin the process of having a "standardized" version of the dBase language, Esber shouted "Go ahead, make my day!"

It was an odd response, given the fact that nearly every other computer language was standardized in one way or the other. For instance, the language we programmed in—C—was standardized in the early seventies. No one was certain what Esber meant by that statement, but clearly he thought Ashton-Tate should have some control over the language.

Regardless, if Ed Esber had visited our booth, we could only imagine what he must have thought when he saw *FireFox* running applications written for dBase IV. We thought he'd be surprised, but we also hoped he'd be a little impressed.

Imitation is a sincere form of flattery, after all.

Chapter 4
Competition and Litigation

On the Sunday night following the end of Comdex, Eric Christensen called me at home. The call surprised me for two reasons. First, prior to that night, I had never been called at home about anything work related. Second, the fact it was Eric was strange because he was the last person I expected to call. He valued time away from work as much as any, and probably more than most.

As I brought the receiver to my ear, though, I was primarily concerned I did something to screw the product up. If Eric found a problem he might be forewarning me. Giving me a chance to get it fixed before others noticed.

I could think of no other reason he would call. Me. On a Sunday.

"Hey Kerry," Eric said, sounding as if he were smiling. "Heard any good rumors lately?"

Weird way to start a scolding. "No..." I said. "Why?"

"Well...I have." He paused. "Dave wants a meeting with everyone in the company tomorrow morning."

I felt my pulse accelerate. Man, what did I do? Is this going to be a public flogging? "Oh...why?"

"Well..." His voice was still smiling. "Last Friday Ashton-Tate decided to sue us."

I was relieved, and then excited. I asked a number of follow-up questions, but I could hardly hear the answers for the thoughts screaming in my mind. What a story!

I took a Computer Ethics course in college. One of the subjects we discussed was the various legal means computer firms have to protect their software. The most common protection was to obtain a copyright on the code.

There were aspects of copyright protection, though, that made it inadequate for software. Copyrights only protect the expression of an idea, not the idea itself. So, I might have ownership of the phrase "I want to go buy ice cream" if it was part of a poem I wrote, but the idea behind the phrase—the fact that I *really* want a frozen treat—wouldn't be protected.

Copyrights weren't originally conceived with computers in mind. They were stretched to try to accommodate programmers' work, but there were inherent difficulties. With computer code, the literal text isn't as important as the ideas expressed within.

It wasn't until the mid-eighties that companies began to test the limits of a copyright's legal protection for software. In a case settled only a few years before I graduated, a company won damages based, not on the literal code written, but on the program's "structure, sequence, and organization." That meant they won on how the software *appeared* to the user, or its "look and feel." Because of this, "look and feel" became a catch phrase in the industry. Any company that wrote software that looked and acted like another company's program did so knowing they might be skating on thin legal ice.

FoxBASE+ looked and felt *exactly* like dBase III+, but it had done so for a number of years. Fox Software started in 1985, after all. If this was a "look and feel" issue, I didn't know why Ashton-Tate hadn't made an issue of it before. Nor why they were doing so now.

I had a hard time sleeping that night. Only months before I studied lawsuits between software companies. Now I was in the *middle* of one. I couldn't wait to hear what Dave would say the next day. Would the developers be witnesses? Was I going to have to testify?

What would happen next?

• • •

Morning came none too quickly. I arose at six-thirty, rushed around the house, jumped in the car, and was at the bank building by seven-thirty. There were more early risers than usual that morning. Even the sales manager Jeff Holth—who never made it in before nine—had already arrived.

At around eight o'clock everyone made their way to the building's largest room, the production facility. We formed a rough circle amidst the machines. While we waited, most of us milled around looking nervous. In contrast, Dave seemed jovial, almost giddy. When he determined everyone was present, he found a place near the center of the room.

"Well folks," he said, "it looks like Ashton-Tate has done for us by litigation what we, as of yet, could not do by competition. For the first time *ever* we were mentioned on the front page of the Wall Street Journal." He smiled and chuckled briefly.

"You know, someone said they saw Ed Esber at our booth at Comdex last week. Well, it's apparent that whether he was there or not, he heard about what we were showing, because last Friday Ashton-Tate filed a lawsuit against us."

This brought a share of gasps. Apparently, not everyone had heard the news yet.

Dave waved away the emotion. "Not to fear," he said, sounding confident. "We have every reason to believe we are in the right." He paused, scanned the room. "You see, they claim they *own* the dBase language and intend to defend that position in court. They also claim we infringed on their 'look and feel' copyrights with our FoxBASE+ product. They are trying to prevent us from selling it along with FoxBASE+/Mac, and the product we've codenamed *FireFox*."

Dave panned the room again, fiddled with the watch on his arm. "Now, let's take a look at what they claim," he said. "We'll start with the language issue. Ashton-Tate is breaking new ground there because *nobody* has ever owned a language before. It's impossible! If it isn't, then I'll take ADA..." He motioned toward our sales manager. "Jeff here can take C, and someone else can have BASIC. Or for that matter English. It's crazy! Nobody can own a language."

He waved dismissively. "So that's a non-starter. A non-issue. That leaves only the issue of 'look and feel'..."

The *big* one, I knew. The one they might actually have a case over. I noticed the shrink-wrap machine again. The stacks of half-finished boxes on the floor.

"Now, I don't know how many of you know this," Dave said, "but there is an old statute of law that says if you encourage someone to do something for years and years, you cannot turn around and sue them for doing the very thing you encouraged them to do." His face gained some color. "At least, not and expect to get anything for your trouble. Yet that is *precisely* the case with the 'look and feel' of FoxBASE+.

"For *years*, Ashton-Tate allowed us, and even encouraged us, to copy the 'look and feel' of dBase III+, hoping our product—along with the other dBase clones—would help grow the dBase market."

Dave brought his arms together and scratched an elbow. "So that's what we've done...and now they intend to sue us for it." He smiled. "Well, my friends, it just don't work that way."

Dave panned the room again. The faces were a little less concerned; some were even smiling. "And while we're on the subject of 'look and feel'...there is no reason why they should be able to sue us for sales of our Mac product or our upcoming DOS product, *FireFox*. The Mac product looks nothing like dBase III+. And *FireFox* hasn't even been released yet."

He frowned. "However, if they can prove they own the language...well...then they *do* have a basis for a lawsuit against those products." He wagged a finger. "Soooo, the language issue is the important part of the lawsuit. But, since no one can own a language, it's hard to imagine them winning on that alone."

Dave smiled again. "So, you may be asking yourself, what is the purpose of the lawsuit, if they can't win?" He paused, panned the room as if waiting for answer.

No one said anything.

"Well, you see...the purpose of the lawsuit, is to do by litigation what they couldn't do through competition. To put an end to Fox Software." He brought a finger up, dagger like. "And, a couple of years ago that strategy might have worked."

The finger lowered. "But we've gotten a little too big for that now. We have absolutely no debt and our overhead is very small. They are betting we are wracked with debt and don't have the capital to defend ourselves. But I assure you—we do, and we will. My partner, Dick LaValley, is already gearing up his lawyer forces to take it to 'em." Another smile. "So, be of good cheer."

I glanced around the room. Most of the concerned looks were gone, replaced by looks of intent. We were going to face the giant.

Dave got serious then. "Now, you are all probably wondering how this is going to affect your lives in the days and weeks to come. Well, for the most part, it won't. These things take a long time—years usually—and we intend to fight it to the very end."

"It *is* the case, however, that those of you on the phones will be asked a lot of questions about the lawsuit. We've prepared written answers for you to some of the common questions." A mischievous grin filled his face. "Under *no* circumstance do I want anyone making comments about Ed Esber having a substandard size penis." He paused, cackled softly. "Whether it is true or not." He laughed louder then and others joined him.

When the laughter ended, Dave surveyed the room a final time. "Now, are there any questions?"

The questions that followed were all predictable in scope; concerns over job security, clarifications of legal matters, and then questions about those questions.

For me, though, it was a great way to start the week. Overnight, my work at this little family-run software company took on new meaning. I was part of a team that was now scowling at the schoolyard bully. Would we back him down or would we flinch?

Only time and the legal process would tell.

• • •

Immediately following the company assembly, Dave called another meeting *for developers only*. All seven of us gathered around his small round table.

"The Command Line is gone," Dave said. "Instead we'll create a Command Window for *FireFox*," he said. "Just like we have on the Mac product."

The "Command Line" was FoxBASE+'s primary interface. Essentially, it was a one-character high line at the bottom of the screen users could type their commands into. The text results of those commands scrolled up to fill the rest of the screen. The rest of the screen—24 lines, each 80 characters across—was referred to as the "Desktop." This Command Line/Desktop interface was used by all prior versions of dBase and FoxBASE. dBase IV was using it as well.

That interface didn't translate well to the window-oriented, mouse-driven environment of the Macintosh. So, for FoxBASE+/Mac, the Fox team replaced it with two separate windows. One, called the "Command Window," was for typing commands into. The text results of those commands were then sent to a separate "Desktop" window.

"We'll bring the ease-of-use of our Mac product to DOS," Dave said. "In the process we'll dodge the 'look and feel' portion of the lawsuit. Then the only area Ashton-Tate will be able to pursue us on is the language. It's the only similarity *FireFox* will have!"

All were leaned close, listening with rapt attention.

"This, of course, means we'll need to add mouse support to *FireFox*."

Eric had a hand to his chin. His thinking position. "We can't count on people to have mice on DOS though, Dave." He flipped up a hand. "On the Mac, everyone does."

Dave nodded his head. "Yes, we'll have to build in keyboard support for everything…" He thought for a moment. "Maybe we can work a deal…throw in a low-cost mouse or something. We'll worry about those details later…"

Dave's proposal would mean an incredible amount of work. To pull it off, the inside of *FireFox* would have to be turned inside out. Instead of just responding to typed-in commands, the product would now have to wait for events— such as the mouse button being clicked or a key being pressed—and handle those as they occurred. But, before all that, *something* would need to actually generate those events.

"…an Event Manager is the important piece, of course." Dave looked at Eric. "Maybe you and your roomie can come up with something there…"

On the Macintosh computer, there was a part of the operating system called the "Event Manager." This entity generated the "events" that application programs, such as

FoxBASE+/Mac, received and then acted on. The DOS operating system had no such animal. Our first priority would be to write our own Event Manager for *FireFox*. Then we could implement code to respond to the events it generated.

That was only the beginning, though. Other parts of the Mac operating system would have to be simulated as well. We would need a "Menu Manager" to handle the creation and operation of menus. Code to control dialogs, and the buttons that sat on them, would have to be written. Thanks to the "SBT by Comdex" drive, we *had* code to create windows, but it was rudimentary compared to what we now needed. A new, more robust "Window Manager" would have to be written. We would need a new text editor; a new tool to create mailing labels...the list seemed endless. Plus there were only six of us to do the work. Marty had his own product to finish and Dave was rarely coding by this time.

Still, the whole thing was exciting. I was eager to help in some way. Maybe I could help Heindel with whatever he was working on. Or help Bill, or Eric...

"Kerry will be working on the Report Writer," Dave said.

The what? I knew Marty was working on something called a Report Writer for the Mac product, but it looked about as complicated as his Screen Painter. Using a similar interface, it allowed users to create printed reports from the data in their databases.

I don't think I can...

Dave went on to explain that Fox purchased a standalone tool for creating reports from an outside programmer. The intent was to release this product as a supplement to *FireFox*.

When we finally got the product in our hands, though, it was found that while you *could* create and run reports with it, its interface and usability were lacking. It worked, but it wasn't pretty.

So, my job was to take all these yet-to-be-created managers, along with the inner workings of this outside product, and turn them into a fully integrated Report Writer with an interface consistent to the revamped, easy-to-use *FireFox*. Create the best Report Writer in the world, out of only sawdust, bubblegum, and dreams.

It was the biggest challenge of my life.

"Any further questions?" Dave asked.

Um, yeah, about this Report Writer...I don't know anything about such things. Are you sure you want to just throw me on it?

Dave checked our faces, paused a moment. "No?" he said to the silence. "Okay gang, let's get started."

• • •

That meeting was the first iteration of what we later referred to as a "five year plan" meeting. (FYP meeting, for short.) The basic meeting structure was simple. First we gave Dave a project status report, then we discussed what remained to be done, and then Dave waxed poetic about the future of Fox Software and its products.

As the weeks went by, though, our *future* would change. So, every week we'd go in for a FYP meeting and come out with a different five year plan—a frustrating situation for most developers. The last thing we wanted to hear, ever, was that everything was going to change again next week.

These meetings *did* have their advantages, though. Encapsulated within them was the ability to change directions quickly. Of them, Dave said "the worst thing a software company could do was to make a five year plan and stick to it."

And he was right.

Guy Kawasaki, the CEO of a rival database company, was

asked once what he thought of Fox Software. His response was "their product might be fast, but dragsters can't turn."

A nice sound bite, perhaps, but it never fit the company I worked for.

If Fox Software was a dragster, it was one that could do more than turn. It could do 180's in the sand, all day, every day.

And the FYP meetings were how those turns happened.

• • •

Following the initial FYP meeting, I struggled with the scope of my new assignment. The creative side of me was excited. I finally had a portion of *FireFox* that was wholly mine. A part nobody else knew a thing about. It was a chance to take a virtual lump of clay and mold it into a tool others could use and appreciate.

It would also have my name on it. I could point at it and say, "Yeah, I did that."

On the other hand, the Report Writer was something *nobody knew a thing about*. Not really. All *I* knew was that it was a tool for designing printed reports; much like Marty's Screen Painter was a tool for designing input screens. Yet only a few months before I watched Marty demo his Screen Painter and thought "I could never do that."

And a few months before *that*, I was happy when the code I wrote to sort a simple list of numbers worked out okay. There were some large projects in college, of course—some that took months to complete. But, in those instances, every other Computer Science student was struggling with essentially the same problem. Plus there was always an instructor to fall back on.

Now I had to work on something just as complicated as a Screen Painter, and I was entirely on my own. Marty was working on a Report Writer for our Mac product, of course, but because of differences between the two machines, no code could be shared.

I know nothing, I thought as I made my way back to my office. Can I do this?

Still reeling, I stumbled into Heindel's domain. He sat staring at the floor, looking a little burdened himself. I undoubtedly looked worse.

"I knew you were going to get the Report Writer," he said.

"Oh?"

Heindel placed his hands over his midsection. "Yeah, I went to Bart's demo of the standalone product. His introduction went something like 'This isn't very good, but here you go'." A brief smile. "I knew that wasn't going to fly with Dave. Pride in the product is essential to his character."

"Oh..." I paused. Crossed my arms. Shook my head.

Time to come clean. "I have no idea where to start with this."

Heindel nodded his head slowly. "Yeah, it's a pretty big deal. In my experience, with huge projects like that, you just start somewhere. Eventually you get it all done."

"Yeah?" I was dealing with a mountain.

He nodded again. "Yeah."

"Okay," I said slowly. "But where?"

Heindel searched the floor. Thought for a moment. "If it were me, I'd start with the global data."

"The global what?"

"The global data. Our product doesn't have a lot to spare. This standalone Report Writer probably uses a ton of it." He gave a comforting smile. "I'd try to bring it all into a handle or something."

Heindel explained that a program like *FireFox* made use of a computer's memory in a couple different ways. Global data—

things with names that needed to be accessed by all parts of the product—took up space in a portion of the computer's memory that was very limited.

A "handle" was a convention used to refer to other portions of the computer's memory—portions that were not so limited. He was suggesting I change the code to move the Report Writer's global data from one chunk of memory to the other. It was a straightforward task, but it would require a ton of code changes. Almost every line of Report Writer code. Of which there were probably thousands.

Still, it would be forward progress. "Okay…" I said. "I'll try that."

"Look," Heindel said. "Try not to get overwhelmed." He looked through me, toward Dave's office. "You saw all the work we have to do. This is going to be a *long* release cycle. Trust me." He turned his palms up. "Just start. You'll get there."

I said okay, nodded my head once, and left.

Just start. You'll get there.

Chapter 5
Adjustments

By the start of 1989 everyone was coding up a storm. Heindel was busy adding commands to *FireFox* to ensure it was 100% language compatible with dBase IV. Bill Ferguson was writing the first cut of the code to allow for the manipulation of controls and dialogs, later known as the Control Manager and Dialog Manager. Eric Christensen was working on the new text editor. Brian Tallman was pulling together code to create and manage windows and menus (i.e. the Window Manager and Menu Manager) and Amy Fulton was constructing a few of the dialogs Dave thought critical. One of these was a dialog to allow users to change the colors *FireFox* displayed itself in. I wasn't sure how this "Color Picker" was essential exactly, but if nothing else, it made good use of the code Bill was still creating.

I, of course, was occupied with the Report Writer, and at weird hours.

The more I got into my new project, the more concerned I felt about getting it done in time. It was a lot like being given a 747 and asked to remove the parts for an essential system—say, everything necessary for navigation—and then told to reconstruct that same system in another vehicle. In this case, though, the other vehicle wasn't another airplane, it was a cruise ship. And the changes to reign in the Report Writer's use of global data was like having to hit each airplane part once with a hammer to make it fit.

It wasn't that I thought I'd lose my job if I didn't succeed—though the thought crossed my mind occasionally—it was just that I wanted to make a good showing for myself. If

I was working on a team of superstars, I didn't want to be the only benchwarmer.

Multiplying my stress was the fact that, as far as I knew, the product was shipping in the spring. I began to have trouble sleeping at night, and at least one night a week I'd fail altogether. I'd just go into work early—sometimes as early as 4 a.m. After a month of that I decided what I really needed was something to look forward to.

I walked into Heindel's office. Heindel was engrossed with a DOS machine that sat on a rolling cart in the center of the room. His chin rested in his hand with his index finger aside his nose as he studied the screen intently.

"How do you get a vacation here?" I asked.

"Just a sec..." He squinted at the screen a few moments longer. Finally, he clicked a couple keys and turned my direction. "How do you get a vacation?" he said. "Well...you talk to Dave."

"Oh..." I was hoping for something a lot less personal. Like drawing a line on a calendar or something.

Heindel noticed my hesitation. "When do you want to take it?"

"Well, I was hoping for some time in May."

"May, huh? Hard to tell how Dave'll take that."

"Well, it's my anniversary with this place..." A year seemed like enough time to me. It was enough to earn a couple weeks of vacation anyway.

Heindel leaned back in his chair slightly and thought a bit. Threw his hands up. "Ask him." He hunched forward again. "Listen, there are no good times for a vacation here. You end up just setting a date and taking it when you planned. Ask Dave. Everyone knows that spring's a pipe dream anyway."

I smiled, thanked him, and turned to follow the outside edge of the inner yellow cubicles to Dave's office. As was generally the case, Dave's door was open when I arrived. I quietly stepped in and took a seat near the circular table. Dave was locked in conversation with a mustachioed man wearing a work belt.

"You're maxing out the system," the man said. "You can either change the system or add another trunk." I assumed he was talking about our phone system. There'd been lots of strange phone behavior recently. Developers getting tech support calls. To protect himself, Marty had started to answer the phone as "Maintenance."

Dave leaned back in his chair and put his feet on his desk. "A new trunk? Well, how much would that cost?"

The phone guy looked tentative. "About a thousand dollars," he said.

Dave didn't even wink. "A grand...? Well, no big deal then."

No big deal? A few months ago I was happy if I had twenty bucks to spend.

The phone guy shifted his stance slightly. "Um...yeah, no big deal."

"Okay, get us a new trunk," Dave said finally. The phone guy nodded once and left. Dave turned to look at me. "Yes, my young friend," he said. "What can I do for you?"

"Hey Dave..." I really wished I could just draw a line on a calendar. "I was wondering if it'd be all right for me to take a week off in May? I'll have my first year in by then and—"

Dave's face turned serious. "May? Oh no, May's no good. We'll be getting ready to ship by then."

"Oh..." I felt like I was turned down for the prom. Still, Heindel told me to *something* on the schedule. I quickly thought of a replacement date. "Okay, how about August?" My birthday was in August. It was the only date I could think of.

Dave leaned back and swept his palm over the top of his

head. "August?" he said, staring at the ceiling. "August should be fine. Yes...we'll have long since shipped by then." He nodded definitively. "Take it in August."

"Okay...good." I stood up and took a few steps toward the door. "Thanks, Dave."

That wasn't as hard as I thought it would be. I didn't get a vacation in May, but I was confident I'd take my first vacation in August. There was a schedule to contend with.

Dave was being as reasonable as he could be.

• • •

During the winter months in my shared conference room office there was one subject that consistently came up.

"It's awful cold in here, Marty." My Mac still occupied my desk space so I had my DOS machine—a new 386s machine—on a rolling stand that faced the door. From my seat in front of it I could see Marty's coat-shrouded back.

"Awful cold in here, Kerry," Marty echoed back.

Marty and I still treasured our living space, so neither of us would complain about anything. But, we'd learned that the room's large windows came with a drawback. They leaked air so bad they might as well have been open. It was beyond the ability of duct tape to fix.

Later in the day, the conversation repeated.

"Awful cold in here, Marty."

"It's d*** cold in here, Kerry!" Marty rolled away from his desk to look at me. "I bet they shut off that heat again."

That was another part of our problem. It was always the case that those who sat in the cubicles near the center of the building sweltered while those of us with offices around the exterior fought off the cold. It led to a constant war over the thermostat that usually resulted in neither group being entirely satisfied. The senior dev members survived by having small space heaters in their offices. Marty and I didn't have one of those, though. It was all we could do to keep our hands warm enough to type.

I flexed my fingers, trying to revive them. The alternative was to try and type with gloves on. And only Marty, who primarily coded using the Mac's Cut, Copy, and Paste functions—which required only two working fingers—was able to manage that.

Marty pulled a screwdriver from his desk and stood up. "I'll fix 'em." He walked past me and I heard the door open and swing shut, making a "thump, thump" sound as it closed.

The thermostat would soon be adjusted to our liking.

Until the support people found out, that is.

• • •

One January afternoon I walked into Dave's office to ask him a question. I found him in the middle of a conversation with a thirty-something man with straight, dark hair—parted neatly on one side. The man had the figure and presence of a young Santa Claus and his blue shirt was clearly monogrammed with the initials "CLW." Their conversation was about some part of the product's interface—a part I knew nothing about. So, I just backed up against the wall to wait. The CLW-man glanced at me as I entered.

Dave acted as if he hadn't seen me at all. He was sitting with his feet on the desk again, a can of soda resting on his lap. "I think you should build in as much leveragability as possible," he said.

CLW nodded, and glanced quickly my direction again. "That way, if Kerry here needs to use some of the components of MODI STRU in his Report Writer, he can." He pronounced

MODI STRU as "mah-dee strew."

I was surprised that this CLW guy knew my name and tried to include me in the conversation. Seems cool.

Dave looked at me and flipped a hand CLW's direction. "Oh yes, Kerry," he said. "This is Chris Williams. He and his team will be joining us. They'll primarily be working on the UNIX port."

I smiled and stuck out a hand. Chris grabbed it and shook it heartily. "Welcome to the team, Chris."

During lunch conversations I'd heard about Chris and his people. Chris owned a Perrysburg local computer consulting business, and recently Dave had negotiated with him to buy his company. As part of that deal Chris, along with two other developers he employed—Sally Stuckey and Carol Garrison— were joining our staff.

I didn't meet Sally and Carol until much later.

Sally was also in her thirties and of smallish dimensions, similar to Amy Fulton. In demeanor she was Chris's exact opposite. If he was Santa, Sally was the dutiful and hardworking elf.

Carol was closer to my age, newly-married, and striking in appearance. She was also very new to programming, much more so than I.

The initial mission for Chris's team was to make *FireFox* work on the UNIX operating system as it was being completed for DOS. Ultimately this would allow Fox to provide a UNIX product without having to rely on an outside company to do the port. Years before, a company named SCO ported the FoxBASE+ product to UNIX, but they were so lax in correcting bugs in that product (FoxBASE+/Unix), they fell out of favor with Dave. With *FireFox*, Chris's group would take their place.

The work on a UNIX product only lasted about a month,

though. By the end of February it was clear we had more pressing matters. *FireFox* was nowhere near ready for release in May, and the Mac product needed help as well. So, Chris's group was pulled in. Carol was put in charge of tracking bugs for the Mac product while Chris and Sally were drafted to help with *FireFox*. Chris immediately took on some of the larger dialogs that needed completing and Sally began working on a tool to create mailing labels.

With eight of us on *FireFox* there was a renewed sense of optimism. The spring deadline almost seemed attainable.

I was even able to sleep regularly again.

• • •

The first outside challenge to our schedule came in the form of a series of marketing meetings held in the first quarter of '89. Present at the meetings was a group of external advisers Dave gathered. What specific criterion he used to select these advisers was beyond my knowledge. All I knew was the back corner office—the one perpetually kept unoccupied "for Dick LaValley"—was suddenly filled with people one day. They were there to offer opinions about the product's new look and suggestions for its final name.

One of the principal attendees was a fellow named Glenn Hart. Glenn was a large, balding man whose appearance suggested "Mafioso" to me. Eric and Bill had a different—less complimentary—name for him, though.

"So, guess what the *Emphysema Poster Child* suggested today," Eric said, a subtle smirk on his face. He took a bite of pizza and looked around the table at Bill, Heindel, Marty, and I. It was lunchtime and we were at a Pizza Hut just across the parking lot from our building.

"What?" Heindel said. "Did they come up with a new

name?"

Eric rolled his eyes. "Well, actually, yes…FoxPro."

"Hmm…," Marty said, nodding his head slowly. "FoxPro..."

"FoxPro?" Heindel said. "Why don't we just keep FireFox? I like FireFox. Fire, burning speed, that's our product. What's wrong with FireFox?"

"It's the codename," Eric said. "Dave wants something else."

"How about FoxFire?" I said. I liked the Clint Eastwood movie of the same name. I also just won the "name the company newsletter" competition with "FoxTrax." I figured I was on a roll.

Eric ignored me. "The name's not the big news, though."

Heindel now had a slice of pepperoni hanging near his face. "What's the big news?" he asked.

"You don't want to know," Bill said.

Heindel looked quickly between the two. "What?"

Eric took a drink of water and smiled. "He wants a new command—SET INTERFACE OFF."

"SET INTERFACE OFF!?" Marty and Heindel said in stereo.

Marty began to chuckle then. "Whoa," he said, "That's a good one."

I was still new to the intricacies of the dBase language. It had a litany of "SET" commands. I had no idea what they all did. "What's that mean?" I asked.

Eric frowned. "It means he wants the user to be able to change the interface back to the old style just by using a SET command."

My eyebrows rose instinctively. We spent several months working on the new interface and were now quite fond of it. We certainly didn't want to give it up for the archaic Command

Line interface FoxBASE+ had.

Marty was still laughing. "That's great," he said. "How'd that go over?"

"Can you say 'Lead Balloon'?" Bill said.

I smiled and took a bite of my pan pizza. Glenn's relationship with Dave was one of dedicated ambivalence. Glenn was well known in the dBase community, and occasionally had a good idea, so Dave tolerated his opinions. But Glenn was a "marketer," and marketing was a source of invariable derision at Fox.

However, in some respects, Glenn's reasoning was sound. Mouse-driven interfaces with pull-down menus and floating windows were virtually unknown in the IBM-PC/DOS world. Most people that owned DOS machines didn't have a mouse and probably wouldn't know how to use one if they did. We were breaking new ground.

Glenn was afraid we were breaking too much ground, especially if we locked the product to it. Better to give users the choice, he thought.

Dave didn't see it that way, though. He knew enough about the internals of the product to know that switching interfaces on the fly just wasn't that easy. Nor, was it the right thing to do. By the time the marketing meetings were over, "FoxPro" was our product's new name, but it would keep the interface we spent so much time on.

We'd survive the backlash if and when it came.

• • •

By March I had *my* Report Writer to the place where it could create and print reports in much the same fashion it did when it was originally designed, except now as an integral part of FoxPro. It wasn't pretty to look at, but it was completely functional.

The code was accessible from two commands. Issuing "CREATE REPORT" with a filename would bring up the design surface where the report could be created, manipulated and saved. Then, once a report was created, a user could use the "REPORT FORM" command to print that report. (There was a third command, "MODIFY REPORT" that could access a report file as well, but it did exactly what "CREATE REPORT" did. It traveled through all the same code internally.)

Overall, I was happy with my progress. I achieved what seemed impossible only a few months before. I integrated two very different products, and they both still worked!

I dragged Heindel to my office to show him. I brought up the design surface, created a simple report, saved it, closed it, and then typed the REPORT FORM command to print it. I smiled as text from the report scrolled up my screen.

"I think you should check it in," Heindel said after my demonstration was complete.

"Really?" Checking my changes in seemed like a big step. At Fox, as was the practice at most software companies, a developer would "check out" the source files that dealt with the part of the product he wanted to work on, and then toil away on them safely on his own machine. During that time the rest of the team would generally have a read-only copy of those files on their machines, meaning they could view it, but not change it. When the developer deemed his code complete enough to expose to the rest of the team, he checked it back into the network.

In my case, most of the files were new, but the process was the same. Once it was out on the network, my code would be fair game for everyone else to see and play with.

"I don't want to mess anyone up," I said.

"You're not going to mess anyone up," Heindel said. "No one else will probably even look at it. Everyone's too busy with their own stuff." He walked around my desk to stand near the room's swinging door. "Besides, if you get it out there you'll have it backed up."

"Good point..." I'd done a lot of work and was getting a little worried about losing it. I had copies of my files on floppy disks in my desk, but there was always a danger of those getting erased or melted to a puddle in a fire. Checking my stuff in would ensure that there was a copy on everyone else's machine in addition to the main network machine—which was backed up regularly. "All right...if you think so."

"Check it in," Heindel said, and then raised a fist. "No fear."

I smiled and said "Okay."

A few hours later everything I'd done was out. Now safely on the network.

• • •

My code wasn't out a day, before Dave swung open my door.

"Kerry, I've been looking at the Report Writer," he said, frowning, "and well—come on—I'll show you!" He turned and made a quick head motion. "I can't get *anything* to work!"

I followed him to his office, and in an hour's time he completely redesigned the Report Writer's interface. It wasn't so much that he couldn't get anything to work, it was that he didn't like the way it appeared while it was working. I returned to my office with a one page, hand drawn mockup of the changes.

I was overwhelmed again.

This looks nothing like what was there before, I thought. How am I going to do this?

Though I'd done a substantial amount of work to get the Report Writer into the product, its inner workings were still foreign. Radical changes, like the ones I was just given, sort of frightened me.

I was also a little confused about Dave's management style.

Before the meeting I was feeling pretty good. In only a few short months I took this large standalone product with its own global data, its own way of interacting with users, its own way of putting out printable data, and successfully folded it into our product. And it still worked. Wasn't that worth at least a quick "good job"? I had no idea whether what I did was appreciated or not.

Or had I underachieved? Was the Fox team so good that my work was inconsequential in comparison?

It was all a mystery.

Chapter 6
Distractions

Sometime in March, Dave called the developers to his office. All ten of us now crowded around the table.

"Now look," he said, "We need to get some people out of this building."

I backed away from the table to give myself more room. No kidding?

Recently, Carol Garrison was moved into the conference room with Marty and me. It was a graphic indication that, while all of us were busy coding, Fox Software was growing. The cozy little bank building of around 6,000 square feet was now trying to accommodate close to 70 people *and* a production facility.

The cubicle area where my first office had been located was now one big open corral filled with technical support personnel. They were packed in like cordwood. In fact, one lady's office was in the entranceway to the men's restroom.

Thankfully, a new home had already been found. A portion of the shopping center behind our bank building was available. It amounted to about 22,000 square feet of space, and previously housed a store, a number of business offices, and a radio station.

"We gave some thought to which groups are most autonomous," Dave said, "which could be easily separated from the rest of the company, and we decided it's the production facility and our group." He crossed his legs and placed a hand on the back of his head. "So, my friends, we will be the first to make the long trip across the parking lot."

A smile. "The builders are hard at work already and as

soon as the bottom floor is complete the two groups will move over. Then, when the upper floor is finished, we'll move upstairs and the rest of the company will move across." He panned our faces. "Sound good?"

Bill Ferguson deliberately hunched his shoulders together. "Great! When do we move?"

Many of us smiled. "In May," Dave said.

I glanced at Heindel. May had been our original release date. There wasn't much talk of *that* anymore. A pipedream...

Still, I was energized by the approaching change of venue. It indicated the company was doing well, despite the lawsuit. I also hoped it meant I would have an office of my own. When I started at Fox, every developer, except Marty and me, had their own office with a door. Now that the Report Writer was functional, I felt like I finally accomplished something significant. A private office seemed like an appropriate reward.

Moreover, the addition of Carol to the conference room significantly increased the noise level. Her task of verifying and tracking bugs for the Mac product brought in scores of chatty people. I needed my quiet back.

The plan for the upstairs of the new building was made available a few days later. In it, I was indeed allotted an office with a window. Then a week later—when a revised plan was posted—everyone *except* Carol and me had offices.

That fed my insecurities. I wondered what I did between one plan and the next to end up out in a cubicle again. There was nothing I could do about it, though. I just shrugged it off and went on with my work.

I'd prove I deserved an office...somehow.

• • •

Finally the day of the move arrived. On a Friday we boxed up our stuff, and over the weekend our boxes were trekked across the parking lot for us, along with our computers.

When I arrived at the new building the following Monday, I found the layout for the offices downstairs slightly different than the final upstairs layout would be. Instead of occupying one of the long walls of the structure, the developer offices hinged around one of the front corners.

There was one obvious similarity though. The machines for Carol and I were set up inside grey-walled cubicles. And my cubicle came with an additional bonus; it was right outside the office shared by Dave, Amy, and their infant son.

The littlest Fulton was part of an unprecedented baby boom at Fox. Nearly everyone I worked with was having kids. Heindel and his wife just had a little girl. Chris William's wife gave birth to a boy. Bill's wife had twins. Eric Christensen's family had a new little boy and so did Dave and Amy. There were fourteen children born to Fox employees from the end of 1988 to the summer of 1989.

I was beginning to wonder if there was something unusual in all that free pop.

• • •

The changes to the Report Writer interface were nearly complete. Dave and I haggled out every detail of the way it should appear, and in the process, it became a useful tool. Like the rest of the product, it could be driven by either a mouse or a keyboard. It allowed users to put text, boxes, and data fields from their databases into a report and change their location simply by selecting and moving them. The Report Writer also performed well. In fact, even though he never told me directly, I knew Dave was pleased. I overheard him calling it "the best Report Writer in the world" to someone on the phone.

One aspect that was never quite right in his eyes, though, was the colors of the Report Writer's display. I would be in the middle of chasing down some complicated bug in my code and Dave would storm over with a minor change to the colors to be put in ASAP. So, I would drop whatever I was doing and tweak the *two lines* of coloring code to match what he wanted.

The rest of the team was experiencing the same thing. It got so the only team meetings we had during a large portion of the development cycle were about colors. Anything that was a hot topic in Dave's mind was instantly important to us all, whether we liked it or not.

These color meetings became such a distraction, in fact, that Amy finally told him to "go off and decide what you want and don't bother the rest of us until you're sure." Dave took her advice, and freed us—for a time—to continue with our work.

• • •

By the beginning of summer '89, FoxPro was turning into an impressive product. As an outgrowth of the new language added to emulate dBase IV, and our new window-based interface, many items present in earlier Fox products were substantially transformed.

One of these was our text editor. Two commands in the language would present this to a user, MODIFY FILE and MODIFY COMMAND. In FoxBASE+, the editor was simplistic. It just filled the screen with whatever file was being edited. Only one file could be edited at a time, and there was a rigid limit to how big that file could be. It was functional for developing dBase programs, but most hardcore users would buy an additional editing program to do real text editing work.

As coded by Eric, though, the new FoxPro editor was an

animal of a different color (no pun intended). It resided in a window and users could have as many text files open concurrently as they liked. They could easily copy and paste text between different files. There was no limit to the size of the file. (No attainable limit, anyway; the actual limit for a text file was larger than most modern disk drives.) It was also blindingly fast. It could open hundreds of files in seconds and scroll text faster than it could be read.

Another command, BROWSE, also got a face-lift. The purpose of the BROWSE command was to present an overall view of the data in a database, much like a spreadsheet. If my database contained mailing addresses, field names—things like "Name," "Address," and "Zip"—would make up the columns across the top and the values (data) would compose the rows. In prior versions, it too was confined to a single window. But, in FoxPro, thanks to Brian and Eric, it resided in a window, data could be cut and pasted anywhere, and it even allowed for two panes (or views) of the data in the same window. It was really, really cool.

Sally's label creation tool was nearly finished, as well. It would replace the simplistic tool from FoxBASE in the same way my Report Writer would replace the earlier reporting tool. Sally was also working with Amy on a useful tool to manipulate any and every file on the hard disk, known as "the Filer."

Bill was busy creating tools to help users debug their dBase programs. Earlier versions of the DOS product provided little help with this, so anything he added was a vast improvement. Our Mac product already included two debugging tools, which Bill emulated in FoxPro. One, called the "Debug Window," gave users the ability to monitor the values of their "variables." (A "variable" is a portion of a program that can change over time.) The other, called the "Trace Window," allowed users to step slowly through their dBase code to find problems as they happened.

For his part, Heindel continued to add dBase IV syntax while working to expand our printing capabilities. Both were mammoth and nearly thankless chores.

The most astounding product improvement, though, was its speed. FoxPro was fast—incredibly fast. It was clocked running code twice as fast as FoxBASE+ and up to seven times faster than dBase IV. (Stop watches were always in use at Fox Software.)

When the product finally shipped, it would be a fully-loaded hot rod.

• • •

There was still much to do, though.

Not many of us were going in weekends yet, but I was. I still felt concerned—like the whole Report Writer was a facade that could tumble down on me any time. Even though it *appeared* to be working, parts of the original code were still mysteries to me. I had to test it—I had to be certain it was right. Plus, the fact that it was considerably quieter on the weekends made them a more desirable time to work

During normal working hours, the carpenters upstairs were a source of perpetual distraction. They were still hard at work trying to complete the top floor and we all knew it. An ordinary day's concentration might be shattered by a loud crash overhead or the sound of hammers pounding away.

Another source of distraction, for me, was the littlest Fulton. A short time after the move, Dave and Amy began bringing him in to work. He was still very young and slept often so this shouldn't have been a problem.

Unfortunately, the Fulton's also brought in this "seat on a spring" thing which they attached to the doorjamb of their office. This meant I'd be sitting in my cubicle, attempting to solve a mystery, and have this "boing, boing, boing" sound suddenly interrupt my thoughts. I'd turn around to find the boy jumping higher than any kid that small should be able and smiling from ear to ear.

Twenty minutes of that and I wished the carpenters would step up their hammering so I could get my concentration back.

• • •

Marty was hard at work as well. The testing cycle for the next version of the Mac product was in full swing, and soon produced another reason for our attentions to be diverted.

I was seated at my desk one morning, staring hard at my computer screen, when I heard a familiar voice behind me.

"Kerry?" Dave asked, sounding serious.

Ah man, not color changes again. I turned to look at him. His face was equally serious.

Uh, oh.

"Follow me," he said with a wave. He led me to the right, past Chris's office, and then Sally's. As we went by Chris's, I noticed his door was closed. That was unusual. Chris was a sociable guy and preferred to leave his door open. The top half of his office was transparent, though. In the split second it took me to pass by, I noticed someone in Chris's office with him, but I couldn't tell who.

We ended at Heindel's office. Marty and Heindel were already inside, waiting.

What could this be about? The only thing Marty, Heindel, and I had any recent interaction about was some printing problems. But that shouldn't concern Dave much.

Dave motioned for me to shut the door, and then took a seat. "I just wanted to let you all know that we decided to let

Carol go," he said, speaking softly.

Whoa. Where did that come from?

Carol was hired fresh out of college. She fit into the low-key environment of Chris's firm really well. At Fox, though, she'd been judged "too untested" to have her hands in the FoxPro code. She was given her bug-tracking job for the Mac product as a first assignment. While that wasn't the sort of thing a developer normally did, I assumed she'd eventually pass the test and become one of us. I had some early tasks that were outside the norm too, after all.

What did she do so wrong that she was now getting fired?

"She just wasn't cutting it," Dave said, shaking his head. "This is probably for the best. She was way over her head here." He looked first at Marty, and then at Heindel and I. His voice got more forceful. "She's personally responsible for the slippage in the Mac product's release date," he said. "She cost us weeks!"

His tone softened again, sounding more apologetic. "I also wanted to assure you three that we're happy with your work. Nobody else's head is on the chopping block. Just Carol. She overlooked some critical bugs..." He shook his head. "Chris is firing her as we speak."

Chris is firing her? That was a little strange too. Dave was technically her boss. Stranger still, was the fact that she was the first developer to be let go. Not the kind of precedent I wanted to see started.

Dave dismissed us then. As I returned to my cubicle I saw Carol walking out of Chris's office. There were tears in her eyes.

I looked away. Was this really necessary?

I found my seat and tried to return to work. Regardless of Dave's assurances, I couldn't say I was feeling any more secure in my job than before. If Carol was fired for losing a bug or two, what would keep them from firing me if I created one? I was one of the guys actually writing the code…

It was also clear from the office arrangements who was *now* the low man. Again.

At my first opportunity, I went to see Marty. "So what was the deal with Carol?" I asked, closing his office door.

Marty turned in his chair and rested his elbows on his lap. "Oh, somehow some bugs got misplaced," he whispered.

I wasn't sure why he was whispering. The door was closed. "Misplaced?" I said in a normal tone.

"Yeah, you know how Carol had that bug tracking program she used?"

I nodded. Carol wrote a program using FoxBASE+/Mac to maintain a list of the bugs that were found. "Yeah, I remember."

"Well, somehow there were some bugs that didn't get entered into the list," Marty said, still whispering. "Consequently, I never heard about them and they didn't get fixed."

"No?"

Marty raised a hand to swat the air. "Well, not until I finally heard about them. It was no big deal though. The Mac product would've been delayed by something else." He shrugged, "I'm still fixing bugs now."

I frowned. "Then why did Dave fire her?"

Marty shrugged again. "He just woke up one morning and decided Carol was the reason the Mac product slipped."

I shook my head.

"She got a raw deal," Marty said. "Especially since there were no clear guidelines given her."

"Unbelievable." I scratched the back of my head. "And he had Chris fire her?"

Marty gave a short laugh. "Yeah, isn't that something? He

had *Chris* fire her." He shook his head. "Poor Carol."

"Poor Carol for sure." I shook my head slowly. My sleep patterns are going to be irregular again…

Management randomness, it's a developer's nightmare.

• • •

In June I was given my second annual review and it was extremely positive—much better than I expected considering what just happened to Carol. Dave told me he appreciated my work and gave me a bonus that, to a recent college grad, seemed obscene. He also informed me that I would, in fact, be getting my own office when the developers moved upstairs.

That final move occurred the following month. We were shuffled upstairs and the rest of the company came over to fill a portion of the new building's space.

Finally, I sat in an office of my own. It had its own window and its own door. No loud conversations. No bouncing kids. No pounding hammers. It was everything I hoped for.

Of course the view wasn't much. Through my window I could see the roof of the adjacent building and the dumpsters that sat behind it. The front side of my office only had a wall part way up. The top half was filled in with Plexiglas that creaked every time someone walked by. It felt a little like being in a fishbowl.

I had the last occupied office on "developer's row"—the exterior offices on the eastern side of the building. It was the furthest from the corner office, Dave's new home. The way I figured it, if anything went wrong, I'd be the last developer he would find.

And the creaking Plexiglas would give me fair warning.

Location, location, location.

Chapter 7

Caves and Beaches

I was in on a Saturday afternoon in the middle of July. I wasn't there because I had to be, I was there because I wanted to be. The Report Writer was proving to be extremely solid. There were few bugs found in it at all. I was feeling comfortable. Like the whole thing *wasn't* going to fall in on me. It seemed I really *had* accomplished the impossible.

A little more testing is always a good thing, though, so I was in to check a little more. I spent a few hours creating reports and watching them print. When I was satisfied, I turned off my machine.

It works. It's time to go home.

I followed developer row toward Dave's office. There was a light on, so I assumed Dave was in as well. He was probably doing a little more testing himself. Our scheduled release date was early August.

As I drew near, I looked in and saw Dave at his desk. In his new office, the configuration had his wooden desk facing the door. To the right of the door as you entered was his round conference table and above it on that wall was a large whiteboard. Along the perpendicular wall to the left were two large bookshelves, filled with books. I moved by Dave's entrance a little more deliberately than I normally would. It's okay for the boss to know you're in on a Saturday, after all.

I was just passing by the adjacent conference room, when Dave called my name.

I shrugged. Must just want to say "Hi." I back stepped to his door.

"Hey Dave," I said. "How are you?"

His face was too serious for a Saturday. "Yes, Kerry. Come here. I need to talk to you about something."

I walked in and sat down.

Dave had the Report Writer up on his computer screen with a typical report already constructed. Our Report Writer was what was commonly known as a "banded report writer." This meant its design surface was divided into a number of sections (bands) and each represented a particular portion of the final printed report. For instance, one band was labeled "Report Header." Anything—database fields, text, or rectangles—placed within that band would print only once, at the beginning (or head) of the report. Likewise, there was a band labeled "Page Footer." Anything placed within that band printed at the end of every page of the report. Another band labeled "Detail" was for information that filled the center (usually the greatest) portion of every page.

In the Detail band of Dave's report he had a handful of the fields from his database arrayed in a couple rows. This particular database was a collection of all the laser disks he owned, of which there were hundreds.

Dave made a motion toward the screen. "I can't create the kind of report I want."

I squinted at his monitor. He had the text "Title:" and next to that a rectangular area as a placeholder for the field named "Title." In that area, the various values for that field would print in the final report. To the right of that he had a similar construct for the "Description" field. The "Description" field was a bit different, in that it was defined as type "memo" in his database, so it could be really long. When it finally printed, the text for it could fill any number of lines.

He had a third field in his report named "Running Time." This was placed beneath the row with "Title" and

"Description" on it.

"That looks okay to me…" I said finally.

"Yes, but watch when I preview it." Dave selected the menu item labeled "Print Preview." The report design screen was obscured by the Preview window, showing a mockup of how the report would print.

I could see all three fields displaying as I expected they would. The titles of his laser disks ran down the left side of the screen. Beginning directly beside those were the descriptions for each one. Some of the descriptions only lasted a single line, others spanned on for a dozen. On the line immediately following the last line of each description, the value of "Running Time" displayed. Its horizontal position was directly beneath "Title," but because the lengths of the descriptions varied, it could be many lines below. "Yeah, that's right," I said.

Dave frowned. "But I want 'Running Time' to always be on the line immediately following 'Title.' How do I do that?"

He couldn't. The report writer we purchased didn't allow for that, so neither did ours. "Well, you can't," I said. "That's how the Report Writer was designed."

Dave's frown deepened. "I think we need to allow a field to be anchored, just like we do in the Mac's Report Writer."

The Mac Report Writer was built by Marty from the ground up. It allowed text, boxes, and fields to either "float" or be "anchored." When placed on the design surface beneath a stretchable memo field the "floatable" fields continued floating down the printed report until the memo field finished printing all its text. Then they would print. That was essentially the way all items in my Report Writer behaved.

"Anchored" fields remained fixed in place no matter what the stretchable fields above them did. That behavior was a part of Marty's design since the beginning, though. I was just working with what I was given. My Report Writer was hardwired to work on only a single line of output at a time. "I don't think I can do that, Dave," I said. "The Report Writer doesn't work that way."

Dave got more serious. "I think we really need to do anchoring, though." He studied the screen. "This Report Writer is unusable without it."

Well, it's been completely useable for the last few months...

I had no idea how to do what he was asking. "I don't think I can," I said. "Not by next month, anyway."

Dave sounded sympathetic. "I really think we need to do this, Kerry." He straightened in his chair. "Listen, you've done remarkably well so far. Our environment here...well, it isn't for just any programmer. You blended in much better than some." He nodded once quickly. "Carol Garrison for instance..." He paused before lifting a shoulder. "Or Sally even."

Sally! What's wrong with Sally?

Dave didn't elaborate and I didn't ask. I stared at the carpeted floor instead. He's really going to make me rip up the engine of the Report Writer only a few weeks before we're supposed to ship. But the thing is solid, so solid.

I looked at Dave again. "But, Dave...you said we were going to ship early next month."

"Well, how long do you think it will take?" he said. "It shouldn't take longer than a couple weeks should it?"

I looked at the floor again, shook my head slowly. "I have no idea. I don't even know where to begin."

Dave was silent for a few moments. "Well, I really think we need to do this," he said. "Maybe I can have Eric come down on Monday and give you some pointers."

I couldn't lift my eyes. The pain in my gut was too great.

"Okay…" I said. "I'll try…" I stood up slowly.

"It needs to be done," Dave said as I turned.

I walked toward the door. "Alright, I'll see what I can do."

I went home, dreading the following week.

The Report Writer hadn't fallen in on me. It was pushed over.

• • •

I was still down on Monday. Defeated before I started. It was nice to know Dave thought more of me than others on the staff. It was surprising really. But I had a feeling the latest turn with the Report Writer was going to change his perception.

Seated at my desk, I brought up the three or four files that composed the Report Writer's engine and started paging through them. It took little time to realize my suspicions were correct. There was no easy way to do what Dave wanted.

As originally conceived, the engine picked out the appropriate information from what the user saw on screen and transferred it to a separate chunk of memory, what the original author called a "literal pool." The next thing the engine did was build instructions (he called it "pcode") that described the precise steps to take to print the report. Then another part of the engine followed those instructions. He called that part an interpreter. The pcode instructions and the interpreter were black boxes to me. Complete mysteries.

One thing was clear, though. They were built to work on one line of the report at a time. There was no mechanism to go back and print something that didn't "float"…or stay with something until it finished "floating." It just didn't work that way.

I noticed movement out of the corner of my eye. I looked

up to see Eric standing outside my door. I waved him in.

"How's it going?" he asked softly.

I shook my head. "It's not."

You must understand. I've been given a task I cannot do.

"Yeah, Dave told me to come and help. I'm not sure how much help I can be, though."

"Hmm," I said. "Okay."

Eric took a seat. He grabbed a pen and a notepad from the top of my desk. "I looked at the Report Writer code a little. Some of that stuff is confusing..." He waved his hands in the air. "There's this literal pool stuff, and this pcode stuff, and this interpreter business." He frowned. "It's really not like Marty's at all is it?"

"Nope." But we're going to try to make it act like it.

Eric drew a few things on the paper. It looked like a bunch of rectangles in a circle connected by lines. "Like I said, I don't know if this helps you or not, but it seems like...well...maybe you can do something to make the Report Writer work on the pool until everything finishes printing, instead of what it's doing now."

I sat quietly. I knew Eric was smart, but he didn't really know much about the Report Writer engine. Nobody did. Not even me. What Eric was saying was about as much help as finding Scotland on a map and telling me to go there.

"Does that help?" he asked, looking hopeful.

"A little."

Eric shrugged and put the paper back on my desk. "Let me know if you need more." He gave a little apologetic smile. "Really, nobody knows this stuff better than you. It's up to you."

"Thanks," I said, forcing a smile.

Eric opened the door and slid through. "I hope I helped a

little."

I nodded. "A little…."

He gave a low, two-note chuckle. "Okay," he said. "See ya."

It was really up to me.

• • •

I accomplished very little the rest of that day and the next. I made a few attempts to alter the part of the engine that interpreted the pcode. It was the only part that really made any sense to me. I thought maybe, if I altered the two places that specifically handled the literals—the elements that printed out—I might have a chance.

My attempts were floundering, though. They didn't work. Either the whole report printed on one line, or it didn't print at all. The only thing I accomplished was I learned a little more about the interpreter portion of the code. It was like holding a single match in a very windy cave.

There was another complication, though. In order to be able to calculate how much space to allow for the Detail (central) portion of the report, the size of the other bands had to remain constant. That meant the anchor/float mechanism *could only occur* in the Detail band. The other bands of the report needed to behave just as before.

However, the pcode really made no distinctions between the bands.

I was still lost.

• • •

Wednesday I floundered around a little more. I thought maybe if I changed the order of the pcode some—if I changed the description of the report the interpreter followed—maybe I could get something to work.

But I accomplished nothing. The Report Writer either froze my machine, or printed a partial report. The day was a total waste.

It felt just like those last couple of weeks before graduation. Me without any job prospects.

I finally decided outright prayer was the best option.

If it was really all "up to me," it was hopeless.

• • •

Thursday I started to have a hint of something. Another match in my cave of despair.

I thought about adding my own pcode instructions to the mix. There would be no harm in that, I reasoned, because the way the pcode/interpreter mechanism worked, there was some room for additional instructions. I could add my own instructions, and try to get something that would work.

I would leave the old ones as they were—and that was good. It ensured the new anchoring behavior occurred only in the Detail band. The other bands should stay as they were. They should be safe.

Or so I hoped.

• • •

Friday I wondered why I didn't start praying sooner.

What I *really* need is a pcode looping structure, I realized. That way, I could have the stuff in the Detail band keep looping until everything printed out. The engine would no longer be tied to dealing with just one line at a time. It would deal with the whole band.

I could have specific pcode instructions for the literals in the Detail band. I would allow for Dave's new "anchored" behavior in those.

It might work.

• • •

That Saturday and the beginning of the following week was spent earnestly pursuing the looping solution I came up with. It was clear that it would work, but it would take some time to clean up all the details. Hundreds of lines of code would need to be altered and tested.

I was carrying a flashlight through the cave, and I had plenty of batteries.

• • •

By the beginning of August I was out of the cave completely. Anchoring worked, floating worked—reports even printed on more than one line.

In addition, I knew everything there was to know about the Report Writer.

I could now call it completely my own.

• • •

The month of my scheduled vacation arrived. As it turned out, it was convenient Dave agreed to let me take a vacation in August after he denied my original request for May. Over the course of the summer, a friend of mine got engaged and asked me to be the best man in his wedding. The date was in August and it was in California—thousands of miles away. I decided to use my promised vacation to attend.

I was greatly looking forward to a trip out west. I'd been working for Fox for fifteen months with only a couple days off during all that time. A week in the sun with friends was just what I needed.

The wedding was August 5th. I already had my tickets purchased, but I still needed to remind Dave. Just in case he went looking for me while I was gone.

I found him hovering over a laptop computer at his desk. Both hands were at the keyboard and he was completely absorbed, but in a negative way. His expression spoke of stomach trouble.

"Yes," he said as he saw me approach. "What is it?"

I hesitated, contemplating coming back later. "Um…I just wanted to remind you of my vacation the first week of August."

Dave looked at me, but his hands clung to the keyboard. "Now? In August? We're getting ready to ship…."

Oh no, I thought. It's just like Heindel said. There's no good time to take vacation. I looked out Dave's window, seeing the old building across the parking lot. In fact, maybe the developers never leave. Has *anyone* been out since I've been here? "But, I asked in March…"

"Yes, yes, I remember." His eyes were back on the screen, "But take only as much time as you *have* to."

"It's for a friend's wedding," I said, "in California."

Dave's face softened a little. "A wedding? Well, that's not the sort of thing you should miss. It's an important event."

"Yes…."

"But take only as much time as you have to."

Since I already had my tickets, "as much time as I have to" was five days off of work. "Okay," I said, backing away.

I returned to my office and looked out my window. The dumpsters were being emptied below.

I shook my head. I'm going all the way to California for a wedding. A week *is* reasonable, isn't it?

Still, I couldn't help but feel a little guilty.

• • •

As soon as I got back, Dave called a FYP meeting in the upstairs conference room. The room was one of the few places in the building where there was any sense of polish. It featured a long oval table, comfortable chairs, and windows that overlooked the parking lot.

After discussing the status of the product, Dave turned to look my direction. "And now that our vacationing developer has returned..." He studied me for a few moments before jerking his head back. "You look tan!" he said.

The rest of the room laughed but I tried not to smile. "Well, I was in California, Dave." The beach was calling.

"Hmm...," he said, looking unconvinced. He forced a subdued chuckle. "No, no, he was there for a good reason—a wedding. Those are important things, the things we shouldn't miss." His eyes stayed on me.

Why is he still looking at me?

"Anyway, now that Kerry is back, nobody should take any *additional* vacation between now and the time we ship this sucker."

He looked away finally. "I'd also like to remind everyone of our eminent deadline. We expect this product to ship by the end of the month, the first of September at the very latest." He repositioned himself so his head rested in one hand while he wagged a finger with the other. "In fact, the product *must* ship by then because we'll be giving out copies at the Developer's Conference."

I checked the faces of the others in the room. On most I saw the same thing I was thinking: the Developer's what?

Dave must have noticed our confused looks. "Oh yes, you probably aren't all aware. The Developer's Conference is a weeklong gathering we're throwing for our users from around the globe. It will be held in downtown Toledo at the convention center. It will be their chance to see some of what we've been doing…" Dave forced a little smile. "…and to ask for their favorite enhancement, of course."

Enhancements?

Someone asked about the price.

Dave scratched his forehead. "The price is six hundred and ninety five dollars. That includes their meals, hotel accommodations, and of course, a copy of FoxPro version one point oh. We'll be handing it out on the last day of the conference."

The last day?

"But that should be no problem," Dave said. "The product will have long since shipped by then."

Chapter 8

Circus

It was noon on a Sunday and my parents and I had just returned home following morning service at our church. Even though their house, the one I grew up in, was surrounded by fields, some things were close by. My high school was only three miles away and the church was less than two.

The town of Bowling Green and college was a bit further out. It was thirteen miles northwest. Perrysburg and work was further still—a little over twenty due north.

On this day I was glad church was close, though. Too much time spent traveling would've been an unwanted distraction. I was beat.

Mom was in the kitchen preparing lunch when I entered. The kitchen and dining room were connected. They had orange countertops, medium-stained cabinets, and similarly shaded wainscoting on the walls. "What are you doing the rest of the day?" she asked.

I dropped into my usual chair beside the slightly-lopsided dinner table. The tilt was the result of an arm-wrestling match many years earlier. It was a family heirloom, though, so it wasn't going anywhere. Despite the tilt. "Sleeping," I said.

"Is my poor boy tired?" she asked without a trace of sympathy.

Dad walked into the room on his way to their bedroom. He held his suit jacket in one hand. "Well, if you guys didn't stay out so late..." He smiled. "What time did you get in?"

I shrugged. "I don't know...three?"

"Three in the morning? What were you guys doing?"

As much as I loved my parents, there were certain

disadvantages to still living at home. "Playing Balderdash," I said.

Dad paused and put a hand on the back of my chair. "In Bowling Green?"

I straightened up a little. Though most of my nights out with my friends were fairly predictable (but entertaining nevertheless), this time had an added bonus. "Yeah, we actually met some girls on campus," I said, smiling. "Three of them. We all went back to their place and played Balderdash."

"Girls?" Dad said. "Really?"

I gave a half-hearted smile, and reached back to give him a mild shove. Dad was the primary critic of my social life. He already predicted that my friends and I would be single our entire lives. He even put money on it.

Dad put up his "fighting dukes" and smiled. "So, no work today?"

I shook my head. "Nah, I was only in for a couple hours yesterday." The Report Writer was finished though—had been for some time. I spent most of my days now just testing the product. "Today, I sleep!"

The phone rang. I stood up and grabbed the receiver from the wall near me. "Hello," I said, voice cracking with fatigue.

"Hi Kerry, this is Janet."

Janet? What is this about?

Janet Walker was Fox's product manager. She essentially played the part of product nursemaid. The list of things she did during the release cycle was long. Aside from managing the beta and verifying bugs, she was frequently a member of developer meetings with Dave. Her knowledge of the product and the dBase community was extensive. If Dave was the father of FoxPro, Janet was—quite respectfully—its mother.

Janet had short dark hair, and a physique that mimicked the burden she regularly had to shoulder. Because of her position and build, I always expected her to be demanding, but she rarely was.

"What's up?" I asked.

"I need you to come in."

Come in? You've got to be kidding. "Is there something wrong with the Report Writer?"

"No," she said. "We just have a lot of bugs to fix before tomorrow."

"Whose bugs?"

"I don't know…just bugs."

"But, I didn't get much sleep last night…"

"We *really* need the help. Heindel and Chris were here most of the night."

Was that my fault? "All right," I said. "I'll be in."

I hung up the phone, and after a quick lunch, drove the *long* twenty miles to work. Heindel, Chris, and Brian Tallman were there, fixing whatever bugs were on Janet's list. My sob story about being out late got me no sympathy. So, I just worked on bugs and prayed the code I was writing in my sleep-deprived condition was halfway decent.

It was September. The product *hadn't* shipped. And the next morning was the first day of the Developer's Conference (a.k.a. DevCon).

Dave's unveiling of our product.

• • •

Monday saw us all draped in polyester, ready to attend the opening session. We slaved long and hard on the product and now had a good share of our individual egos invested in it. Everyone was curious to see how the conference attendees would view our creation.

The only exception was Sally. When I stopped by her

office, I noticed she was wearing the usual jeans and a cotton shirt.

"You're not going?" I said.

Sally shook her head. "Uh-uh. I can just see Dave when something goes wrong." She straightened in her chair. "There's something wrong with the blankity-blank Filer!" She brought her hands up and flailing them in the air. "Sally! Where's Sally? Get her up here!" She returned her hands to her lap and shook her head again. "No way. No thanks. Enjoy yourself."

I smiled and gave a little wave as I stepped back into the hall. Though Sally worked like an ox, she sometimes had the nature of a fawn. I went to join the others, who were gathering near Heindel's office. Soon we split into car-sized groups and were on our way.

When we arrived at Toledo's convention center, the conference attendees had already formed a large mob outside the room where the demo was being held. I watched the crowd press against the closed doors. They were excited, expectant.

This is wild, I thought. People are lining up to see something I worked on.

I was nervous. The feeling was akin to what parents feel the first time their child goes onstage. You're excited and proud, but also not exactly sure what's going to happen.

I saw similar feelings reflected in the eyes of the other developers. Each of us was worried our part of the product might misbehave during Dave's demo. The wait was intolerable.

The doors finally opened then, and we flowed in with the rest. Some of the more ambitious attendees raced to the front while the majority, numbering in the hundreds, silently filled in the remaining seats.

The room—a converted ballroom—was decorated in deep shades of red. In front was a stage with a computer-bearing desk placed to one side. Behind this desk was a huge projection screen. On it was the image of what a user would see when they first started our product—a menu bar and large letters that spelled out "FoxPro" on a blue background.

The developers remained near the back of the room. "There are only enough seats for the paying customers," we were told, and that didn't bother us in the least. If anything went wrong, we were close to an exit.

Dick LaValley, the company's other co-owner, took the stage. Dick was a large man with gray hair and the bearing of most farmers I knew. "I just want to welcome you all..." he said in a casual, drawn out manner. He meandered on for some time before making a quip about Fox being located in the heart of "Silicorn Valley."

Heindel stood near me. "That's my line," he whispered excitedly.

I smiled. I'd heard Heindel use the phrase before and knew he was proud of it. Perrysburg was, after all, on the edge of farm country.

The suit-wrapped Dave now mounted the stage, and after a brief greeting, seated himself at the computer. As the crowd quieted, he used the keyboard to navigate through the menus and open the "Command Window," all of which was visible to the room on the projection screen.

The FoxPro version of the Command Window was roughly 2" x 3" square, but resizable to any dimension. It hovered above the blue background surface that displayed the product's name. Functionally, whatever command was typed into the window, the product would execute. It also kept a record of all previous commands; making it simple for the user to check everything they did since starting the product.

The first command Dave entered was "USE VIDEO," a command to open one of his databases. He quickly followed this with "DISPLAY STRUCTURE," a command that caused the layout of his database, in this case "VIDEO. DBF," to list out onto the blue background. As it appeared on the big screen, the results of the command, a long stream of text, were partially obscured by the Command Window itself. The attendees were squinting to see what the command had done.

"Can you move the Command Window?" someone finally shouted.

That surprised me. I assumed most of the attendees were business people, usually a low-key, respectful lot.

Dave seemed unruffled by the request. "Oh, you want me to move the Command Window?" he said. "All right...."

He carefully waded through the menus to locate the proper item to move the Command Window. After finding it, he nudged the window over using the arrow keys on his keyboard. This brought a smattering of recognition from the audience. The output from the DISPLAY STRUCTURE command was now fully visible.

Dave clicked the window using the mouse pointer and moved it slightly. Following this—in an act worthy of a showman—he clicked the window again and shook it all over the screen. The crowd exploded with applause.

"Heh, heh, heh," Dave chortled. "Can I move the Command Window..."

From there the presentation took a turn into the surreal. What followed was somewhere between a rock concert and a pagan ritual. Heindel later said that there was "rhythmic clapping, feet stomping, and the calling for a human sacrifice..."

Dave proceeded to demonstrate nearly every facet of FoxPro. The minutest addition brought gasps and sighs from the crowd. Even a simple function we added to remove the spaces from both sides of a character string, ALLTRIM(), brought a thunderous round of applause.

Yet through it all, the developers remained tense. Each of us caught our breath as Dave demoed our part of the product, and then exhaled as he moved on—thankful our area of responsibility performed without incident, yet fearful the product would crash in the next section of code we'd written.

The worst, by any measure, was Chris. He seemed to be on the verge of a nervous breakdown. And the things he was most concerned about weren't necessarily things he worked on.

"No, Dave!" Chris yelled as Amy and Sally's file management tool was brought forward. "Not the Filer! Don't bring up the Filer!" Chris had both hands on his face, nearly shielding his eyes. "Get out of there! Get out!" He turned and paced away from our group nervously.

Over the months since I met him, I saw hints of melodrama in Chris before. But this time he was at a new level. Thankfully, the attendee commotion was loud enough to drown him out.

Chris turned around again, and after glancing toward the front, said, "He's bringing up the Report Writer."

I checked the screen and, sure enough, my child was on display. I felt confident, though. There hadn't been any problems reported with the Report Writer in quite some time. I watched as Dave put a few database fields on his report surface, and then selected the "Print Preview" menu item. The Preview window opened, giving him, and all the attendees, a glimpse of what the printed report would look like. Everything appeared to be working fine.

He tried a few other things. He drew out a rectangle, typed in some text—everything behaved as expected. Then he brought up the dialog for one of his database fields and changed its format, effectively altering how the field's data would display when it printed. When he finished with that, he previewed his changes again.

At that point, I saw something weird. Most of the display looked normal, but some of the output for the fields Dave changed looked garbled.

Oh crap, I thought. I glanced at Chris and the others, who were all still staring at the screen. I checked the exit. So near, so inviting...

I looked at the stage again. Dave, who undoubtedly noticed the misbehavior, was closing up the Report Writer and continuing on. He only had a few things left to show.

Heindel leaned my way. "What was that?"

I frowned and shrugged my shoulders. "I have nooo idea." The behavior almost didn't seem possible. The code that would exhibit the weirdness wasn't that complicated, and it got a lot of prior testing.

Of course, it was possible that by that point in the demo the product was reaching of state of "unreliability." The Report Writer wasn't the first thing that exhibited some unusual behavior. There were some weird things with the Filer and debugging tools too.

Thankfully, the crowd didn't seem to notice. When the demo finished, they rose to their feet for a standing ovation. They loved our work and couldn't wait to get their hands on it.

For a kid just out of college, it was an amazing feeling— something I wouldn't have felt if I was locked away with a mainframe somewhere.

Now, all we had to do was get the finished product in their hands.

• • •

By Thursday we knew it wasn't going to happen.

Part of the Fox Software credo was "no product shipped

with known bugs in it," and at the end of the day Thursday, everyone was still fixing bugs. Finally, Dave decided the version we gave the conference attendees would be a very, very late beta. It would be shrink-wrapped in a box like the final product, but it would really just be a beta. A work in progress.

Thursday night was a gathering at the Toledo Art Museum for the conference attendees. The developers were allowed to go as soon as the last fixable bug was out of their code. I was one of the first to be released and over the span of a couple hours everyone made it to the party.

Back at the office, a version of the product was built and left with the production group. They would work through the night to spin out 600 copies.

• • •

The following morning was the closing session. Dave took the stage with a boxed copy of FoxPro in his hands. The box was white with the outline of a fox head on it. Behind the head were six bands of color from the red part of the spectrum. A red-shifted rainbow.

After some initial comments, Dave held up the nine-pound burden and looked at it. "For those of you who were disappointed you weren't a part of our beta program..." He surveyed the audience and chuckled softly. "Well...you're about to get your chance."

He went on to explain the situation and apologize for any inconvenience it may cause.

"We think the product is really close," he said. "We'll wait on you to make the final decision."

• • •

Shortly after the conference ended our phones were ringing off the hook. Evidently, everyone ran home with their "late beta" copy of the product and immediately tried to run their favorite piece of dBase IV code.

What many of them found was in those places of the product where it was hard to emulate exactly what dBase IV did, or if we found a better way to do something from how dBase IV did, we always ignored the precise dBase IV syntax. This meant that much of their straight dBase IV code would not run without minor changes. Our workalike was more of a work-it-might.

The developers were summoned to the conference room again.

"These incompatibilities are intolerable," Dave said. "We lost our focus." He pushed his head forward and looked sternly around the table. "We should have always allowed the dBase IV syntax, even if it was in addition to what we already had."

It was difficult to hide our consternation.

Although Dave's conclusion was true—we should have allowed the additional dBase IV syntax—few of us agreed with the "we" part of his statement. Whenever any of us approached him with one of these dBase IV dilemmas, he always said we should "do what makes the most sense." Usually, what "made the most sense" was to ignore what dBase did. We were just following orders.

While I listened to Dave scold us, I started to theorize about the possible explanation for him forgetting his prior instructions. It wasn't the first time I'd seen such behavior. On more than one occasion I encountered a situation where Dave would tell me to do something, I'd go off and do the very thing he told me to do, but when I finished with what he asked, he would turn around and ask me why I did it that way.

Maybe he has one of those pods from the "Invasion of the

Body Snatchers" in his closet? One that switches with the real Dave every so often?

Regardless, we now had new marching orders. We trudged into October fixing incompatibilities in what was starting to feel like the "product that wouldn't ship."

Fortunately, since the Report Writer was a new entity, I had few incompatibilities to deal with. So, I kept myself busy fixing the random bugs on Janet's list—a task that actually wasn't too bad. I got to find and fix problems and didn't have to feel responsible for putting them there in the first place.

• • •

Around this time Fox hired another developer, a fellow named Brian Crites. Brian was engaged to marry one of our most promising technical writers, and partially to encourage her loyalty, Dave offered Brian a job. Or so I heard.

Brian was a clean-cut guy with an understated, frequently serious personality. He was about my age, and like everyone on the development team—except Marty and Sally—he graduated from BGSU. He was given an office one door down from mine, and his initial assignment was to add commands to the FoxPro language for the next version of the product, a starting point with which I was familiar.

That wasn't Brian's only form of initiation, though. Less than a month later, Dave was sitting quietly in his corner office when his wife Amy walked in.

"Brian Crites checked in an mmm.h!" she said. "What is he doing checking in an mmm.h!?"

Mmm.h was a file nearly every C source file in our project utilized. Usually the changes one would make to it were harmless—things that wouldn't affect anyone else in the group. It *did* contain some vital information, though. None of us, even the most experienced, would ever change that. I know Brian didn't.

Dave leapt to his feet in response. "Brian changed mmm.h! Well, I'll see about that." He marched the full length of developer row, passing my office, to Brian's. He swung open the door and without a word, grabbed Brian by the wrist. Heindel and another employee were present in the room.

"What?" Brian said as he was led past my office again.

Dave said nothing. He continued past Sally's office, past Chris's, past Heindel's, all the way up the chain of seniority until he reached Eric's office.

"Yes?" Eric said as Dave and Brian marched in.

Dave looked at Brian. "Brian, this is your new Mom. Don't do anything without asking him first." He then addressed Eric. "This is your new son. Watch him." He squinted for emphasis. "Carefully."

Dave left the office and turned right toward his own.

Ring leader of Fox Software's high-flying extravaganza.

Chapter 9
Fireworks

Around the beginning of October, in another FYP meeting, Dave asked which of us would like to attend Comdex. He was looking for two volunteers.

There was silence for many moments. As a junior member of the team, I assumed two of the senior members—Eric, Bill, or maybe Heindel—would go again. Last year's event certainly seemed climatic, with Ed Esber visiting our booth and all that followed. This year we were going to have a new product to show. It should be exciting shouldn't it?

The senior members stayed quiet, though. A few even groaned.

Finally Chris brought up a hand and nodded his head vigorously. That didn't surprise me much. Vegas seemed to match his personality.

"Anyone else?" Dave asked.

I looked around. No one else seemed even remotely interested. Not Marty, not Sally, nobody.

"I'll go," I said. Why not? It's a free trip to Vegas.

And anything could happen.

• • •

The airline ticket I was given a month later said that I, Kerry Nietz, was flying out for Comdex on November 11th—a Saturday afternoon. That got me there two days before the conference started on Monday. I would return the following Saturday after everything was finished.

The product still hadn't *quite* shipped, but on Wednesday

the 8th we had a version built we thought could be the one. After weeks of infrequent bug fixes, the trickle of changes had nearly ceased. The intent was to sit on this build for a couple days, see if anything major came up, and if nothing did, ship it on the final day of Comdex. This would allow us to announce FoxPro was "now shipping" while our booth was still standing.

Wednesday afternoon I recognized the top of Norm Chapman's hairless head in the lower part of my office Plexiglas. Then I heard a knock on my door.

"Hi, Kerry," Norm said, walking in.

Norm was Amy Fulton's father. He started at the company a few months before as the Vice President of Administration, or as he liked to call it, "the man in charge of everything." He was a diminutive older gentleman with glasses who usually dressed in polyester pants and a light button-down shirt. Rumor had it he was the best person to take with you if you were shopping for a car.

I returned Norm's greeting and smiled. I didn't know him well yet, but I respected him. Even if I didn't, he was a member of the owner's family. I had to be nice.

"Do you have that airline ticket we gave you?" he asked.

It was still in my desk drawer. "Yes," I said, nodding my head.

"Good, give it to me. Janet is going to be you."

I raised an eyebrow. "Huh?"

"Yeah, she needs to stay here an extra day. We're going to switch your tickets."

I reached into my drawer and took out my ticket. My name was printed clearly on the front. "Are you going to call the airlines?" I asked.

"No," he said, smiling. He took my ticket and handed me back another. "There you go. You fly out Friday with the first group." He turned as if to leave.

I glanced down at the ticket. It had "Janet Walker" printed on it. Is this legal? I looked up to see Norm's back as he left. "Can I fly on Janet's ticket?"

Norm paused, turned slightly. "Sure," he assured me. "You could be a Janet."

My eyebrow rose higher. "Okay...."

Norm made a calming motion. "It'll be fine. Don't worry about it." He then walked away.

I sniffed. Fox was managed like the owner was Scrooge McDuck. First aid supplies were under lock and key. Our office chairs were little better than sitting on rocks. Support technicians who brought me sample code illustrating bugs would wait until I copied the offending code to my machine so they could get their floppy disk back.

It was almost comical.

But under Norm's supervision the company actually got *more* frugal. He was a master at getting the better deal. Our suppliers were so squeezed they were afraid to talk to him. Norm opened all the mail that came to the upstairs offices. We suspected it was because he was looking for money.

Now I'd witnessed his act first hand. I smiled and tucked Janet's ticket into my drawer.

Anything could happen.

• • •

That night an organizational meeting was held regarding the upcoming event. Because Chris and I were new to the experience, we stayed late to attend. We were the only developers in the building. The rest of the meeting's attendees were volunteers from other groups in the company—support technicians, writers, and salespeople. Together we would help man the booth at Comdex.

Dave Fulton was there too. It wasn't unusual to find him hanging around Fox Software late in the evening. Like a captain who is most at home on the bridge of his ship, Dave seemed most comfortable within the four walls of the company's building. Important things happened there daily. It was where the key decisions were made. Where the product's course was charted. The livelihoods of over eighty employees were now dependent on him making the right decisions, on his following the best course. And on the week FoxPro was to *finally* release, Dave's feelings were undoubtedly magnified.

The Comdex meeting was relatively short, covering what our responsibilities would be, how to dress, hotel arrangements—what things *not* to say and do.

At the close, Janet Walker invited everyone to her office for a run-through of what we'd be showing. "I'm going to take them through the self-running demo," she said, looking at Chris and me. "You two probably don't need to come."

Chris and I exchanged looks and then shook our heads. We were quite familiar with the demo program because we tested with it for weeks. It was a dBase program Amy wrote to showcase FoxPro. Left unattended, it would steer a spectator through the product's important features. It could be directed to show specific portions as well. Its primary interface was a checklist of features to view, and each item could be set on or off manually. The checklist was probably the most inventive part of the program. It used our enhanced BROWSE command to present its list of items.

Janet led the rest of the group—about ten people—away to her office while Chris and I returned to his. I hovered near Chris's door chatting, but over the grey cubicles walls I could see the group at the far end of the building. Gathering closely around Janet's computer. I also noticed Dave making his way through the central aisle that ran between the two banks of cubicles, presumably to join those watching the demo.

Dave used the Demo program for testing too. You'd think *he* would've seen enough of it, as well.

I shrugged, and walked in to sit with Chris.

A short time later there was the sound of a small commotion. Then—over the fray—we could hear Dave say, "There's an internal consistency error in BROWSE!"

I looked at Chris, and stood up to peek through the Plexiglas. I could see Dave circling Janet's office like a shark. He was livid.

I turned toward Chris. His face paled and he reached for his keyboard.

I could only guess at what happened. An "Internal Consistency Error" was the severest form of error our product gave. It essentially meant FoxPro encountered something it didn't know how to deal with and couldn't continue. Shortly after this error occurred, the product terminated and anything the user was working on was lost. End of story and good night.

If it happened in BROWSE, it was probably the BROWSE the self-running demo invoked. The product we thought "ready to ship" had a very serious and blatant problem.

Dave's mantra of "There's an internal consistency error in BROWSE" continued, growing louder with each iteration, until finally he was shouting it at the top of his lungs. I saw him leave Janet's office and start marching our direction.

And he wasn't losing any steam in the coming. Four-letter words became part of his ICE chorus. Things were not good.

I ran around the desk to stand next to Chris. Safety in numbers, plus Chris was a larger target than me.

We then tried to find out who was responsible for the crash. Since the problem was in BROWSE—one of the most frequently used product features—the change would have been recent. Otherwise someone would've noticed. We made a quick scan through the day's changes.

By the time Dave tramped through the door we were fairly certain Brian Tallman was the culprit. He changed BROWSE's code that very day. Poor Brian.

"There's an Internal Consistency Error in BROWSE!" Dave said as he entered. He noticed us hovering over the computer. "Who's responsible?!"

I backed away from the desk, shuffled along the wall past Dave, and stood near the door.

"We think it's Tallman." Chris's voice was hesitant, yet even—in the manner you might use with a barking dog.

Dave hit a new level of mad. Brian's name was added to the verbal inferno, along with threats to do things to Brian's body I didn't want to imagine.

I quietly slipped away to call Brian. I had a good idea he wouldn't be home, though. It was a church night and that's where Brian would be. The phone rang six times before I gave up. Things were definitely not good.

I returned to Chris's office and stood quietly near the door. Dave stopped kicking the side of Chris's desk to turn and glower at me. "Did you reach him?" he asked.

I shook my head. "He's not there. It's Wednesday night, he's probably—"

"Do you know where he lives?"

I'd been to Brian's house once, and I hadn't been driving. "Um...not..."

"Go to his house!" Dave said. "Find him!"

I sprinted from the building to my car. I had no idea where I was going. I had no address. I had no map. There wasn't time! I drove out into a town I barely knew, looking for a house I only saw once. My only plan was to head in the general direction of Brian's neighborhood and hope for the best.

I had to find him. Things were desperate. Time was short.

After many minutes circling, I found a neighborhood that seemed familiar. I began searching for his house. I remembered a brown house and a curved roofline, so I looked for a house with those features.

Eventually I found one. It was brown. The roof was curved. Things began to click. Yeah, this is it, I thought, I know it is.

I stopped the car and ran to the door. I rang the doorbell, peered in the windows, pounded on the door, but nobody answered. The windows were dark. As certain as I was that I found the right house—I was equally certain no one was home.

Now I had to go back and tell Dave I couldn't find Brian at all.

I returned to my car and contemplated just going home, retreating to the farm. Things would get sorted out in the morning. If Dave got mad at me because I didn't return, no big deal. He was mad already.

But why risk it?

I sighed, and reluctantly, turned my car for the office again.

When I arrived, Dave was hovering near his secretary. She was doing her best to calm him down. "It'll be all right," I heard her say.

Dave only glared at the floor, shook his head, and grumbled.

My news wasn't going to help at all.

The floor squeaked and Dave looked up and saw me. "Did you find him?" he asked.

I shook my head. "He wasn't there."

Dave's face reddened. "That g** d*** Brian Tallman!" he said. "I'll burn his house down!" Things were still not good.

I didn't stay to chat. I instead went to check on Chris.

I found him alive. He looked a little flushed, though. Eyes wide.

He was still sitting at his desk, and his computer appeared to be in the process of building our product. Lines of text pausing, then scrolling up the screen.

"What happened while I was gone?" I asked.

"It wasn't good."

I saw a few books on the floor. Chris noticed my eyes and nodded his head. "Yeah, he threw them."

"Threw them?" I shook my head. Crazy. "So what did you do?"

"Called Eric. Figured out what Brian did. Backed it out." He indicated his machine. "I'm building a new version here. If it runs the demo, I'll check my changes in and start the build machine building."

I nodded. Then everything would be as good as ever. All fixed.

I looked at the fallen books again. "You did all that with the…" I fanned the air. "…flying overhead?"

He nodded his head. "It was pretty…" His eyebrows rose and the nod quickened. "Yeah. Pretty bad."

"Wow." I thanked him and headed for home.

Happy to be alive.

• • •

I stopped in to see Brian Tallman early the next morning. He was in his usual polyester pants and button-down shirt. Completely unruffled. Normal.

"Howdy, howdy," he said as I entered. "What can I do you for?" Brian had a large supply of cache phrases. I just heard two of them.

I smiled and took a seat. "So…is your house still standing?"

Brian cocked his head slightly. "Come again?"

I proceeded to describe the events of the previous night. While he listened, Brian frowned, rolled his eyes, and occasionally shook his head. "That's sad," he said finally. "Just sad."

"Yeah…" I said and stood up. "Well, just so you know…"

Brian shook his head again. "There's no reason for that." He groaned and gave a little wave. "See ya."

Later in the day I stopped by to check on him again. Nothing was ever said.

The storm had come and gone.

• • •

The next day, six of us met at the office to carpool to the airport. I rode with Norm, his wife, and one of our tech guys, a Syrian native named Bassel. The other two—our lone internal marketer Richard and a support technician named Bart—went ahead of us in another car.

"We'll take the luggage," Richard said. "No problem."

Along with everyone else, I handed over my bags—a small suitcase, a garment bag, and my carryon.

After we arrived at Detroit's airport, Norm parked in the long-term parking lot and we began our trek to the terminal. Along the way we saw the other two. I was surprised to see they were empty handed.

"Where's the luggage?" I asked when they got in range.

Richard—a balding man who always wore his jacket with the collar turned up—looked at me and shrugged. "We checked it," he said.

"Checked it?!" I exclaimed. "One of those was my carryon."

He looked at Bart and gave a little chuckle. "Sorry. We checked them. That's what we do."

Great, I thought, shaking my head. Aside from reading material, my brand new Sony Discman was in my carryon. Like many in development, I had purchased one for my office. Then I remembered something else.

"My ticket is in that bag," I said as we reached the terminal doors. I glanced at Norm. "Well, Janet's ticket, actually." I frowned. "But it's in that bag."

Norm glanced at the Northwest ticket counter, and then at Richard. "Go see if they can get the bag back."

The answer to that question was "No." The clerk at the counter just shook her head sympathetically.

Richard placed his credit card on the counter. "All right, we need to buy him another one."

Norm came up behind me. "Give me that other ticket when you get your bag in Vegas," he said and smiled. "I'll come up with something. You had a doctor's appointment or something."

I gave a half-hearted smile. "Okay...." The clerk handed me my new ticket. It had my name printed boldly on the front. I may have lost a Discman, but the flight attendant wouldn't be calling me Janet.

• • •

Vegas is a long way from Perrysburg, Ohio in more ways than can be easily counted. As unusual as it was to have a database software company in a sleepy suburb of Toledo, it seemed more unusual that the world's largest computer conference was held in Sin City. The flashing lights and glitzy shows seemed to contrast with the warm glow of a computer screen and the hum of a hard drive. But, every November, those two worlds collided in the trade show called Comdex.

As a testimony to the size of the computer industry, the

event maxed out Vegas every year. Every hotel contained booths from one computer related company after another, each booth a shrine of company wares. Every niche was represented, from video games and joysticks to mouse pads and pocket protectors. For one week only, the desert city became a geek boy's paradise.

In '89 the pavilion of the Las Vegas Hilton was reserved primarily for database products. On the central main floor, the colossal booths of Ashton-Tate, Nantucket, and WordTech dominated the landscape.

The Fox booth wasn't nearly so prominent. Down a side hallway—just a short walk from the main floor—was a 25' by 40' room for our use. Our display divided the room into two halves with cloth panels. Each side had a specific purpose. On one side were nine computers set up on square, carpeted pedestals. Booth attendants, of which I was one, used these machines to give personalized demonstrations to guests who straggled in.

The other side was arranged like a small auditorium, with about thirty seats in five rows and a stage with a projection screen and a computer. Here, Chris and Janet presented a scripted run-through of the product, one show per hour.

It was a busy week. The side of the booth I was on—the personalized demo side—was constantly crowded. Pockets of humanity swarmed around each machine from early in the morning until late in the afternoon. It was exhausting work; we had very little free time, and my feet constantly ached.

Still, it was great to see so many people had a genuine interest in our work. And occasionally, something interesting would happen.

• • •

"Hey Kerry," Janet said to me one day, toward the middle of the week. "I'd like you to meet someone." With her was a young Asian man, dressed casually.

"Yes," I said, painting on my exhibition smile. My feet were already aching. Nobody told me to buy comfortable dress shoes and the desert air had done something weird to my knees. They were sore too.

"Kerry, this gentleman worked on the Report Writer for dBase IV. He doesn't work for Ashton-Tate now, but I thought you might like to show him the product."

"Sure!" I stepped over to one of the machines. I took the former AT employee through the product, ending with a customized presentation of our Report Writer. "How many people did you work with?" I asked finally.

"On the Report Writer?" he said. "Seven." His attention was primarily focused on the screen. He couldn't see my raised eyebrows.

He glanced at me. "How about you?"

"Just me," I said. "We had seven on the whole project."

He looked at me a little longer that time, and then back at the screen. "You guys did a good job," he said, and then nodded. "A very good job."

• • •

On Chris and Janet's side of the booth, things were busy as well. By midweek the word was out on their flashy presentations, and people were starting to flock in to see them. During the busier hours, every seat was filled and standing observers spilled out into the hall. Excitement for the product filled the room.

Of the two presenters, Chris clearly had the most showmanship. His demos were great fun to watch, and regularly brought cheers and laughter from the audience. When I was in the room, he often gave me credit for the things I worked on.

One didn't have to watch too many of his presentations, however, to notice something else.

During one such session, Chris filled his demonstration screen with a number of windows—each belonging to one of FoxPro's "Desk Accessories." In general, these accessories were useful tools that were added to the product as an afterthought. They included things like a calculator, a calendar, and an ASCII chart.

"All you see here," Chris declared, indicating the screen. "I did."

Chris often had a hard time separating product-promotion from self-promotion. I was beginning to understand why his shirts were monogrammed.

• • •

The remainder of Comdex went well for the company. The crowds continued to pour in and wherever you walked, you could overhear "Fox" or "FoxPro" being mentioned. The company had made it to the big time—and to solidify that fact—FoxPro was released on Friday as planned.

With bright smiles still carved into our demo-wearied faces, we announced to all that could hear: "FoxPro is now shipping!"

FoxPro Color Support

General

A-T's implementation of colors has the following shortcomings:

- using the same color settings for their system interface as for user objects, and

- not giving users complete control over colors which are used.

FoxPro's color management facility provides users with full control of the colors used by both system and user menus, popups, windows, dialogs, alerts, etc. yet avoids the above difficulties. This is accomplished using the notions of color scheme and color set together with extensions to the COLOR clause which allow user-definable color schemes and sets.

Terminology

Here are some terms used below:

Color
: This consists of a foreground and background color. Encoding is identical to that of FoxBASE+, except blink settings will be interpreted according to the current state of SET BLINK (see below).

Color Scheme
: A color scheme consists of a set of ten colors, each specifying a foreground and background color.

Color Set
: This is a set of 24 color schemes which together describe completely how FoxPro will assign colors to objects. Different color sets may be used to utilize the capabilities (or lack thereof) of various types of display hardware (e.g. monochrome, CGA, VGA, etc.) as well as permit developer or user adjustment of the interface's appearance for aesthetic reasons.

Color sets are identified by a name up to 10 characters long which adheres to the same rules as other FoxPro language names and are stored in the FOXUSER resource file.

Color sets also contain the current state of the SET BLINK option. Therefore if a color set is defined with BLINK OFF, that will also be the state when the color set is loaded.

The attached table shows the precise manner in which each of the 10 colors making up a scheme is used in drawing various FoxPro system objects.

Color Schemes

At present, FoxPro supports simultaneous utilization of 24 different color schemes. These schemes, numbered from 1 to 24, fall into four general categories.

First page of Dave's color document

Chapter 10
Missing Pieces

FoxPro 1.0 was a very useful—and in many ways— revolutionary product, yet it still lacked some of the functionality of its rival, dBase IV. One missing component was a built in Screen Painter. Our Mac product had this type of tool since the summer of 1988, but there just wasn't time, or able bodies, to get one into the first cut of FoxPro. So, we planned to remedy that in the next version.

There are inherent similarities between a Report Writer and a Screen Painter. They are both tools with a design surface where *things* are manipulated. They both allow things to move around, have their sizes altered, and other properties changed. They both save information about these things, such as size, color, and position to a file and restore information from that same file.

There are some differences too. The types of things being manipulated are different between the two tools. In a Report Writer they are database fields, boxes, and text. In a Screen Painter this list grows to include interface elements like radio buttons, check boxes, and push buttons—also called "controls." A report is primarily intended for paper while a screen is intended to be part of an application's interface. The things in a report turn into printed data, the things in a screen ultimately interact with a user.

The similarities were the reason I was chosen to add a Screen Painter to FoxPro. "Just leverage what you learned from the Report Writer," Dave said, and that was the only initial direction I got.

It was enough, though. The parameters for FoxPro's

Screen Painter were easy to discern. It needed to have the functionality of the one Marty made for the Mac, yet live within the confines of the DOS operating system. My experience with the Report Writer gave me enough knowledge about FoxPro and its interface to do quite a bit without needing further instruction.

In fact, working with minimal guidance was almost part of the job description. When it was a feature with a high margin of flexibility, like the Screen Painter, Dave just gave us an idea about what it was supposed to do, we came up with a design, and then started coding away. Usually, we ran the gist of our design by Dave before we started coding, but sometimes not. We knew we could count on him to drop in to see how things were going as we progressed.

That's when Dave was at his best—when he had something visual to work with; something tangible he could see. The developers laid the foundation and started nailing up the boards, knowing full well the plans could change mid-construction. Rooms may be moved and walls torn down, but most of the time, the foundation stayed the same.

So, following Comdex '89, I began work on the first feature that was wholly mine. The land was clean and bare, and the plans were still mostly in my head.

And I loved it.

• • •

By the end of 1989, Fox had grown to be a fair-sized company in the sleepy town of Perrysburg. We employed over a hundred people. The bottom floor of our building was completely filled by the MIS, Accounting, and Production departments. The top floor was about one quarter full, and was occupied by Sales, Tech Support, Writing, and Development—each growing toward the center of the building from their own respective corners.

In that bustling crowd of people, though, I realized there was one face I hadn't seen in a while.

"Hey, Heindel-man," I said one day when I was in his office. I'm not sure at what point I appended "man" to Heindel's name. Somehow, it just felt right. "Where's Kevin?" I asked. I was referring to the Kevin I met my first day of employment. He and Heindel both commuted from Bowling Green and knew each other from social circles.

Heindel shrugged. "I guess he got fired."

"Fired! Really? What for?"

Heindel's shoulders rose again. "He took home some pop from the fridge. Dave heard about it. Fired him."

Kevin was a walking billboard for Fox and its products. He was also a very hard worker. I couldn't believe he was terminated for taking home a few cans of pop. "Without a warning or anything?"

Heindel frowned. "Yeah, it probably wouldn't have been a big deal," he said, "but he took home Diet Coke."

I glanced skyward and smiled. That made a little more sense. Diet Coke was Dave's favorite in the old building. Since the move he was more of a diet Vernors man, though. "Unbelievable. Kevin was the most…"

Heindel turned up a hand. "Yeah, I know. Dave fired him."

• • •

By late December much of the Screen Painter was functional. Unfortunately, the only place that Screen Painter could be *seen* was on my machine. Our network source files were in a state of limbo.

This is how the source code of FoxPro was handled normally. (…to reiterate, and expand.) On their office computers every developer had a copy of all the files needed to build the product. In addition, there was what we called a "canonical" copy of these files out on the network's file server. When a developer wanted to work on a particular part of the product, he would "check out" the files he needed and make changes to them on his computer. During that time, the files he checked out were marked as locked by him on the network, and everyone else was prevented from checking them out.

When a developer deemed his changes complete enough for the rest of development to have (minimally to the point where no one else's work would be impeded), he would "check in" the files he changed. This process would place his new versions of the files on the network. The other developers—Dave included—could run a small "update" program to pull them down and build a copy of the product with the changes included.

In practice this worked as follows: I check out a source file for the Report Writer called Report.C and make a change to it. I "compile" the file on my machine—a process that takes the human-readable source file and turns it into a machine-readable form. Another process called "linking" joins the machine-readable form with the other compiled files of the product to produce a new product with my change included. I verify the change works as I intended. When I'm certain it does, I check Report.C back into the network. Another developer, say Heindel, could "update" from the network and get my changed file. He would compile that file on his machine and build his own copy of the product with my change included.

Following the release of FoxPro 1.0, though, the typical process was suspended. It was important that a version of the source code remained identical to what the product was like when it shipped. There were several reasons for this.

First, for localization. When we created the interface, we did so using English words, and it was thus usable by Americans and others (such as Canadians, UK, Australians) with English as their native language. However, in order to sell product to those who spoke other languages, we translated the interface to those languages, such as German and Spanish, and natives of those countries had a version of FoxPro in their native tongue. This process of translating the interface to another language is called localization, and we needed to translate from the master source code for the current shipping version.

The second reason was bug fixes. The company policy, from the beginning, was to address immediately the bugs users reported, and then mail them a special build of the product with the fix included. For obvious reasons, these fixes had to be made to the master code for the current shipping version. We wanted to give them a slightly newer version of 1.0 with the fix included, not a half-finished version of 2.0 with the fix— and a ton of additional bugs.

So, the canonical sources of FoxPro 1.0 were restricted; a file could only be checked in if it was a bug fix or was necessary for localization. As the weeks following 1.0's release went by, though, fewer and fewer of us were working on those issues. Most of us were busy adding features for the next release of the product, FoxPro 2.0.

There were no official "canonical" sources for 2.0 yet, though. The job of creating a new network source tree was a huge undertaking, and those that knew anything about it— Chris and Heindel—were otherwise occupied.

So for months, those of us doing 2.0 work made whatever changes we needed to make *only* to the copy of the 1.0 sources that resided on our personal machines. This allowed us to proceed with our new development work, while keeping in step with any 1.0 bug fixes that came along.

There were dangers to this though. The developer who didn't keep a careful backup of his work ran the risk of losing it if his machine died. (A tragic circumstance, but one you could only blame yourself for.)

In addition, there were many instances where one might have a file checked out for new development work and another developer might suddenly need that same file for a 1.0 bug fix. In that case, the first developer was obliged to undo his check-out for that file without checking in his changes. We called this process "going rogue" and the altered version on the first developer's machine became a "rogue" version. From then on, the rogue file didn't play well with the whole updating process, and if you weren't careful, your changes might get inadvertently overwritten when the second guy checked his bug fix back in. A major pain.

Aside from all that, though, there was another reason the code's limbo state was starting to annoy me. Since the only functioning Screen Painter was on my machine, Dave became a regular visitor to my office. This was fine initially, because I was usually happy with my latest change and glad to show it to someone.

But by December, he started bringing random people with him, many of whom were company visitors he was trying to impress. This created pressure for me to have something in a demonstrable condition at all times, and that wasn't easy. It's difficult to *always* have a product to show when you're also making changes to it.

Other developers ran into the same situation, and solved the problem by setting aside a demonstrable version every day that could be whipped out at a moment's notice. I never thought of that. I was too busy trying to make forward progress.

I was frequently caught with my product's pants down, so to speak.

It usually went like this:

The door swings open and Dave's body frames the doorway. Behind him is...someone...

"Yeah, Dave, what's up?" I just made a change and my version of the product just finished compiling. I'm working on adding a new control to the Screen Painter. There are about five different parts to the process. Add code to internally create the control, add code to draw it, a dialog for the user to specify details on the control, code to save information about the control to the disk, and code to retrieve that information. I like to complete them one at a time. I just added the code to create the control. At least, I think I did.

"This is Leroy Davidson," Dave says. "I want you to show him the Screen Painter."

The person with Dave is someone I've never seen before, and will probably never see again. He looks excited about seeing something new. Something other people haven't seen. Something from the inside. He's probably someone Dave is trying to impress.

"Okay...." I reach for my keyboard and type "F-O-X-P-R-O."

The two of them move close to my chair. There's a hint of excitement in the room. Dave has his hands in his pockets. His pocket change jingles.

The product starts up. A good sign. In the command window I type "CREA SCRE". That's short for "Create Screen"—the command that brings up the Screen Painter.

"Ah yes," Dave says, "here comes the Screen Painter now..." Both he and the visitor lean in expectantly.

The window for the Screen Painter opens. Then, less than a nanosecond later, my machine is back at the DOS prompt. The product has quit. Abnormally. Apparently, I broke something. Bad. Maybe a few more pieces of the puzzle need to be in place.

Nobody says anything for a time. "Um...shoot," I say. "I was in the middle of adding something..."

"I see..." Dave's face is expressionless. The visitor's eyes move between Dave and the screen. Both faces say "Can't you fix it?" but I hear only silence.

"Sorry," I say. "Maybe if I..."

Dave starts to move around my desk slowly, reluctantly. I embarrassed him. The visitor follows him out. He looks back at me once, disappointed.

I'm grateful when the door closes.

• • •

In January, I was finally given the news I was waiting for.

"Chris and I are going to split the sources tonight," Heindel said with a smile.

"Yes!" I said, lifting both hands in the air.

That night, after everyone went home, the two of them "split the sources." This meant they took the 1.0 source files on the network and created an additional (duplicate) set of sources. This second set would be used as the work-in-progress sources for 2.0, while the initial set would stay as a "frozen" version that reflected the product's state when 1.0 shipped.

When they finished, they performed the same operation on everyone else's machines and started them building. The entire process took them until two o'clock in the morning.

The next day the fresh 2.0 sources were open for check-ins.

• • •

Two days later, after everyone else checked in the changes they were holding, I was ready to put my Screen Painter out. I came into the office early and looked over everything I'd done. After assuring myself all was good, I circled around to the developers' offices telling all who were present that I was about to put a big change out and to "not update unless you mean it."

This last step was important because I made changes that would cause every source file in the product to compile, a process that could take hours. A person who unknowingly updated and got such a change (what we called a "destructive" change) would sit for a long time waiting for their machine to finish. Since such changes routinely happened during the course of the day, many of us didn't update until we were ready to go home for the night. Still, to be on the safe side, I warned everyone I could. I returned to my office and spent thirty minutes checking in my stuff.

An hour later, Dave stopped me outside of Chris's office.

"I saw you put out a change this morning that causes everything to be recompiled," Dave said, his face unreadable.

I made the turn toward my office. Two thin cubical walls now separated us. I was happy that my changes, some twenty or thirty files, were finally safe on the network. I accomplished a lot in two months. Now anyone could see what I'd done. Or, in Dave's case, demo it to visitors. "Yeah, I put the Screen Painter changes out…"

Dave's face reddened. He stopped and hooked an elbow over the side of one cubicle. "You should've coordinated your check-in with what Chris and Heindel did."

I took a step back. I can't believe he's mad about this…

Unfortunately, Dave was the one person who didn't

update only before he went home. He would update and build constantly throughout the day in order to be *right on top* of changes as they were made. This habit came with many risks. One was that he would update while a developer was in the middle of putting out their changes. He'd get only half of what he was supposed to and then be mad because *something* didn't work right.

The other drawback was the destructive change. He'd get something that caused all his files to compile, and for some reason (perhaps because he feared everyone else was waiting too) this situation really ticked Dave off. It was part of the reason he dragged a naïve Brian Crites to Eric's office and made Eric his new "Mom."

Brian walked a tight line with the network sources following that experience. Apparently, so should have I.

Still, Dave had been anxious to get my changes before. Maybe if I explain. "That was two days ago," I said.

Dave pushed away from the cubicle wall, becoming this angry disembodied head. "That doesn't matter," he said. "You should've worked with them."

I turned slightly, wanting to run. "But they were here until two in the morning."

He wasn't listening. "It should've been coordinated!"

I frowned. There were no rules or guidelines about coordinating check-ins. I probably could have worked something out with Chris and Heindel, *if* I wanted to complicate all our lives further. Dave was just hacked off because there was another large compile. He was being unreasonable.

"Okay…," I said. "Sorry." I wasn't really, though. I was just confused.

I took the remaining steps to my office, essentially ending the conversation. Nothing I could say would've mattered, anyway. Dave was mad, he found someone to blame, and just let them have it. This time, I was the guy.

Ever since the infamous "Internal Consistency Error in Browse" incident before Comdex Dave seemed more intense, more demanding. It was as if he was losing touch with how hard it was to write solid code. Little by little, he was becoming more of a manager and less a developer. Less one of us. Others noticed the change too.

This scolding was the hardest, though. It marked the beginning of a new phase of my existence—one with a recurring cycle. Dave would chew me out for some inexplicable reason. I retreated to my office and tried to return to work. Instead of working, I would contemplate how nice it might be to work somewhere else. My contemplation would continue for some time, but before the end of the day, I would convince myself to stay.

There were many reasons to stick with it. The work was interesting, and there weren't too many opportunities for similar work in northwest Ohio. The pay was decent, especially for the area of the country where I lived. I was close to my friends and family...

Any other workplace would be missing one of those things.

But, most of all, I felt like Fox was the place I was supposed to be.

• • •

A few weeks later Chris swung open my door, tossed a couple sheets of paper on my desk, and then acted like he was going to leave again.

"What's this?" I reached for the paper. Whatever it was, it had a lot of text on it. The sheet looked almost full.

"Just FYI," Chris said. "A resume for someone Dave's interviewing today." He stood in the doorway with a hand on the doorknob and the lower part of his body still out in the hall. He clearly had other places to be.

"Really?" An interview with Dave was always big news. I glanced at the first page. The name on the top was "Dave McClanahan." Has the quota on Daves been raised? We already had about a half dozen. "What's he interviewing for?"

Chris already had the door partway closed, but reluctantly reopened it. "Developer..." He frowned. "Listen, I have to circulate the rest of these. I'll be back." He straightened back into the hall and closed the door.

I looked at the resume. It was two pages single-spaced. It brimmed with facts on the candidate's knowledge and experience. I also noticed a few spelling and grammar errors. It violated everything I was taught about writing resumes.

Chris returned. "Any more questions?"

"What's he going to work on?" Aside from the Screen Painter, there were other key dBase IV features that still weren't a part of FoxPro. Most of those were spoken for already, though.

Chris paced into the room. "SQL," he said.

That made sense. SQL, or Structured Query Language, was a set of commands that allow for the definition, control, and manipulation of data in tables. It was also something of an industry standard. The perceived advantage was that no matter what product was used to manage a given database, the same SQL commands could be used to retrieve data from it.

I nodded my head and glanced down at the resume again. "It looks like he has a lot of experience... he has a PhD?"

Chris widened his eyes and nodded his head quickly. "Yes, that's the kind of person Dave wants. He decided not to hire any more kids fresh outta college for a while."

Huh? I raised an eyebrow.

Chris's tone changed. "Well, not that those haven't worked out before...it's just for SQL he feels we need an expert."

"Oh." I frowned slightly. Chris was not helping me feel secure. I was the only recent college grad who'd been in trouble recently. Was I to blame for our change in hiring standards?

Chris walked back toward the door. "I better go. See ya."

McClanahan was hired that same day. Short and timid, his appearance was similar to Willy Tanner, the befuddled father from the TV show *Alf*. He had a strong theoretical view of programming, and as soon as he had an office, he was concealed within, filling his whiteboard with hieroglyphic symbols, and typing away frantically.

I didn't understand any of it, but I was just one of those college kids.

The kind we weren't going to hire anymore.

Object-Oriented FoxPro

Introduction

This document describes the proposed addition of object-oriented features to FoxPro. The goal of this proposal is to allow programmer access to all of the FoxPro interface.

This document focuses on the dialog-like elements and menus. However, it provides a common method to access MODIFY FILE/COMMAND windows, BROWSE sessions, report and label writer sessions, as well as menus and dialog elements.

Perhaps the most important part of the scheme presented here is that it merges with the existing language, it does not require replacement of existing constructs. Therefore, existing programs will not be broken and existing programmer techniques need only to be augmented, not replaced.

The model chosen for these additions is based on industry standard object-oriented language terminology and concepts. Wherever possible the terms and concepts presented are exactly those used in OOP systems.

This document begins by defining the necessary concepts and concludes with complete syntax and semantics for the language enhancements. This document does NOT discuss the Interface Builder or Code Generator, as they will just be natural extensions and interfaces to these concepts.

Object Concepts

Objects, in the context of this proposal, are interface elements, such as text edit fields, push buttons, etc. Formally objects are defined as being made up of either atomic objects or group objects. Group objects can consist of any combination of atomic objects and other group objects so long as the definition is not self-referential.

Atomic Objects

The currently available atomic objects are:

- Static text
- Editable text
- Push buttons
- Check boxes
- Radio buttons
- Popup menus (as currently used in dialogs)
- Scrollable lists (both single and multiple selection)
- Graphic items (initially boxes, later pictures and ...)
- User-defined objects

These objects will be discussed in detail in the sections ahead.

First page of the infamous OOF document

Chapter 11
Objects

Dave stopped me in the hall outside my office. His hands were buried in his pants pockets, change jingling incessantly. "Just wanted to give you a head's up. I've got Chris and Heindel working on a proposal for some changes to the language that will affect you."

"Oh?" I opened the door to my office and walked in.

Dave followed. "Yes, we're looking at adding some language extensions to FoxPro."

I nodded my head slowly and circled around to sit at my desk. It felt more comfortable to have my chest partially concealed by the bulk of my monitor. "What sort of extensions?" I asked.

"Some 'Object-Oriented' extensions."

I nodded my head again. The expression "Object-Oriented" was the catch phrase of the industry. Every magazine was touting the benefits of some amazing new product with "Object-Orientation" built in. I had no idea what being "Object Oriented" really meant, though. And from some of the articles I read, I wasn't sure the journalist knew either.

So how does this affect me?

"We're also hoping to remove some of the redundancy in our code," Dave said. "Like in the Dialog Manager and READ, for instance."

That part I understood. There were portions of our product doing similar things, but using disparate sections of code. The Dialog Manager and the READ command were prime examples. Both had code to manage the interaction between controls.

Redundancy in code was undesirable for the same reasons two separate engines were undesirable in a car. It made the final product bigger, there were more parts that could fail—and therefore more to test—and there were no guarantees the two engines (or code) would work in harmony with each other.

I still wasn't sure how the language changes would affect me, though.

Standing just inside my office, Dave glanced to the right and spotted the poster that hung there. It was of two bikini-clad women.

"Eric and Heindel hung that up," I said quickly. "I guess they think it's funny." Taking a shot at the single guy.

Dave studied the poster for a moment. "Ah…Skippy, Skippy…" he said softly.

Skippy was the name used for Eric during his impish moments. His usual trick was putting two fingers up behind people's head. He branched out with the bikini poster.

Heindel helped, of course.

Dave gave a little clucking sound. "Obviously virgins," he said to the poster. He turned to look at me again. "Anyway, you should keep abreast of what those two are doing."

Chris and Heindel, I assumed. "Okay…"

Dave bounced his way through the doorway to the hall. "Yes. The Screen Painter will have to support whatever they come up with."

Ah. Now I see.

• • •

By February the Screen Painter was essentially complete. As Marty had done years earlier on the Mac product, I created a tool allowing users to visually construct an input screen. Functionally it would play the same role as his Mac version.

Coupled with a yet-to-be-written "generator" program, it would make building database applications a snap.

In appearance, however, my Screen Painter was quite different from Marty's. No cutesy palette of pictures ran down the left side of its design surface, nor were there any dotted grid lines to help with the placement of controls. Instead, my design surface was solid blue and it had a utilitarian status bar in the upper left corner that gave the position of the cursor (the spot where controls could be placed).

As a part of our DOS product, my Screen Painter had to deal with the inherent restrictions of that character-based environment. It couldn't have as nice an interface, nor allow for the cool graphic elements (like pictures) common to the Mac. It was just as usable, though, and completely my own.

Meanwhile, Chris and Heindel toiled away on a document to describe the new "Object-Oriented FoxPro" (or "OOF"). Their work was now essential because I couldn't really call the Screen Painter finished until it supported whatever new language syntax they created. I *thought* it was done, but it was only with respect to the way FoxPro 1.0 defined an interface. Their new OOF document could change all that. I might even have to abandon everything and start over.

In the meantime, there was nothing specific for me to do. Dave told me to spend my time mapping out the changes to the Screen Painter that would be necessary for Chris and Heindel's new syntax. That was hopeless, though, because their syntax was changing by the day. As confident as Chris and Heindel were they'd have *something* great to show us, even *they* thought it was a waste of time to try to design based on speculation. So, I continued to wait—almost to the point of distraction.

Eventually I started to tinker with things, rolling my own features for the Report Writer and Screen Painter and adding them without discussing them with anyone. I added a "marquee" that let the user select more than one object at a time. I made it easier to increase and decrease portions of the Report Writer's surface (the "bands"). I added an auto-scroll feature that would scroll the screen if the user dragged an object beyond the screen's boundaries—something even the Mac Screen Painter didn't do yet.

I spent more than a month adding things I thought were useful and no one told me to stop. Everyone was so involved with their own projects, they never noticed.

So, I stayed out of sight, and kept adding stuff.

• • •

Finally the day arrived when Chris and Heindel were ready to unveil their "Object-Oriented FoxPro" document. The bulk of the development team was summoned to Dave's office and given a copy of the text. It was about twenty-five pages long and described in detail how nearly everything in FoxPro—menus, windows, controls, and the like—would be defined and manipulated as an object.

In my mind, the primary weakness with their new syntax was obvious. It was extremely wordy. In the current version of the language, the code to define a single push button took only one line. Like so:

```
@ 0, 0 GET ok FUNCTION '* OK'
```

Using the "Object Oriented" syntax, though, a push button definition took at least five lines. It went something like this:

```
DEFINE PUSHBUTTON ok;
```

```
FROM 0, 0;
TO 0, 10;
PROMPT 'OK'
DEFAULT;
```

The problem multiplied if you wanted to create a group of buttons. (And buttons were commonly presented in groups).

A group of two buttons in the current language:

```
@ 0, 0 GET okcancel FUNCTION '* OK;Cancel'
```

But in the "Object Oriented" syntax, a group of buttons looked like this:

```
DEFINE GROUP okcancel AT 0, 0
    DEFINE PUSHBUTTON ok;
        FROM 0, 0;
        TO 0, 10;
        PROMPT 'OK'
        DEFAULT;
    DEFINE PUSHBUTTON cancel;
        FROM 2, 0;
        TO 2, 10;
        PROMPT 'CANCEL'
        ESCAPE;
```

It meant more typing for our users, and more complexity for our generator program. That seemed like a big drawback to me.

On the other hand, there was a certain descriptiveness to the OOF syntax that I liked. It was easy to tell what it was you were defining. In addition, the new syntax for controls was very similar to the way menus were defined in our product already.

Of course, our users already complained that our menu

syntax was too wordy...

The wordiness issue didn't get much talk at the meeting, though. Instead, someone (usually Dave) got hung up on an apparent trifle and we would discuss it to death. The worst instance, by far, was when we spent the better part of an hour debating whether the syntax for the command to initiate an object-oriented interface should be "Activate" or "Execute."

I should have stayed on the farm.

Finally, after we frittered away most of the morning, Dave reached a decision. "While I'm pleased with the work Chris and Heindel have done," he said, "I think it needs Amy's touch to smooth out the rough edges."

Then the meeting adjourned.

I followed Chris back to his office, and Heindel came too. Chris was clearly not happy. Whispered expletives escaped his lips.

"What's wrong?" I asked. "You just got out of work."

Chris eyes weren't blinking. He looked at Heindel and flipped his hands up. "I can't believe that."

Heindel took a seat and slid down slightly. "That's fine," he said, sounding ambivalent. "If Dave wants to give it to Amy, that's fine."

At least *he* seemed pleased. I couldn't get anything more from Chris, though. So, with a last look at Heindel, I shrugged and walked next door to Sally's office.

Sally always worked with her back to the door. When she heard me, she turned and smiled. "That was great!" she said.

I returned the smile, not completely sure why we were smiling. "Well, Chris isn't happy."

"Of course not."

Sally was more of a student of human relations than I. And having worked with Chris for years—even before joining Fox—she did a good job of being his barometer. "Why do you say that?" I asked.

"Chris hates it when someone takes credit for his work," she said. "*Hates* it!"

I nodded my head. So…even though Chris might give someone the impression he worked on something he hadn't, if someone took recognition for *his* work…

"And the fact that it was *Amy*," Sally continued, "makes it all the worse."

If there was a hierarchy to the development staff, it flowed mostly along seniority lines, with Sally and I somewhere in the middle and Chris probably just ahead of us. Amy held the top spot, though. As the spouse of the boss she had unrivaled power and we all knew it. She was adept at both cooling Dave off when he was upset, and heating him up over a seemingly trivial matter—Eric's forced adoption of Brian Crites was a good example.

And because of her special position, Amy had her share of perks. She took days off whenever she wanted, even when we were close to a product release. She was responsible for less of the product than most of us, and in general, the parts that *were* hers weren't as "mission critical."

Amy also had a certain aloofness to her personality that didn't help. She hardly left her office during a normal workday—and when she did—it was rarely to speak with the rest of us. So, even though she was part of the development team, it never really felt like it.

Amy's detachment was evident in her work. The coding style she used in her areas of responsibility was different from the rest of the product, and the way those areas behaved was often different as well. It was as if she never bothered to see how anything else worked. She just did things the way she wanted and left it at that.

Furthermore, her connection to Dave just complicated

things. I liked her as an individual. She was always pleasant to me, and I found her more sympathetic and rational than her spouse. I still limited my interaction with her, though, for fear of gaining more of Dave's attention. I got an ample portion of *that* already.

Now Amy was in charge of a document that was supposed to change everything.

• • •

Nearly two weeks later Dave called us to the conference room to discuss Amy's revisions.

I was overjoyed. Since the OOF handoff, I was *supposed* to be designing dialogs for the Screen Painter using Chris and Heindel's version of the syntax. What it amounted to was more time coming up with things to do. Consequently, the list of creative additions to the Report Writer and Screen Painter grew.

Finally, some direction in my life.

We took our seats around the large oval table, each with a copy of the current OOF document clutched tightly in our hands.

Legs crossed and looking casual, Dave glanced around the room. "Okay, is everyone here?"

Heindel, Chris, Amy, Marty, Sally, and myself. Yep, everyone who cared was present.

Dave raised his copy of the OOF document slightly. "I've looked over this document, and let me tell you, I think it's a great piece of work. Once again, many thanks to Chris, Amy, and Heindel for their efforts. You've pulled off a virtuoso stunt."

He placed the document on the table slowly. Tapped it twice. "However...after a little talk with Marty this morning, I made a decision." He paused and gave a nearly straight-line smile. "I decided we aren't going to do it."

What? I looked around the room—all eyes mirrored my surprise.

The dragster had turned.

Dave put a hand on the back of his head, a posture he frequently took. "Marty had a lot of good points, but his best point was this—if it is so hard to spec this object stuff, how are we going to explain it to our customers?" Dave became more animated. "We spent what?—the better part of two months—trying to come up with this thing and we're still not sure how it is all going to work. I'd hate to be in Tech Support trying to explain it after we've finally figure it out."

He shook his head. "No. We just can't do that," he said. "I appreciate everyone's work, but we just can't do that." Dave frowned. "This product is complicated enough already."

I couldn't believe it. Somehow, Marty talked Dave out of the whole thing. I tried to contain a smile. The Report Writer and Screen Painter were essentially done; all they needed was a little fine-tuning and a little more testing and they were ready to go out the door. It should be smooth sailing from here.

Right?

• • •

A few days after the final OOF meeting, I called the desk of one of our receptionists, named Denise. A few months earlier we started dating. When I needed a break from adding my "home rolled" features to the Screen Painter, I often called her desk. A sympathetic female voice was a welcome diversion to the life I now lived.

Another receptionist answered the phone, though.

"Oh…sorry," I said, not giving my name. Sometimes the

receptionists switched desks—I figured this was one of those times. I started to place the phone back on its cradle.

"Is this Kerry?" the receptionist asked, now a little distance from my ear.

When I admitted it was, she proceeded to tell me that Denise was fired the day before.

"What?" I felt my stomach begin to turn. "Why?"

"I don't think it was about you," she said. "She had problems with our boss." There was a short pause. "I'm pretty sure it wasn't about you."

The pain in my stomach grew. Assurances aside, it very well *could* have been about me. Many of the non-development employees at Fox had the same uneasiness around developers as we had around Amy. Sally suspected this was an encouraged behavior, though certainly not by development. It seemed like management was telling the new hires to treat us like royalty.

I gleaned what more I could, and then hung up the phone. No sooner did my hand leave the receiver than there was a knock on my office door. I glanced up (through the Plexiglas) to see the top of Amy's head.

Amy *never* came to my office.

This is it then, I thought.

Amy walked in and shut the door. "Kerry," she said softly, "I'm just here to tell you that Denise was fired yesterday."

"Oh?" I said, frowning. I wonder what Carol Garrison is doing now...

"I also wanted to assure you that it has nothing to do with you," Amy continued. "Denise had some tardiness issues." Amy smiled pleasantly. "Your job is as safe as ever. You're not next on the hanging list."

"Okay," I said. "Thanks." I was sure I'd heard that speech somewhere before, though.

Amy left and I felt my pulse begin to normalize.

Concerned, I tried to call Denise at home. What I heard shortly after her "Hello" was the dial tone again.

I shrugged and returned to my machine.

So much for dating girls from the office.

• • •

As it turned out—in a separate meeting with Heindel—Dave made a decision that created additional work for me. It was decided my Screen Painter would no longer create a special file to be used by a template generator (like the CodeGen program used previously in the Mac product) to generate code. Instead—Heindel proposed—the Screen Painter could simply create a database file and the FoxPro language itself would serve as the new "template" language.

Why did we need *two* languages in the product, really?

It was an idea so straightforward and elegant we were amazed it wasn't thought of before. Everyone loved it, and Heindel and I soon got busy implementing it. My part was to switch my tools from writing out the tab-delimited files required for CodeGen to writing out database files instead.

This would be the last change, though. Then I'd finally be ready to ship.

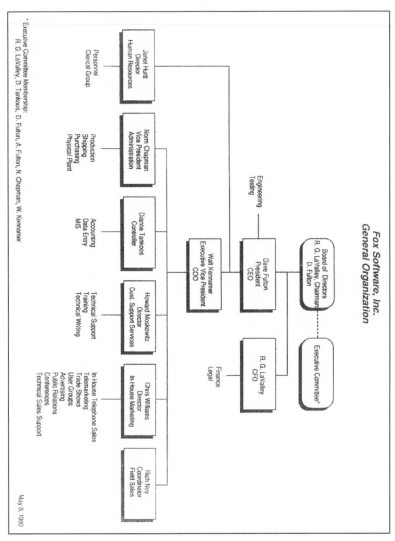

Fox Software, Inc.
General Organization

Board of Directors
R. G. LaValley, Chairman
D. Fulton

Executive Committee*

Dave Fulton
President
CEO

R. G. LaValley
CFO

Finance
Legal

Walt Kennamer
Executive Vice President
COO

Engineering
Testing

Janet Hurtt
Director
Human Resources

Personnel
Clerical Group

Norm Chapman
Vice President
Administration

Production
Shipping
Purchasing
Physical Plant

Dianne Tankoos
Controller

Accounting
Data Entry
MIS

Howard Moskowitz
Director
Cust. Support Services

Technical Support
Training
Technical Writing

Chris Williams
Director
In-House Marketing

In-House Telephone Sales
Telemarketing
Trade Shows
User Groups
Advertising
Public Relations
Conferences
Technical Sales Support

Rich Ney
Coordinator
Field Sales

* Executive Committee Membership:
R. G. LaValley, D. Tankoos, D. Fulton, A. Fulton, N. Chapman, W. Kennamer

May 8, 1990

Org chart (May 1990)

156

Chapter 12
Marketing Effects

In the spring of 1990, Dave conducted an interview in his office. Joining him around the table were some of the more senior members of the team—Amy, Eric, and Chris. The person to be interviewed was another graduate of Bowling Green, a master's student this time.

Her name was Gloria and she exuded competence and intelligence. Dark hair, glasses, immaculately dressed. Dave briefed his fellow interviewers ahead of time that they probably should hire her. They still weren't quite sure where she fit, though. She took some programming courses, but that didn't seem to be her area of expertise *or* preference. She had business experience as well...

Perhaps sales or technical support?

The interviewers peppered Gloria with questions for well over thirty minutes—and at times, she reciprocated. Then she found a subject that surprised everyone.

"So, tell me about your marketing department," she said.

Dave—who sat cross-legged with his coffee cup resting on one knee—shot a quick glance at the others, and then exploded into laughter. "Marketing department?" he said. "You want to know about our Marketing department!"

His laughter grew until his coffee finally shook free of the cup, spilling down his shirt and pants. "Sh**!" Dave exclaimed. "Sh**!"

• • •

Prior to May of 1990, the marketing department of Fox

Software was virtually non-existent, and management was fine with that. The company sold its product entirely by word-of-mouth and the positive press received from magazine reviews. The prevailing opinion was that our products were good enough to sell themselves, they were selling just fine, so why let marketing screw that up? In fact, our in-house "Marketing Department" consisted of one person, a thirty-something man named Richard.

Richard was a friend of the LaValley family, and Dave barely masked his disdain of him. There were multiple reasons for Dave's feelings, but Richard's profession as a "marketer" was at least one strike against him.

Another strike was doubtless Richard's connection to the LaValley family. Over time, I noticed a strange, often-antagonistic rapport between the two ownership families. Every other week or so, I would see Dave and Mr. LaValley chatting amicably in Dave's office. But, in lunch conversations, I'd hear Eric or Bill marionette that LaValley was a "bottom-feeder" or warn that "the company would soon be knee-deep in LaValley's" and I'd wonder.

I saw anti-LaValley sentiment in Dave too. It was obvious he didn't think much of our company payroll clerk, one of Dick LaValley's daughters. Dave once bounced three rigid juggling balls hard into his floor because she did something to anger him...and her office was directly below his.

It made me wonder how the partnership originally came to be.

In addition, Richard had at least one character flaw that was certain to get him into trouble. He suffered from a terminal case of "hoof in mouth disease." I witnessed that condition first hand.

After lunch one day, I went to the upper floor men's room. The facilities of the room were typical. Aside from a sink and a mirror, there were two stalls and two urinals, a sufficient quantity for the forty-plus men with offices upstairs.

The room had an additional bit of discomfort over most restrooms, though. Originally designed to have just one urinal, at some point late in construction the builders ripped out the one urinal and crammed two into the same spot. These remaining urinals were so close together that two people intending to use them would have to stand touching shoulders. It added a new dimension to an already uncomfortable situation.

I tried to avoid using the upstairs urinals.

In this instance, I had no need to. I was there to brush my teeth. While I stood at the sink, Heindel and "Marketing" Richard came in. Since both required a urinal, they went through the usual exercise of relieving themselves—side by side and shoulder to shoulder.

Heindel finished first and turned to pry himself free. "Sorry Richard," he said. "I hope I didn't mess you up there."

Richard laughed. "No, no, I'm okay," he said. "But if you think *that's* funny, you should've seen the time Dave and Chris were in here. I thought those two would never get unstuck!"

Still brushing, all I could do was grin at the joke. Both Chris and Dave were men of considerable girth. That *must* have been tough.

Richard and Heindel continued laughing as they washed and left the room.

I emptied my mouth and glanced up into the mirror. I could see the door of the stall behind me, and through the crack I noticed the shadowed edge of someone sitting within.

Who is that?

Whoever it was, they hadn't said a thing during Richard and Heindel's conversation. I bent forward to wash my hands and glanced back at the crack again. I could just make out the shine of a bald head.

There were scant few balding men on the Fox staff. Norm Chapman was one, but his head was squat, angular, and slightly colored with age. This head was none of that. It was round and consistently white. It was one I saw nearly every day of my development life.

It's Dave! He's been here the entire time!

I quickly collected my things and returned to my office, which was directly opposite the restroom on the far side of the building. From there I watched for Dave to leave through my office Plexiglas. When he finally came out, he had a mischievous little grin on his face.

In that instant, I was glad I wasn't Richard.

• • •

Despite Marketing being a perpetual joke, management apparently realized that state couldn't last forever. The push to create an internal marketing team began, and the position of "Director of In-house Marketing" was created to lead it. The biggest surprise came, though, when we heard who was chosen to fill that position.

"He'll be back," Sally said, shaking her head and smiling. "This is just like him."

"Why's that?" I asked. We'd just learned that Chris was going to take the new Director position. Even though it was unexpected, it seemed like a good move for him.

"The grass is always greener with Chris. He'll be back, trust me."

I shrugged. "We'll see…"

For the first time, we were going to have a real marketing department, and Chris was going to lead it. I had no idea how any of it would affect the company as a whole, but mostly, I hoped it wouldn't affect me too much.

• • •

Chris's first marketing event—"the Fox Reunion"—occurred in late June. It took place over a long weekend and was an event to which only Fox "gurus" were invited. "Gurus" were a small subset of the dBase community who were recognized as its most outspoken leaders. Many of the names were familiar to me now—Tom Rettig, Adam Green, Pat Adams, and so on—but I had only met a few of them. This Reunion was another chance for Fox to learn what users needed from our product.

It seemed strange to me to ask what people wanted from FoxPro 2.0 eight months after we started working on it. We already made significant additions—many of which derived straight from users' requests. Shouldn't that be enough?

Optimistically, if we tied up everything we started and fully debugged the new code, we could get the product out by the end of the year. We'd then have a shipping product that offered everything dBase IV did, a complete work alike, and could worry about moving ahead from there.

Dave and the new Marketing department didn't see it that way, though. As the Fox Reunion commenced, my singular wish was that the features it brought would either be trivial, or things that could be postponed for a later version of the product.

• • •

The Monday following the Reunion, Dave summoned me to his office. He was conspicuously gleeful. Feet up on his desk, he smiled brightly as I entered. "Ah, my young friend," he said, "you are going to *love* what I have in store for you." He cackled then—a sinister sound.

Janet, who sat in front of his desk, just smiled softly. She clutched some papers in her hand. She was always carrying a list of…something.

I frowned. The Screen Painter was finished and I had nothing specific left to do, aside from testing. If we let that be, I *could* help finish other parts of the product.

Dave placed his hands behind his head. "Read the list, Janet."

She bowed over her papers. "They want an easy way to create menus."

Dave nodded. "Creating menus is egregiously complicated," he said. "Kerry will do that."

Janet glanced at me, wrote something down, and then squinted at her list. "They want more control over the way information in groups in the Report Writer spans over page boundaries."

Dave wagged a finger. "Ah, yes, that's a good one. The ole Widow-Orphan effect. We need to do something about that." Another nod. "Kerry will take care of that."

The Widow-Orphan what? I frowned deeper. What's *this* all about?

Janet consulted the list again. "They want to have multiple windows interacting in READ." She glanced at Dave. "That's probably a Heindel thing, though…"

"Multiple windows in READ?" Dave stretched back on his chair, looked pensive. "That makes sense, I guess." He thought for a full minute. "Yes, I could see why they'd want that." He smiled, looked at me, and then turning to Janet, spoke seriously. "Kerry will do that too."

What the…? Was the sole purpose of this event to find work for me?

And READ had *always* been Heindel's thing.

I started to panic. "I don't know anything about READ."

Dave cackled. "I know, but Heindel's busy adding generator commands. It would be good for someone else to know what's going on with that READ code."

"Okay…" I said, but I wasn't really.

"That's all for now," Dave said, waving me away. "Let me know when I can test it." He laughed as I stood and made my way to the door.

I returned to my office, feeling ill.

• • •

Of these requests, the most burning issues for Dave were the Report Writer changes, so shortly after I recovered from my shock, he called Marty and I back to his office.

Put simply, the gurus' problem was that sometimes they didn't get all the information together on the same printed page as they liked. The problem stemmed from the use of two special purpose bands called "Group" bands. Unlike other bands that printed continually throughout the life of the report (e.g. The "Page Header" printed at the top of each page and the "Page Footer" printed at the bottom) *Group* bands only printed if the value of a specific condition—specified by the user—changed.

A common grouping condition might be "State". The effect on a report with that condition would be every time the value of the database field "State" changed, the information in the Group Footer would print (closing out the information for the last State), a new Group Header would print (for the new State), and then the Detail information for that State would begin.

Now say that report printed the value of the State field (like "Ohio") in both its Group Header and its Group Footer, and in the Detail section just listed the employees that worked in that State.

Sometimes, depending on the number of employees, the size of the Detail section could span out *just* long enough to push the Group Footer to the next page by itself—leaving it "orphaned." This was the problem we were looking to solve. Dave's "Window-orphan effect." Somehow we needed to tie what printed in Group Headers and Footers with the Detail information they surrounded. It was a problem few report writers handled well, but Dave vowed ours would be the one to "do it right."

Dave, Marty, and I spent some time discussing the problem. Finally, we reached a point where Dave felt the need to offer up suggestions on how we should fix it, not from a designer's standpoint, but from a developer's.

"Well, I'll tell ya what you're gonna do," he said, stretching out the "well" for a good three seconds. "You allocate some memory…"

Now, that suggestion wasn't much help, really, since almost *everything* we did involved allocating memory. It was a surprise though, because Dave had no idea how our Report Writers worked internally.

"Let's call it a buffer…," he continued.

I glanced at Marty who was nodding his head attentively. But I sort of knew what he was thinking behind that deer-like stare: A buffer? Does it really matter what it's called?

"Well, maybe two buffers…" Dave said, drawing out the "well" again, "…two *big* buffers…."

The rest of what he said isn't important. What *is* important is those first few lines became legendary among the developers from then on. If any of us had a question on how to do something, most likely the response would be, "Well, you allocate some memory…let's call it a buffer…."

The "Widow-Orphan" problem was solved eventually, but in a way that didn't cause me to allocate a lot of memory (or buffers, for that matter).

It marked the start of a long summer, and I had Chris's new marketing department to thank.

• • •

The next burning issue was the menu design tool.

In the FoxPro language there were *many* ways to define a menu—to put it mildly. This surplus of commands stemmed from the fact that FoxBASE+ (in response to user requests) had a way of defining menus before dBase IV (and its multitude of language additions) came along with another way. Then, after we added the dBase IV syntax, we found there were problems with it, so we added *still more* commands to compensate.

Altogether, it made it unclear what method of defining menus was preferable for what situations...and even which commands were intended to work together. Our users got confused, and justifiably so. Even when one knew precisely what commands and functions to use, there was still a large amount of typing necessary to get the desired system of menus.

So, to address all that, we were going to add a new tool to the product. This tool—later called "the Menu Builder"—would allow users to create menus with very little effort. It would also relieve them of the burden of knowing what specific commands to use when. It had the potential to make their lives a lot better.

The first step in the development process was for me to investigate what other products did. If there were good ideas out there, I'd use them, and if I saw something terrible, I'd know what to avoid. Like every project before, I knew the final phrase to describe our Menu Builder had to be "the best." Now I had to figure out what was best.

I went to our company's small library and gathered up every competitive product I could find. I also raided the personal software collections of other developers. I then started installing products on my machines.

With the Report Writer and Screen Painter, I spent a little time studying the competition, but most of that was after the fact. Just to make sure I didn't leave out anything useful.

This was the first time my research was done before coding began.

What I found, though, was most products hadn't done anything at all. There were few examples of a menu design tool anywhere, especially among DOS products. The only examples I found were on the Macintosh, and they just weren't appropriate for our needs. They used cute interface tricks to bring a menu to life, but in the end the process took more time than creating a menu by hand.

So, the full design burden fell on me. I had to come up with something that fit the way our menus worked, minus the tediousness and complexity. It was a tall order, but as I settled in to design *something*, I found I enjoyed the challenge.

The basic syntax for defining a menu system using our preferred method looked like this:

```
DEFINE PAD _msm_file OF _MSYSMENU
    PROMPT "File" COLOR SCHEME 3;
    KEY ALT+F, "";
    MESSAGE "Create, open, or quit"

DEFINE PAD _msm_edit OF _MSYSMENU
    PROMPT "Edit" COLOR SCHEME 3;
    KEY ALT+E, "";
    MESSAGE "Edit text"
```

```
ON PAD _msm_file OF _MSYSMENU
    ACTIVATE POPUP _mfile
ON PAD _msm_edit OF _MSYSMENU
    ACTIVATE POPUP _medit

DEFINE POPUP _mfile MARGIN RELATIVE;
    SHADOW COLOR SCHEME 4
DEFINE BAR _mfi_new OF _mfile
    PROMPT "New...";
    MESSAGE "Create a new file"
DEFINE BAR _mfi_open OF _mfile
    PROMPT "Open...";
    MESSAGE "Open an existing file"
DEFINE BAR _mfi_quit OF _mfile
    PROMPT "Exit";
    MESSAGE "Exit"

DEFINE POPUP _medit MARGIN RELATIVE;
    SHADOW COLOR SCHEME 4
DEFINE BAR _med_cut OF _medit
    PROMPT "Cut";
    KEY CTRL+X, "Ctrl+X" ;
    MESSAGE "Put selection on the clipboard and remove it"
DEFINE BAR _med_copy OF _medit;
    PROMPT "Copy";
    KEY CTRL+C, "Ctrl+C" ;
    MESSAGE "Copy selection to the clipboard"
DEFINE BAR _med_paste OF _medit;
    PROMPT "Paste";
    KEY CTRL+V, "Ctrl+V" ;
    MESSAGE "Paste clipboard contents at the insertion point"
```

This snippet of code would create a menu bar (the words across the top of the screen) that says "File" and "Edit." The "File" item would open (drop-down) a menu with the items

"New," "Open," and "Exit." The "Edit" item would open a menu with the words "Cut," "Copy," and "Paste" on it. Each item had messages that would display along the bottom of the screen when it was selected, and some had special key combinations (like CTRL+X for the "Cut" item) available in addition to the mouse.

This syntax was straightforward in many respects, because each item in the menu system was defined one at a time. The syntax for defining the top level, the "menu bar" level, was a little different than the subordinate popup menus, but there were many similarities.

Ultimately, what stuck out most to me was the tree-like structure of a menu system. A menu bar could have 1 to N menus attached to it, every menu could have 1 to N items attached to it, and those items could, in turn, attach to another menu, which itself could have items attached to it, ad nauseam. Inherently it was like a tree, with the menu bar representing the first level of branches, the next set (the top level) of menus representing shoots off those branches, and so on.

The other thing that struck me was the many properties of these items that had to be defined—names, numbers, prompts, etc. Each required a lot of text to be typed in, which would be the case no matter what interface I eventually created.

To me, the whole thing screamed for some sort of list-like interface. From there the Menu Builder sort of created itself.

What I drew on my whiteboard was a window with a list in it that represented one branch of the menu system at a time. Also on that window was a control that indicated where the user was in the menu system currently. If he was working on the _mfile popup for instance, "_mfile" appeared in that control and the information for the individual items of the _mfile popup appeared in the list.

I showed Dave what I had, we discussed it a little, and I

started coding. The Menu Builder went from whiteboard to keyboard in only a few days, and from there to nearly functional in less than two weeks.

• • •

Aside from marketing, there was still one other team that, until mid-1990, was noticeably absent from our roster. Unbelievably, through the entire cycle of shipping FoxPro 1.0 and another Mac product, we had no in-house testing department. Regular employees and outside beta-testers continued to be our only testing source.

To correct that deficiency, Dave hired a former programmer from SCO (the company that provided our UNIX version of FoxBASE) to start a new testing department.

The programmer's name was Jim Simpkins and he was highly respected by all who knew him. In appearance he was around six feet tall, thin, and looked in his mid-twenties, although he was actually well into his thirties.

His youthfulness carried over into his demeanor as well. Though usually sedate, he had a cocky confidence about him that was atypical for our group.

I liked Jim from the start—and that was a good thing, because I soon needed his help.

DBASE IV and UI2 Programmer. Neither of them comes close!!!

#: 69223 S12/Fox Software
31-Dec-89 15:15:14
Sb: #69186-XBase Benchmarks
Fm: George F. Goley IV 71140,3527
To: Paul Ferrara [CONSULT] 76702,556 (X)

Paul - The report writer in FoxPro is outstanding. Personally, I hate report writers, screen writers, and code generators. However, after one of our programmers developed a client in one day using FoxPro, I became a convert. 92% is a fairly high number, but you can do a lot with FoxReport.

George.

There is 1 Reply.

#: 69235 S12/Fox Software
31-Dec-89 15:40:47
Sb: #69223-XBase Benchmarks
Fm: Paul Ferrara [CONSULT] 76702,556
To: George F. Goley IV 71140,3527

That's good feedback. Thanks.

I never tried R&R because it didn't output source code. Now, I'm almost tempted, but will wait to play with FP when the myu version ships.

But straying even farther from the subject... <grin> if you don't like screen generators, what do you use: screen design forms for COBOL? That's one tool I couldn't live without. Used SED for the longest time and cleaned the output up with my editor. Now I'm hooked on SCI*MAGE.

Paul

#: 69290 S12/Fox Software
31-Dec-89 17:05:52
Sb: #69186-XBase Benchmarks
Fm: Walt Kennamer 74025,514
To: Paul Ferrara [CONSULT] 76702,556 (X)

I've done several reports, some of them pretty elaborate, in FoxPro. It might not do all reports, but it's pretty nice for most. I think it would be worth your time to learn it. It "does" take some time to get used to, especially if you want to use its advanced features.

#: 69222 S12/Fox Software
31-Dec-89 07:49:34
Sb: #69179-XBase Benchmarks
Fm: George F. Goley IV 71140,3527
To: JEFF WINCHELL 76066,533 (X)

Jeff - dBASE IV is about 1/2 as fast as FoxBASE+ in almost all areas. That failing, and its lack of reliability, are the reasons why I waited for FoxPro.

George.

#: 6937/7 S12/Fox Software
01-Jan-90 15:43:38
Sb: #6919?-XBase Benchmarks
Fm: Pat Adams 75146,312
To: JEFF WINCHELL 76066,533

The code that the dBASE IV report generates usually works but it is pretty badly constructed. While I do occasionally use the IV report writer to

churn out code for me, I always go thru and clean it up. Whoever wrote the code generator obviously was not a Dbaser because it stops to do things like testing whether the printer is on or off and then issues SET PRINT ON or SET PRINT OFF commands, etc. When there is no need to do the IF/ELSE/ENDIF but, rather, just issue the command.

R&R is a good product but with large files it is very, very, very slow - especially if several large files are related. Also, when working with tight memory constraints - especially in LAN situations - and with large files, R&R often requires more memory than is available, even when using the runtime. The code generating module solves that problem, however. Here again, you are sure to want to go in and beef up the code that R&R churns out.

My approach is to do as much as possible in the FoxPRO report writer and then resort to the other options when that is not possible.

#: 68949 S12/Fox Software
29-Dec-89 13:41:13
Sb: #68835-Index Arguments
Fm: Steve Davies 75410,322
To: Jerry Hare 76247,2672

I need the BROWSE PLEASE command, too. My programs have been getting very argumentative lately.

<CHeeers>
<Steve>>

#: 68969 S12/Fox Software
29-Dec-89 14:03:05
Sb: #68835 Insects
Fm: Y. Alan Griver 71541,3150
To: Fox Software 70004,1651

Kristine,

I found two of the little critters today.

1. In the color picker, if you pick help when in the save dialog you hang up the machine with it beeping at you.

2. If you BROW NOMODIFY MODIFIELD and define an ON KEY LABEL to put you into an append routine, the appended records can be modified and deleted.

Also, I've been modifying the command line because clicking on Save then picking an already defined color set (COLOR) and clicking Save again doesn't seem to work...

Thanks alot for the help. BTW, I'm using version 1.0 - the original, no updates since the betas got the correct 1.0.

yag

#: 68955 S12/Fox Software
29-Dec-89 14:15:25
Sb: #68835-Editors
Fm: John Bauman 71140,3122
To: Y. Alan Griver 71541,3150 (X)

TAG-
I'm not sure what dBRIEF's "preprocessor" is and would appreciate further explanation... I'd bought 1 in an older version of dBRIEF that I bought. I DO agree with Martin, however...and have not even considered going back and upgrading dBRIEF after seeing QF macros.
As for your other two examples: database structure in window (ALT-?)

CompuServe traffic, with a compliment circled

Chapter 13
Acting

Dave pushed the keyboard of his DOS machine forward so hard it slid into his coffee cup, disturbing the fluid within. "You're just asking me the same questions over and over," he said, eyes wide.

I searched the faces of the others in the room...Marty, Jim, and Brian. They all looked as stunned as I was. Completely speechless.

There had been a number of issues with the Menu Builder lately. Mostly with the code it generated. I thought our questions were legitimate though.

"You're trying to make things difficult," Dave said, wagging a finger in the air. "But I won't put up with it. You four just go on...get out of here. Figure it out yourself!"

I moved to hide in front of the others as we made our way to the door.

• • •

The following day there was a quick knock before my office door opened. A curly-haired head extended through the opening and smiled softly. It was Jadzia Carlson, one of the testers Jim Simpkins hired. Though a relatively recent Polish immigrant, her voice had only the hint of an accent. "Can I ask you a question?" she asked.

I returned the smile. "Sure...what's up?"

During the course of the summer Jadzia was drafted to write much of the template code for the product. Similar to the templates I wrote years earlier on the Mac, her templates would take the information stored by our design tools and produce dBase code. In August—while I was still finishing the Menu Builder—she was busy constructing its template. Jadzia was the nicest person I ever met…who also knew how to assemble a machine gun.

"Yes," she began politely, "I still can't get the Edit items in my menu to work right."

I frowned. By "Edit items" she meant the Cut, Copy, and Paste items in a menu she was trying to create using the Menu Builder and her template. Thus far, she'd been very thorough in testing her template. So thorough, in fact, she turned up a half-dozen holes in our menu creation process. They weren't bugs in the design of the Menu Builder, per se; they were problems with what happens *after* a user designed a menu. How do we go from the information in the design tool, to actual generated code? And then, will that generated code actually work?

In Jadzia's latest scenario she was trying to create a duplicate of FoxPro's Edit Menu. In FoxPro, like many products, when you selected some text in an editable area of any window, the "Cut" and "Copy" items were enabled. After a user performed one of those two operations, "Paste" was then enabled. Jadzia wanted the same thing to happen in her menu. It was a reasonable request. Our users might want to do that.

I thought we had it fixed, though. Recently, Brian Tallman added a feature called "System Menu Names" to address it. This feature meant that every item in our menu system had a name and our users could reference each item by that name. They could even give their own menu items those names and have the enabling and disabling done for them automatically. Jadzia *should* be able to get her menus working now.

Even if she couldn't though, it probably wasn't an issue with the Menu Builder. It was probably a problem in our Menu Manager, with the way the System Menu Names were implemented internally.

But just to be sure... "Show me," I said.

I followed Jadzia from my office and turned right. All of the testers sat in a bank of cubicles just behind Dave's secretary and across from the senior developers. Jadzia's spot was just outside of Tallman's office.

When we reached her cubicle, Jadzia ran the program to create her menu. Her menu was defined so it would be appended to the end of our System menu bar. She did this so she could compare what her Edit menu did with what our Edit menu did. So, while her program was running it actually looked like FoxPro had two Edit menus. It was kind of weird, but our users had a penchant for doing weird things. It was a good test.

Her menu appeared and it seemed to be working fine. She then took the steps necessary to end her program.

I shrugged. "Looks like it works to me," I said.

"Ah-ha!" Jadzia said, sounding like a detective making an important discovery. "But look at this!" She pulled down FoxPro's own Edit menu.

Something about it seemed strange.

"No Cut, Copy or Paste items!" she said.

She was right. When her menu went away, it apparently took items from *our* Edit menu with it. "Where'd they go?"

Her eyes were wide. "I don't know!"

"System Menu Names" were Dave's answer to Jadzia's original problem. I never really liked that solution. It seemed like it opened up a lot of new functionality just to solve one little problem. Like we opened a fire hose when all we really needed was the garden variety. That commonly happened at Fox.

There was only one person to talk to about menu matters, though. I cocked my head to one side. "Let's talk to Brian."

• • •

Brian Tallman was now master of everything window or menu related. Since the early days of FoxPro, he worked tirelessly on these two crucial, complicated, and often thankless areas. With hardly a complaint. If there was an award given for "heart of a servant," Brian should have a dozen.

Plus his door was nearly always open. "Brian!" I said as we entered his office. "Jadzia has a problem."

Brian turned toward us and smiled softly. Another thing he maintained over the years was business attire. He didn't go so far as to wear a suit, but he still always wore dress slacks and a button-down. "Okay…" He grabbed his brown pants at the knees and straightened them slightly. "What is it?"

Alternately providing information, Jadzia and I described the behavior we were seeing. Through all of it, Brian sat with arms crossed and nodded his head attentively.

"Yeah," he said finally. "That doesn't surprise me."

"Why not?" I said. "Those System Menu Names don't access our real menu items, do they?"

Brian gave a quick nod. "Sure do."

"What?" Now it looked like my original concern was well founded. It appeared that in trying to allow one small bit of functionality, we gave our users complete access to our menus. It was the kind of situation we called "helping them shoot themselves in the foot."

"Is that what Dave wanted?" I asked.

Brian shrugged. "Don't know," he said. "It's the way it has to be, though." He chuckled. It was a boyish, full-of-joy laugh. It didn't seem right coming from a man whose house was nearly burnt down once.

"We could do something different," he said, "but…" He uncrossed his arms and turned his hands face up.

"What?" I asked.

He smiled. "You'll have to talk to Dave first."

I frowned and glanced at Jadzia. That wasn't the answer I wanted to hear. The last couple weeks had produced an endless stream of Menu Builder complications. Only the day before Jim, Marty, and I so frustrated Dave he sent us away. *If we bothered him again…*

"Oh, no," Jadzia said, giving voice to my fears.

Brian chuckled again.

I brought a hand to my chin, and then looked at Jadzia. "Why don't we talk to Jim first?"

• • •

During his short time of employment, Jim Simpkins built a distinct rapport with Dave; one that none of the rest of us even approached. My suspicion was it had something to do with Jim's former employment at SCO, but even that reason didn't fit completely. Dave hired Chris and Sally originally because he decided to dump SCO, after all.

Perhaps it was just something about Jim's demeanor. SCO stood for Santa Cruz Organization and a lot of California came with Jim to Fox. Brash and confident, he wouldn't take flak from anyone—Dave included. Jim routinely told Dave to go off and do unmentionable things to himself and Dave would just laugh raucously. Dave not only tolerated Jim's behavior, he seemed to admire it.

And, as the head of the testing department, Jim was officially Jadzia's boss. I figured we needed him.

Jim's office was one of the exterior offices at the south end of the building. When Jadzia and I arrived, Jim was seated at his computer with his legs crossed like a yogi. The posture had nothing do with any religious dedication though. It was just

Jim, being consistent in being different. His dress was atypical too. He wore a loose-fitting button-down shirt and pants a couple shades lighter than the shock of brown hair that lived on his head.

Noticing the concern on our faces, Jim laughed and said, "What's up?"

"Well...you know how Dave has been lately." I then explained Jadzia's problem. "I'm afraid Dave's System Menu Name idea might not be a good one. In fact, we may need to talk him out of it completely." My eyes drifted to Jim's office window. He actually had something to see aside from roof and dumpsters. There were houses back there. "But considering what happened last time..."

Jim nodded his head slowly. "Yeah, he was pretty extreme."

To put it mildly. "So, what do we do?"

He uncurled his legs, stared at the floor for moment. "Well, here's a thought—"

I held up a hand. "Wait, whatever it is—will you go with us to see Dave?"

He gave a short exhaling laugh. "Sure."

I nodded once. "Okay. What's your thought?"

He smiled. "What if we scripted out exactly what each of us will say when we're in with Dave." Jim put out hands to mimic the movement of scales. "We'll try to weigh out ahead of time what Dave's response will be. Try to come up with the best way to avoid an explosion...like a play...or an opera."

I hesitated. Don't most operas end in tragedy? I glanced at Jadzia again. She didn't look convinced either.

Still, we needed to do *something*. "It's worth a shot," I said, frowning.

• • •

Trying to plan for a meeting with Dave was like trying to plan a child's sporting event. All you were *really* certain of were the players. Everything else was pure speculation. And governed by randomness.

When Dave was in a placid mood, he had a number of mannerisms he performed while thinking I found distracting. Sometimes he removed his wedding band and twirled it slowly on his head. Other times he would hold a coffee cup or soda can on his head while tapping on the top with his free hand. Or, he might take his earlobes between his forefingers and thumbs and twist them repeatedly. In more reflective moments, he might simply stroke the back of his head with his hand or hold his head in his hands, right hand at the chin and left hand at the top.

There was also usually some food consumption going on. Dave's great loves were popcorn, coffee, Sen-Sens, and diet Vernors. Throughout the day, he could be found eating or spilling any one of them. His office floor was a graveyard of missed attempts at getting food into his mouth.

Other meetings were more combative in nature. Dave was very opinionated about the product and forceful with those opinions. If he didn't like something, he told you—and more often than not—he told you straight to your face and at high decibels.

As part of this, he had a library of catch phrases he loved to use. A statement that he didn't agree with might bring a "No, No, NO, NO, NO" with each "No" accompanied by a rap on his desk. The last "No" bringing the loudest rap of all. A bug he found could illicit a "You know what the problem is...I'll tell you what the problem is...," or it might just bring an order to "Heal it—quickly!" with a wave to get you on your way. Sometimes this statement was followed by "Today would be a good day. Now would be a good time." Or, if one of us didn't understand Dave's meaning we might hear "Do you want me to say it again...in Chinese?"

Personally, I found this latter type of get-together difficult. Programming for me was almost an art form. Harsh criticism was hard to take, like someone pushing over my sandcastle.

Dave's style just wasn't the sort of thing they taught you in programming classes.

In this case, it was even worse, though. *We* needed a meeting and Dave didn't want one.

I hoped Jim was a good director.

• • •

"I think you should start us off, Jim," I said.

Jim brought a leg close to his chest and wrapped his arms around it. "Alright, I'll go first," he said. "What if I say something like 'Dave...um, we have some questions about the Menu Builder....'"

I shook my head. "That's how we got in trouble the last time."

Jim's head moved up and down. "Right, right...okay, I'll say some issues have come up that we'd like to discuss."

"That's a little better," I said. "Now what?"

Jim looked at Jadzia. "Well, then I think Jadzia should talk. You know, use the feminine angle some..." Jim chuckled a little, and then got serious again. "No, I mean, Jadzia, just be factual. Tell him what you're trying to do."

"Just the facts," I said.

Jim glanced at me, smiled. "That's right, the facts. Then, Kerry, you should tell him why the problem exists. That it's because these menu names are tied to the actual items, and according to Brian that's the way it has to be." He waved a hand. "I wouldn't elaborate too much more than that. If Dave wants to pull the feature or whatever, we'll make that *his* decision. We'll try to lay it all out there. See what happens."

"Okay," I said.

"And we need to have a few solutions to present. Like I said, make it *his* decision."

I nodded slowly. "What if..."

The scripting and rehearsing lasted for close to half an hour. Finally, we thought we had something that might work.

• • •

One aspect of life at Fox I came to appreciate was the fact that there were rarely any scheduled meetings. When one of us needed Dave's time we simply walked to his office and talked to him. Anything other than a discussion-in-progress with another developer would be put on hold to answer our question.

On this occasion, the three of us arrived to find Dave alone. His desk faced the door, but his feet were up and he was absorbed in studying the screen at the right end of his desk. When he turned to look at us, he didn't look pleased.

Oh, man. This was a bad idea...

As we closed in on the chairs in front of his desk, he just grunted.

A really bad idea.

"Dave...um...some issues have come up with the Menu Builder we'd like to discuss," Jim said, reading straight from the script.

This is *so* preposterous. I resisted shaking my head. Now, who speaks next?

Jadzia described the problem and how we discovered it.

Dave gave the predicted response: cautious

acknowledgement.

"It's because the menu names are tied to the real items," I said. "I talked to Brian..." I continued with my lines, being as factual as possible. Not wavering, not sounding like I'm whining, and definitely not smiling.

When I finished speaking, Jim listed off the possible solutions. "So, now we're wondering what you think. We really need your decision to proceed."

Dave sat quietly for a few moments, staring over our shoulders.

I was nervous. I've seen that look before and I knew. He's going to get mad again.

"Ah..." Dave said. Then more silence.

Still not looking good.

A few more moments went by.

"Yes, yes," he said finally. "I can see the problem now."

I can't believe this actually worked.

From there we discussed the possible solutions and eventually dragged Brian into the mix. In the end, the greatest part of the work was in Brian's code; many of the huge problems with the Menu Builder had the same result.

The solution, in this case, was to add a new command to the language. One that would let users restore the entire menu system to its original state, no matter how much they screwed them up.

Essentially we added a fire hose, and then gave them a large weight to shut it back off again.

Regardless it was out of my hands now. I guess everyone gets a chance to be an actor sometime.

Chapter 14
Wombats and Eggs

A few weeks later, the Menu Builder was finished. But then I had a new problem.

I entered Heindel's office, and after the usual "Hey Heindel-man" greeting, I got to the heart of the matter. "Dave wants me to add multiple windows to READ," I said. "I was hoping you could give me some advice." Heindel had his desk positioned so he faced the door. I walked left to stand near the end, next to his black guest chair.

Heindel's face tracked me as I moved. At the word "READ" his cordial expression suddenly turned sober. "Be very careful," he said. "And don't break anything."

I shook my head. "Thanks." At times, Heindel had the wit of a first-grader.

Heindel turned back to study his computer screen. "Don't mention it." He then squinted at the screen as if the conversation was over.

There was a stuffed Cleveland Browns football placed prominently on Heindel's desk. I contemplated whether using it to bean another employee was against company policy. Probably not.

Heindel turned to look at me again and chuckled. "I'll give you a walkthrough of the code for READ, but I warn you, it ain't pretty. And be prepared…every time I touch that code, I break something."

"Really?" I eased myself into the guest chair. Why can't it ever be easy? The chair caught on the carpet. I fought to bring it closer to Heindel's desk.

"Really." Heindel cupped a hand and jerked it forward in

the air as he talked; one jerk for each point. "Try as you might, no matter what, if you change *anything*, somewhere, somehow, someone's dBase program won't work right anymore."

Not what I wanted to hear. "Well...I don't know if I want to...."

He made a calming motion. "You're the creator of the Screen Painter, you can do it. Just be prepared to test. *A lot.*"

Great. What have I been thrown into now?

• • •

Though only a single command, READ was one of the most intricate and convoluted commands in our product. The purpose of READ was to animate an application's interface. A user, when creating such an interface, typically defined its elements by using a list of @SAY/GET commands. At the end of the list, they would issue a single READ command to make the whole thing live. Like so:

```
USE dvds
@3, 13 SAY 'Title:' GET dvds.title COLOR gr+b, r/w
@4, 13 SAY 'Description:' GET dvds.description COLOR gr+b, r/w
READ
```

This program uses a database (dvds) created to hold an inventory of DVDs. When run in FoxPro, it would present a blank screen with the string "Title:" on one line and next to it a rectangle of text displaying the actual title of one of the DVDs in the collection. The string "Title:" is the SAY portion of the command and the presented title is the GET portion. The user of the program could change the value presented in the GET portion. Directly beneath the "Title:" line would be a similar line for "Description:" and a corresponding changeable (GET) rectangle of text next to it.

READ also allowed for more complex interface elements. Things like push buttons, radio buttons, and checkboxes. Anyone who uses a computer encounters these regularly in windows and dialogs.

To me, it *seemed* like the code to implement the READ command should be relatively straightforward. All it had to do was handle the interaction of a few interface elements. We had code in our Control and Dialog Managers doing similar things and that was all accessible to me. Easy to read, easy to understand…it didn't take much studying to comprehend. I could even make changes if necessary. READ shouldn't be much different.

How bad could it be, really?

Heindel's walkthrough hinted at the answer. And later, when I was in my office with the code for READ in front of me, I knew for certain.

The answer was: really bad.

My college instructors drilled into my head the rules to follow to write "structured code." A few of the important ones went like this:

1. A single subroutine (a self-contained portion of code) should have one purpose. This is the programmer's version of "A place for everything and everything in its place." Create a routine to do one thing, and use it for just that. If you need it to do something slightly different, write another routine.

2. Every routine should have only one entry point and one exit point. This means that as the computer makes its step-by-step way through the code it should have only one place to begin a routine and only one way to finish it. Just like reading a book…you start at the beginning and end at the end. No shortcuts.

3. If you find yourself writing the same lines of code more

than once, you should create a routine that consists of those lines of code and call it. This is essentially like speed dial on your phone. If you dial a number regularly, you should probably put it on speed dial.

4. Document your code. This means put comments around any code you wrote to tell the next person your intent. Anyone who has put together a child's toy knows this one. The better the instructions, the easier it is to understand. For programmers, comments are the roadmap to another person's mind.

Unfortunately, the only thing READ had in common with this list was that it didn't follow any of them.

Heindel gave me a utility to maximize the amount of C code I could print on a single sheet of paper. Using a very small font, it printed about seventy-five lines per sheet. Printed that way, READ still spanned nearly twenty pages.

And the code read like a horror novel.

It contained one huge decision structure (called a "case" statement in C lingo) with multiple entry and exit points and several looping structures (constructs that tell the computer to do a section of code repeatedly) that spanned all twenty pages. Nearly everyone hired before me had touched it, indicated by their initials near individual lines of code. Yet there were no additional comments, and none of those developers would claim responsibility if asked.

READ was what my friend Rusty would call a "can of wombats."

And I was right in the middle of it.

• • •

In the first version of FoxPro, a user could only define their interface (@SAY/GET) elements in a single window. This behavior emulated what FoxBASE+ and dBase IV did, so there was no immediate pressure for us to change it.

Neither of those products were really windowing environments, though. DBase IV allowed for the definition of windows, but the primary interface of that product was still very much like its predecessors. (As was FoxBASE+, of course.) Each tool—the editor, the BROWSE command, the Report Writer—was confined to a single screen and didn't interact much with the rest of their product.

FoxPro wasn't like that, though. Our windows were sizable, they moved, and they could overlap each other. Our tools lived inside windows of their own.

So, having a READ command that didn't allow our users to provide *their* users with a similar experience just didn't seem right. My mission was to give them that ability.

I also thought I could clean up the READ code a little before adding the changes to make it support multiple windows. In my first glimpse of the main READ routine, I saw dozens of places where the exact same lines of code were written. If I could break those places out into separate routines, I'd not only get my feet wet in the ocean of code that made up READ, but I'd help the code itself. Shrink it. Make it a little more structured. Closer to those ideals I learned.

I could then press on to make it obey some of the other rules of structural programming. My hope was that when I finished, READ would be a concise, well documented—purely structural—routine. From there it would be easy to plug in the multi-window changes.

So, I created a few new routines to replace the duplicate code and made the appropriate changes in the READ code to call them. I built a new version of the product and did some testing.

And READ worked fine. I was confident it would, though.

The changes I made were about as innocuous a change as could be made. Usually, if your product will build with them in, they work.

After more testing, I checked in the first round of my new and improved READ.

• • •

The next day Janet was at my door. "I'm seeing something weird," she said, looking perplexed. "Come look at this."

I followed her to her office. She was situated in the back of the building, just behind the cubicle hive of tech support. It was typically a busy place, and the interior of her office looked like it. Lots of opened boxes and printed lists. In fact, there was no room for her computer on her desk, so it lived on a small rolling computer stand.

She motioned toward her computer screen. On it was a relatively simple READ in action. It had a couple of database fields displaying data in GET rectangles, some text, and a couple push buttons.

"Now watch this..." She hit the tab key a number of times. As she did so, the color of one GET at a time would change to show it was the currently selected one. When she reached a particular GET, instead of the entire rectangle changing color, a line cursor appeared.

"Yeah?" I said.

"Well, yesterday that GET would be completely selected," she said. "*Today* it is just showing a cursor." Janet looked at me. "Heindel said you were working on READ now, so..."

I hooked my fingers on my belt loops and glanced out Janet's window. Like Jim Simpkins, she could actually see trees and houses. Nice.

I looked at the screen again. "And it didn't do this

before?"

Janet shook her head. "Do you want the code to reproduce it?"

Not really. "Okay…"

I took a disk back to my office. After putting Janet's files on my machine, I brought up my version of FoxPro and ran her program. I saw the same behavior I saw in Janet's office.

I next took the steps necessary to temporarily "back out" the changes I made the day before. I rebuilt the product and tried Janet's program again.

It worked differently. Just like she said it would.

"Well for all the—" I shook my head. "How?"

I spent the better part of an hour figuring out "How."

Every GET element in a READ may have a number of "clauses" associated with it. The description of the syntax for the style of GET Janet was using (and there were many styles) went like this:

```
@ <row, column>
    GET <memvar> | <field>
        [FUNCTION <expC1>]
        [PICTURE <expC2>]
        [DEFAULT <expr1>]
        [ENABLE | DISABLE]
        [MESSAGE <expC5>]
        [RANGE [<expr2>] [, <expr3>]]
        [VALID <expL1> | <expn4>
            [ERROR <expC6>]]
        [WHEN <expL2>]
```

Every line after "GET <memvar>" was what we considered a "clause" and every one of them could—in some way—affect the behavior of a GET, if included. With my changes I inadvertently altered the behavior of one of those clauses.

Once the problem was known, though, the fix was straightforward. One of my new subroutines needed to act *slightly* different when it was called from one place in READ than it did in all the other places it was called. It wasn't a big enough difference to elicit an entirely new routine, so I brought out another tool from the coder's toolbox. I made it so I could send a flag (a simple "YES" or "NO" value) into the routine. A "YES" meant it was called from the place that needed to act differently, a "NO" from all the others. I made that change to the READ code, tested it, and checked it in.

• • •

Later that same day, the writer named "Dave" (Venske) arrived at my door. In his late thirties, he had a full, slicked-back head of hair, and an easy smile.

"Janet says you're in charge of READ now," he said. "I have something that's acting weird for me today."

"Do you have the code?"

He handed me a disk and gave me a short explanation of the problem.

"Let's give it a shot..." I copied his dBase code to my machine. "Maybe I've fixed it already." Maybe the changes I made for Janet...

I ran his code and GETs filled my screen.

He chuckled. "Nope. Still there." He pointed a finger, indicating the problem. Another place where something worked slightly different than it had before.

I looked heavenward, frowning. "Okay, I'll take a look."

An hour later, I figured out his problem. A different clause and a different side effect of those same trivial changes. I made another—more complicated—fix. Checked it in.

The next day, *another* person appeared at my office door. "I heard you're in charge of READ…"

"Yeah…?"

After about a week of similar occurrences, I *finally* had my initial changes to READ working. I also came to realize that READ was not just a "can of wombats." It was what the senior members of the team called "a tower of eggs." You could construct the tower once, but after it is built, it is best looked at, and *never* touched again.

I decided not to press ahead with any more READ renovations. I'd just make the multi-window additions Dave wanted and get out. The odds that I could make those changes without breaking something were already incredibly slim.

Why push my luck?

• • •

I managed to finish the multi-window READ changes by the end of September, but by then, Dave had *another* list of enhancements he wanted added. Those changes came with another level of complication.

"Look at this!" Dave said after he hauled me into his office. He brought up the Screen Painter and started pointing at his screen. "I can't seem to find the places in the Screen Painter where I can set a control's DISABLE attribute. Where are they?"

The answer to that question was easy. "They're not there yet," I said.

The corners of Dave's mouth turned down. "Why not?!"

My heart began to pound. I now not only had to add features to READ, I had to add the means for accessing those features to the Screen Painter as well. This round-robin approach was in direct opposition to the way I liked to work. I liked to code one feature at a time and test it until I was confident it worked. Consequently, I liked to be responsible for one under-development portion of the product at a time and work on that until it was finished.

Working on two large and complicated portions of the product, both undergoing frequent changes, with some interdependencies, but no code being shared, was a lot to keep my arms around.

"Well...I haven't had time," I said. "I've been working on adding it to READ first."

I glanced at a set of juggling balls Dave kept within arm's reach of his keyboard. Many in the development team took up juggling as a hobby—Dave especially. I didn't know how to juggle, and frankly, I didn't care to. One ball in the air alone was enough for me.

Dave studied me quietly for a few moments. Then, out of the corner of my eye, I saw Heindel pass by Dave's door.

"Oh, David!" Dave said.

Heindel, who just made the turn toward developers' row, quickly walked back to Dave's door. "Yeah, Dave?"

"How's your stuff coming?"

"Pretty well," Heindel said, shrugging. "Should be done soon."

"Good...good..." Dave drummed his fingers on his desk. "There are some READ changes that need made."

Heindel glanced at me. "Oh?" He thought he'd left READ behind.

"It *is* your bailiwick," Dave said. "Kerry has Screen Painter changes to make."

I remained silent and expressionless, but inside my emotions were mixed. Part of me felt like a failure for not being able to handle both areas concurrently. But the other part of me—the larger part—was feeling really good.

"Okay," Heindel said hesitantly. "I'll work on READ…."

Dave waved us away, so I followed Heindel back to his office.

"Dave wants me working on READ," he said, mostly to himself.

"Sorry." And I was. I hated others having to pick up my mess.

Heindel flipped up a hand. "Dave wants me working on READ. Fine…fine…"

Heindel was a proficient juggler. For that, I was grateful.

• • •

The following weekend I took our family friend, Marlene, to see where I worked. Like she had many years before, it was now *my* time to share.

Few people were around that day, but in the middle of the tour, Dave strolled out of his office. He clutched a bag of popcorn in one hand.

"Hey Dave," I said. "This is a friend of mine, Marlene."

Marlene smiled. "Yes, I sort of motivated Kerry into the computer field. Into programming."

"Oh really?" Dave smiled and stuck out his empty—and doubtless butter-clad—hand to clasp Marlene's. He then bounced a little and cackled loudly. "Maybe I should hire you…to motivate him now!"

This isn't a question or a bug or a complaint. This is just to say that
using your prg files from Foxapp, modifying the startup, creating a
database, compiling and debugging I created an beautiful working application
in 45 minutes today, including the time it took for the client to explain
what they wanted in the database. The client was duly impressed, and I
marvelled at just how much 2.0 had made programming fun and had increased
my potential income. I am now taking on programming jobs that would have
been painful in the past, and find that I can afford to do some pro bono
work knowing that with Foxpro 2.0 and my distribution package I can whip up
a quick database for the church or the school or anybody who just can't
afford custom programming.

I've been hacking PCs since I bought an Apple at the Homebrew Computer Club
in Palo Alto from a couple of kids who were building them in a garage.
(In those days they were talking about marketing them as a multilevel, like
Amway). I've played with a lot of software, ranging from user-hostile to
stuff that curls up on your lap and talks dirty in your ear.

But Foxpro 2.0 is something special. What you folks have created is an
elegant solution. When you finally go public, may you all cash out as rich
as Bill Gates.

Please thank all the Fox folks for me.

Charles

Letter from a FoxPro admirer

Chapter 15

Devotion

In the middle of September 1990, Dave called us to the upstairs conference room. "As you are all undoubtedly aware," he said, "the second Developer's Conference is fast approaching…"

Bill, who sat near the table with his elbows on it, covered his eyes and groaned. Eric snickered and the rest of us just smiled knowingly. Though the prior year's DevCon had its share of rewarding moments, the push to get a "final release" product into the hands of the attendees was borderline chaotic.

I suspected Dave loved that kind of chaos, though.

"Yes, yes, I share that sentiment whole-heartedly," he said, his face serious. He brought a hand up to scratch the back of his head. "Because of our experience last year, this year we decided to take steps to insure that our lives will be considerably easier."

Now there's a switch.

Eric was across the table from me. He sat with legs crossed and his face partly buried in his hand. He nodded his head slowly as Dave spoke. I guessed that Eric and Bill were involved in whatever it was we were about to hear.

"Two things will be different," Dave continued. "First, we will *not* give out product this year. This version of FoxPro is still a good six months from shipping, with many features yet to be completed." He reached out to take his metallic "no-spill" coffee cup from the table and rest it on a knee. "I see no reason to risk our sanity by handing out a half-finished product. Undoubtedly, some of the attendees will be disappointed…" He forced a smile. "…but they will learn to live with it."

He moved closer to the table and rested his arms on it. "In

addition, at some point, probably a week or so before the start of DevCon, we will *freeze* the product. This means after some predetermined time, no one will be allowed to check in any change that could interfere with my demo at the opening ceremony. Any development work completed after that point will just stay on your personal machines until the conference is over."

Dave panned the room. "It will be a stress-free, pain-free event this year," he said, sounding sincere. "Now, any questions?"

There was silence for a few moments. We developers looked at each other while trying *not* to look at each other. The plan seemed too good to be true. Highly improbable. But no one would say that.

Eric stuck up a hand. "Well, I have a question," he said. "Won't this code freeze interfere with your preparations for the demo?"

There was some murmured agreement from around the table. How could Dave restrain himself?

"Now look," he said, "a good presenter can demo a non-functioning product and make it seem wonderful. And our product is more than functional." He wrapped a hand around his chin. "It will be just like I said: Stress-free and pain-free."

• • •

Immediately following the meeting, I stopped at Sally's office. Though she normally worked with her back to the door, she was still turned toward it. Expecting me to arrive. She sat a little hunched in her chair, with a leg crossed beneath her. I just leaned at the door.

She smiled when she saw me.

"So, what'd ya think of that?" I asked, returning her smile.

She shook her head. "It'll never happen."

I shrugged. "Seemed like he meant it." I was trying to be hopeful.

"Yeah, but you know how it'll be. The code will be frozen until Dave needs something *for the demo,* and then…"

Our frozen code would be liquid again.

Sally brought a pen near her mouth. Many of her pens bore the evidence of nervous chewing. "Besides," she said, frowning. "The demo means Dave will be playing with the product."

I nodded. An activity *known* to be dangerous, Dave's prolonged use of the product could lead to almost anything at any time. And unfortunately, more of my "children" would be in the spotlight this year than the year before. Not only would Dave be showing the Screen Painter, he'd be showing the enhancements to the Report Writer, the new Menu Builder, and the multi-window READ changes as well.

"We're doomed!" I said, quoting a line from *Star Wars.*

Sally laughed.

I smiled, and with a sigh, rolled around the corner to my office. "We'll see…."

• • •

DevCon was the first weekend of October.

As planned, the code freeze happened the Monday before.

As predicted, the freeze lasted about a day.

Dave found some SQL issues that needed to be addressed, and since SQL was a crucial part of his demo…

I made it until Wednesday before I felt the trickle of "code thaw" run down my back. I made two separate trips to the corner office that day, and both resulted in code changes that *had* to be in the product.

The first trip was because Dave didn't like the way multi-window READ behaved. That was a minor issue and the changes to make it work "right" were straightforward. I got them done within an hour's time.

The second trip was for one of Dave's perennial hot topics—colors. In this case, there were some minor inconsistencies between the way the colors of certain controls were defined in the Screen Painter versus the way they were defined in READ. These inconsistencies were present for months and went unnoticed, but *now* they had to be fixed for the show. Heindel and I would have to make some significant code changes, and make them perfectly, for fear of breaking the demo.

After the scope of the changes were laid out, I returned to my office and contemplated what to do next. It was nearly three o'clock in the afternoon. At four-thirty I had an appointment with an allergist (I decided I'd suffered long enough) so I would have to leave a little early. Following that, the rest of my evening was completely planned out. None of it included time spent at the office.

It was nearly impossible to plan anything outside of work. Deadlines and ship dates were ever changing. One's workload might be multiplied tenfold in the course of a day, an hour or—in this case—a matter of minutes. A feature supposed to be put off until later might all of a sudden be given "show-stopper" status. My workplace was tense and volatile. Difficult to schedule around.

Now I had these color changes to deal with. By conservative estimates, my portion about two days of work. I had to change a handful of dialogs, tweak the code that drew the controls on the Screen Painter's design surface, and make sure the enhanced color information was saved and restored from the file correctly. It was a nice-sized little project.

The code for the Screen Painter, though, was like an old friend; most times the work didn't take me as long as I initially thought. Plus, DevCon didn't start until the following Monday—a whole four days away. I had all that time to write the code, test it, and get it out into the build. Dave didn't say we needed to stay until the work was done *that night*. Was there any reason I couldn't leave at four as planned?

I could come in real early and work on this stuff.

So, I updated my machine at four, started it compiling, and got up to leave. When I reached my door, I pondered briefly which way to leave the building. From my office there were three directions I could go, but only one that allowed me to avoid Dave completely.

The first and boldest exit was to turn right, follow developer row to the corner where Dave's office was, turn left, pass his secretary, and then cross the front of the building to the door located on the opposite corner. From there, it was straight downstairs to the front door.

The second was to follow the row past two offices (Sally's and another) and turn left. There was a large division between the cubicles there I could use to cross the building. I could then turn right and—using the cubicle walls as partial cover—walk to the front and out the door. This had lower risk, but there was still that limited exposure near the front of the building. If Dave left his office while I was still out in the open, anything could happen.

The final route came with a downside, but the risk of detection was very low. From my office I could turn left, pass Crites's office, then McClanahan's, and finally arrive at the rear of the building and the door at the leftmost eastern corner. This door led down the back stairwell. From there I could pass through the ground floor offices to the front door and freedom.

The stairwell itself was the downside, however. The smokers in the building used that cold collection of cement steps as a break room, so it was a bit like being part of a night league at a bowling alley. I usually held my breath the whole way down.

Option three, I decided finally. I don't have time for confrontations tonight.

• • •

The next morning I was in before six, and by nine, I accomplished quite a bit. I felt comfortable and in control. Confident I'd have everything done in time, well before the weekend.

Then came nine-thirty.

I reached over to drop a CD into my newly-repaired (but still unreliable) Discman when I heard the distant sound of moving footfalls. Due to our building's less-than-adequate construction, the larger members of the company caused this thunderous booming sound when they walked the outer circle. I did my best to ignore it while I worked, but pounding footsteps shrunk the set of potential walkers to a small handful.

The footsteps were getting closer. They were past Marty's office, and then Heindel's. They crossed over the dissecting hall and didn't make the turn. Closer, still closer...in front of Sally's office now...slowing...

Slowing!

My door swung open. Dave filled the doorway wearing a white FoxPro polo and beige pants. He didn't look happy.

Oh, man. Not again.

I remembered the window behind me. Wondered if I could get it open. Escape to the roof.

"Why did you leave before the color changes were done

last night?" Dave's voice was controlled and steady, but that didn't mean anything. An explosion could be imminent.

Because I want a life outside of work?

"I had a doctor's appointment last night." Honest.

Dave paused. He wasn't expecting that.

I hoped he thought I had a terminal illness and would go easy. Or just go away.

"Oh, a doctor's appointment, huh?" His voice accelerated. "Well, why didn't you come back afterwards?"

No such luck. "I had plans last night." That was the truth. I was busy until nightfall.

"What plans?"

I knew he was going to ask, but I was hoping he wouldn't. There were a number of us on the team who considered ourselves Christians—"an inordinate amount for a group so small" according to Chris, our resident agnostic.

None of us were just the church-on-Sunday types, though. Most of us attended a midweek service or Bible study. That's where I was the night before. I was never in the position where my work conflicted with my faith before.

That was about to change. "I was at a Bible study," I said.

Dave paused again, but only for a second. "Bible study? Well, sometimes we have to put our work in front of our personal engagements."

I suspected that would be his response. Although many of us were believers, Dave wasn't one of them. From the little background I heard, Dave's father was some sort of setup man for a traveling evangelist and the whole experience left Dave bitter. It was like a scene out of Robert Duvall's film, *The Apostle*.

Dave's went into full rant mode. *He* stayed late. *Heindel* stayed late. *Janet* stayed late. I acted irresponsibly and endangered the demo. I shouldn't have left before the changes were done and checked in. (Even if they took me a couple days, apparently.)

I stayed quiet and waited him out. He finally finished with a scowl, closed my door, and boom-stepped away.

As the footsteps grew fainter, I fought with reverting to my typical response to one of his "ego-adjustment seminars." I contemplated other professions. Could I work on the farm again? How about lifeguarding?

Maybe just random violence followed by resignation?

When the offer to work for Fox originally came along, it seemed like an answer to prayer. The job description was perfect and I had no other immediate options. I was having a hard time finding the blessing in it now, but sometimes those take time to see.

If nothing else, my Fox experiences would make a great story someday.

• • •

By the weekend, Dave decided there were too many design issues involved with the color changes. We would leave them out of the build for DevCon.

My portion was within hours of being complete, though.

• • •

Monday brought the start of DevCon. For the second time Fox users from around the world converged on Toledo, Ohio, anxious to see our latest and greatest. And there was much to show.

Thanks to the work of Heindel, Eric, and McClanahan a good working set of the SQL syntax was in place. In addition, Amy Fulton created a tool—called the Query Builder—that made generating that SQL syntax easier. Though not yet complete, it was near enough to be demoed.

Another amazing new feature was FoxPro's "Rushmore Technology." Devised by Eric and McClanahan while laboring over SQL optimizations, Rushmore was an internal mechanism to get information back from ad-hoc queries at blinding speeds. For example, a SQL query to retrieve a few dozen records out of a database of over a million took only a few seconds.

Our favorite demo involved a table that contained every street in the U.S—over 2 million records. The user could look for every instance of a street named "Abercrombie" and FoxPro would return the answer before the user had time to take their hands off the keyboard. Our closest competitor's product took about forty-five minutes to return results for the same query. It was incredible. FoxPro could retrieve information on a personal computer at speeds only ever attained before on a room-sized mainframe.

Of course, since my design tools and Jadzia's templates were so interface oriented—easy to grasp in a demo setting—they would provide much of Dave's presentation.

Altogether, we thought our updated FoxPro would make the attendees ecstatic. Remembering how fun the demo was the year before, everyone—including Sally—decided to attend.

When we arrived that morning, though, we found things were different than the prior year. The number of attendees, now close to a thousand, forced Dave's session into a much larger room. And while the additional space allowed everyone, dev included, to have their own seat, it changed the atmosphere entirely. As the demo progressed it became clear there would be little rhythmic clapping, no foot stomping, and definitely no calling for a human sacrifice. The reception was cool, almost business-like.

The only thing I worked on that received any applause was

the "selection marquee" I wrote during my time waiting for the Object Oriented FoxPro document.

It was a complete letdown.

• • •

Two days later, I was part of the "FoxPro Feedback" session.

This session was held in a smaller room than was used for Dave's demo, but it was still fairly large. Large enough for three to four hundred people. The seating was divided into two equal sections with an aisle down the middle. In that aisle, near the front of the room, was a microphone stand.

Also in front was a long table and chairs for the panel of developers. The members of the panel were Eric, Heindel, Amy, Brian Tallman, and me; all shrouded in polyester. Itching and uncomfortable.

Janet Walker sat with us as well. Her job was to make introductions and field any questions the rest of us couldn't handle. Chris Williams hovered nearby, looking as if he regretted his decision to leave development. Marty and Brian Crites—now affectionately known as "The Mac Dweebs"— were seated in the audience.

Usually, being in front of a large crowd isn't my favorite place to be. But as Janet described the session when recruiting me, it was strictly question and answer format. No speeches or demos. It was an opportunity for our users to tell what they liked or disliked about the product. And to ask for their favorite enhancement.

I figured I could handle that.

When we first took our seats, the room was maybe one sixth full. No big deal. But by the time the session was to start, the place was completely packed.

I was really hoping nobody asked me anything.

Janet leaned into the microphone.

"As you all probably know, I'm Janet Walker, the product manager. To my right here is Amy Fulton. She's responsible for the Filer, the Color Picker, and most recently, the Query Builder...."

I watched the audience. Tried to minimize their size in my mind. There was a polite round of applause for Amy.

"Next, is Brian Tallman. He's responsible for the BROWSE command, the menuing, and our windowing..."

The applause increased. There was some movement toward the back. A few people got to their feet.

"Next to him is Kerry Nietz. He worked on the Report Writer, and now the Screen Painter and the Menu Builder..."

Now everyone was standing.

Wow. I glanced at the other developers, then gave a tentative smile to the audience.

Okay, I can do this...

Janet continued the introductions and the audience remained on their feet throughout, clapping loudly.

Then the question and answer portion began. People lined up behind the microphone and took turns asking questions or making suggestions. In general, the feedback was positive. No one asked me anything. I mostly just smiled and nodded.

Finally, after almost an hour, a female attendee reached the microphone. She had short, light-colored hair and was casually dressed. She looked like someone's mom. "I'd just like to say, I listened to all that's gone on here," she said, nodding, "and I think it's all good stuff. There have been a lot of good answers and good suggestions."

Her eyes scanned our faces. "But, I waited in line for a different reason..." She paused, smiled. "I'd just like to thank those of you on the panel. You and your product really changed my life. Before FoxPro, I was living in a tent on the street, unsure of where I'd get my next meal. But now I'm a highly skilled and well-paid consultant…and I have you guys to thank." She nodded once. "So thanks!"

Okay. That was a little weird.

I glanced at the other members of the panel. Their faces mirrored my thoughts.

The audience erupted into another standing ovation.

I wasn't sure what to think. Here we thought we were busy creating a simple computer program, when in actuality, we were starting our own cult. I saw Marty and Crites applauding and laughing at the same time.

Still, it was difficult to leave the session without feeling appreciated. It gave me a renewed sense of purpose. Someone *really* cared about what we did, and from what we heard, made a good living using it. Whether we were actually getting people off the street or not, we were helping people. Making their life easier.

Sometimes the blessings take time to see.

Chapter 16
Snippets

Dave had the product running on his computer with a Screen Painter design window open. He was mindlessly creating controls on the surface and clicking through their dialogs. An example of what we called Dave's "dinking with the mouse."

I was sitting in the chair at the end of his desk, the proverbial "hot seat."

"What the Screen Painter needs, my young friend, is the ability to attach snippets of code to controls."

I leaned forward and squinted at his computer screen, trying to see what brought about this new revelation. "Snippets?" But the Screen Painter is finished…

Dave looked at me. "Yes, little snippets of code. For the GET clauses…WHEN, VALID, and the rest. Instead of putting in an expression, they'd be able to type in the actual code. The generator would take care of matching it all up at code generation time."

My stomach began to ache, and lunch was still a few hours away. Apparently, Dave was adding something to the Screen Painter the week after we demoed it at DevCon.

Now granted, the conference existed—in part—to gather information on what our users wanted from the product. *Most* software companies would use that information to design features for the *next* version of their product, though. Not one they'd been working on for the greater part of the year.

And I didn't hear *anyone* at the conference mention "snippets." This must be all Dave.

"Did someone ask for code snippets?" I asked, sounding innocently curious.

Dave was staring at his screen again, mouse aflutter. "No…but they wouldn't know how to. Being able to attach snippets of code would give them the same functionality we were trying to achieve with that object-oriented stuff." He nodded his head slowly. "Snippets…yes…we need snippets."

• • •

Essentially, every control (push buttons, checkboxes, etc.) a user placed on the Screen Painter's design surface had a number of "clauses" associated with it. This was because, when code for that control was generated, the resulting GET command *also* had clauses as part of its definition. These clauses had a litany of names, such as VALID, WHEN, or MESSAGE and each had what was called "an expression" associated with it.

As part of the READ mechanism, these expressions would be evaluated (have their values checked) at different times in the life of the interface. For instance, the expression for the WHEN clause of a control was evaluated when someone first selected that control. This evaluation process was also called the time the clause "fired." So, if a dBase program defined a push button control, the WHEN clause of that control "fired" when a user first tried to push on it.

There were some rules for these expressions, but what they did was really in the hands of our users. In their most complicated form, an expression could actually be another chunk of dBase code they wrote. This chunk of code was called a User Defined Function (or UDF, for short) and it was another instance where we allowed our users to customize the performance of their program. With that power and flexibility, we also gave them the ability to "shoot themselves in the foot" if they wanted to.

In the current incarnation of the Screen Painter, when our users wanted a clause to have an expression that was a UDF, they needed the actual code for that UDF defined elsewhere— in a separate file outside of the Screen Painter. They just used the name of the UDF as their expression in the Screen Painter. The generated code then would use that same name to call their UDF when the clause fired. It was up to the user to make sure that the separate file was available when the generated code was run.

Dave wanted to change that, though. He wanted the Screen Painter to hold and manage all the code for the UDFs, eliminating the need for a separate code file. Furthermore, Jadzia's templates would have to somehow take care of naming those chunks of code.

For me, it meant the wombats broke free from their can and were now living under my desk.

• • •

Downtown Perrysburg is a quaint little historical area. Its principal dissecting street, Louisiana Avenue, ends at a statue of Captain Oliver Hazard Perry, the naval captain famous for his exploits in the War of 1812 and responsible for the phrase "We have met the enemy and they are ours." The Maumee River is just beyond that statue to the north. To the south, the street is lined with a handful of Victorian buildings that contain shops and eateries.

Of the restaurants, a couple were on the "regular visit" list for the Fox developers. Principal of these was Kwongs, a small Chinese place Heindel dubbed "the best lunch deal in the free world." On any day, you could purchase a full plate of food for less than five bucks, and lunch came with tea and an egg roll. Kwongs was the choice the day of Dave's snippet epiphany. At lunch with me were Eric, Heindel, and McClanahan.

Menu in hand, Eric leaned close to me. "What part of FoxPro do *you* like the best?" he asked, using a distinct hillbilly twang. He used that phrase and dialect often. I'm not sure why. *Tallman* was the one who grew up in West Virginia. Eric came from Ohio.

I sniffed. "Not the Screen Painter," I said.

Eric feigned astonishment. "Do I sense a little animosity?" He then looked at the others and chuckled.

I buried my head in my menu. I really didn't want to talk about it.

The waitress, an elderly Caucasian woman, arrived gripping a pen and a small notepad. "What can I be getting you boys?" she asked.

"Szechwan special," Eric said, returning his menu.

McClanahan was next. "Um…yes, I'd like the Szechwan too…" He pointed at the menu. "Vegetarian. No chicken, and um…no MSG." Aside from a first cousin, McClanahan was the only practicing vegetarian I knew. In the heart of farm country, he was determined "to not eat anything that ever had a face." Our lunch group just called him a "picky eater."

The waitress turned to Heindel.

"I want the Szechwan too," he said, slapping his menu shut and passing it like a baton. "And I'd like a bucket of MSG on the side." He formed his hands into a large circle. "Yeah, a big bucket of MSG. Just put it right here on the table."

Laughter ensued. The waitress just stared at Heindel with a polite smile on her face. Waited. "Are you serious?" she asked finally.

Heindel, now almost to tears, gave a little wave. "No, I was just kidding."

McClanahan chuckled along softly and pointed a threatening finger at Heindel.

After the waitress left and the laughs subsided, Eric turned his attention to me again. "So, what is Dave adding this time?"

I looked skyward. "Snippets."

Eric looked at Heindel. "Snippets? Que signife 'snippets'?" Occasionally, one of those two would drop into "French mode." It was a form of mental illness.

"Snippets," I repeated. "He wants little code snippets for people's VALID clauses…well, for all the clauses really." I shook my head. "It's a mess," I glanced at McClanahan, and then Heindel. "And I thought the Screen Painter was finally done." I turned to stare absently out the front window at the street beyond. It was completely empty. "I wish I could talk him out of it."

The waitress returned with a pot of hot water. Eric took it, began filling our cups. "Well, good luck," he said.

Heindel put some sugar in his cup and stirred it. "Yeah, Dave has definitely reached the point where you can't talk him out of something because it's hard to do."

I took some ice out of my water and dropped it into my tea. What Heindel said was true, but I didn't like to believe it. When I started with Fox in 1988, Dave was still occasionally coding on the product, so he still had a good idea of what was involved in adding a feature.

Now he was far removed from the product's inner workings. Plus development had pulled off many seemingly miraculous things. Dave no longer cared *how* something was done. He just came up with features and we had to add them.

Heindel continued. "He just doesn't want to be bothered with implementation details anymore. The only way to talk him out of something is to convince him it is a bad idea."

Which was hard, especially when it was *his* idea.

There was something about snippets I didn't like, though. It seemed like a lot of work for very little gain.

The waitress arrived carrying plates. *I have to get out of this…somehow.*

• • •

I wasn't good at persuading Dave. I just couldn't come up with compelling arguments for *why* something shouldn't be done. The only reasons that usually came to me were: "This is really hard" or "There's something about this I don't like," and neither of those worked anymore. They definitely wouldn't help with "snippets." Dave *loved* the idea.

So I had to disprove the concept somehow. The only avenue I really had was to get snippets working and hope that when he finally saw what they were like, he'd realize the deficiency of his idea, and drop it. That was my only chance.

Less than a week later I had the first cut of "snippets" added. And I was still hopeful.

Previously, every clause that the user could define would bring up a dialog called "the Expression Builder" where they could construct an expression for it. With my new additions, though, there was now an intervening dialog where the user chose between bringing up the Expression Builder, or just typing their snippet code into a small, six-line editable text area. The size of a snippet was limited to 64K of memory space. (Roughly equivalent to the size of this chapter.)

The new dialog wasn't very flashy though. In fact, I thought it was butt ugly.

There was a certain amount of awkwardness to the process, as well. Reaching the Expression Builder now took an extra step, so those who liked to do things the old way would be slowed down. And for those who *wanted* to use snippets…well, trying to put code into a six-line editable area was awkward too. Our users were accustomed to using the text editor for editing dBase code. They were spoiled.

Yet my new dialog was fully functional, and everything was just as it had to be. I was giving Dave the functionality he wanted in a dialog that was consistent with the rest of our interface. If the process was clunky, it was clunky because *snippets* were clunky.

They were a bad idea.

And he should be able to see that.

• • •

Dave's hand rested on his chin. "This dialog looks okay…" he said as he studied my changes for the first time. "But there needs to be a way for them to edit their snippet in our editor."

I shook my head quickly, as if to clear it. "Huh?"

Dave glanced at me. "Yes, for small sections of code this dialog works fine. But their snippets could be any size."

I checked the definition of "snippet" in the dictionary. It meant "a small part." But our editor could edit a file nearly as big as a computer's hard disk could store.

And I had no idea what a snippet window that was an actual editor session would entail. All the sundry clauses were self-contained from the Screen Painter's perspective. They were carried around in memory as character strings and theoretically had the same size limit I gave the code snippets—64K.

I was stalled. "An editor window?"

Dave nodded. "Yes, an editor window. In this dialog somewhere should be a button they can push to open an editor session."

That was unheard of. No interface I ever saw allowed a floating, sizable window to come up on top of a fixed dialog. It just wasn't done. "You want me to open an editor window on top of this dialog?"

Dave paused for a moment. "Well, maybe not on top. Maybe *behind* the dialog."

That seemed even weirder. "Okay…" I stood up to leave. "I'll look into it."

Though this editor window twist was unexpected, I felt a blossom of good feeling.

I may have found my way out.

• • •

My next stop was Marty's office. As the resident Mac whiz he was sort of the resident interface whiz, as well.

"Hey Marty," I said as I entered. "Got a question for you."

Marty hated the office chairs we were given, so he'd pilfered a straight, non-rolling chair from the conference room. When I entered, he turned around, hooking an arm over the chair's square back. "What's that?" he asked.

"Have I told you about snippets?"

He shook his head. "No…"

I summarized the genesis of snippets. "But that's not the best part," I said finally.

Marty was watching me attentively. For months he'd worked on the Mac code with minimal input from Dave, so he liked to hear what he was missing in the spotlight. "Okay, Kerry," he said, "what's the best part?"

"Dave wants a snippet editing window to come up behind the dialog that opens it."

Marty moved in his chair slightly, causing it to thump on the floor. "What?! Behind the dialog that opens it?" He glanced at his Mac screen. "How are we going to do *that* on the Mac?"

It was the response I hoped for. "I don't even know how I'm going to do it in DOS," I said, shrugging. In general, our Window Manager was built to open a new window in front of other windows. I would need Tallman's help to get around that somehow.

And I didn't even want to think about the editor issues yet.

Marty shook his head. "Snippets. What the heck is a snippet?"

I shrugged and moved toward the door.

• • •

Mentioning Marty's reservations did me no good, though.

"The Mac?" Dave said. "Well, let's not worry about the Mac now." He frowned, scratched the side of his neck as he thought. "Eh...I don't know what we'll do in FoxPro Mac." He paused, slid his wristwatch up his arm a little. For some reason, his watchband always seemed a size too big. "We'll do something else. Something more Mac-like."

"Okay..." Darn it! He's punting.

Dave leaned back in his chair and laced his hands behind his head. "And I was thinking...we need snippets in the Menu Builder too...."

"In the Menu Builder?!"

"Yes, they should be able to attach snippets of code to their menu items."

I felt my face begin to flush. The last I knew our Beta cycle was going to start near the end of the year. Two and a half months might be enough time.

But Dave had a knack for constructing deadlines. It seemed there was always something—some show or demonstration—we needed to prep for. "When do we need this stuff done by?"

"Comdex," he said. "It must be done by Comdex."

The second full week of November. Less than a month away.

Oh, the pain, the pain.

• • •

Lunch the following day was at the local Burger King, a place manned by automatons. "Hello. Welcome to Burger King," the woman monotoned as we reached the front of the line. "May I take your order?"

A few minutes later we were seated in the solarium portion of the building, soaking up whatever sun we could get on a chill October day.

"This snippet stuff is going to kill me," I said. "Dave now wants snippets in an editor window. And I have to add them to the Menu Builder." I scowled and pulled a fry from its cardboard container. "Oh yeah, and it has to be done by Comdex."

Eric sat across from me, picking toppings off his sandwich. "Well, I'll tell you what you're going to do." He moved his hands so it appeared he was holding a small rectangular box between them. "You allocate some memory…"

I just glared at him. Now was not the time for jokes.

He saw my look. "Call it a buffer?" he asked, still clutching the imaginary box.

I stayed silent. No jokes.

"No?" Eric watched me for a moment, and then took a bite of his sandwich. "You know," his voice was now even, signaling he was in advice mode, "I used to get frustrated with some of the things Dave asked for." He popped a fry in his mouth. "But I've learned to do what he wants even though I don't like it." He glanced over at Bill and Heindel before looking back at me. "He's usually right."

"Does that mean he's right now?" I wanted to ask, but didn't. I knew my boss was a gifted man. You couldn't start a college Computer Science department *and* a successful software company without having a few things on the ball.

And there was undoubtedly much about running a company I didn't appreciate, many decisions and hidden pressures.

But was it wise to add a feature just because you could?

Snippets? Why snippets!?

Still, if Eric was telling me to "shut up and just do it" it was probably time to do just that. End my complaining and just work.

It was going to be hard, though. The snippet ball was rolling downhill, and it felt like it was picking up steam.

• • •

The next week I succeeded in getting the editor windows to open up behind the snippet dialog (actually, behind the snippet dialog and whatever dialog brought up the snippet dialog) but there were *many* difficulties. It turned out the editor liked to be the "top dog."

Dave seemed happy with the change. Until...

"Look," he said after I arrived at his office. "When I edit this snippet..." He went through the motions to open a snippet editing window and paste a huge amount of text into it. Following this, he closed the window and went through the entire process to open up the editing window again. When he reached the place where the editor's window was open, he scrolled down to the end of his "snippet" of code.

"It's truncated!" he exclaimed. "Part of my code is missing!"

That 64K limit I mentioned. "Well, yeah Dave, those things are stored in handles. The limit is 64K."

Dave looked at me with eyebrows raised. "What!"

"You know, handle-size, Dave. The limit is 64K."

"A 64K limit?" He straightened in his chair. "That's unacceptable."

For a snippet of code? "I thought these things were just snippets." Now, granted, I took the path of least resistance, but time was short. There were only a couple weeks until his contrived deadline.

What does he expect?

"Unacceptable! We will not have a 64K limit!"

He was getting heated. It was time to talk implementation. Even though it wouldn't help. "Dave, here's how the Screen Painter works…" I summarized the Screen Painter internals, explaining that it didn't have anything to do with a file on the hard disk after the file was initially opened. Allowing for snippets of any size would change that. In fact, it would change a lot of things.

"And if I have to do this for the Menu Builder too, and before Comdex," I said, talking as fast as I could. "I can't get it done. No way. I just can't."

Dave stared at his screen, thinking. Making me wonder if he understood my dilemma. Or even cared. "What's Sally doing?" he asked finally.

Last *I* knew she was working on functions for the manipulation of arrays. But shouldn't *he* know, really? "I don't know," I said.

"Well, maybe Sally can help," he said. "But a limit of 64K is unacceptable."

• • •

Sally was happy to get involved. "Alright," she said, throwing my office door open. "What did you get me into?"

"I'm sorry," I said. "Really."

Her look of disdain changed to one of futility and surrender.

We divvied up the snippet tasks. She would create a "Snippet Manager" to handle the operation of snippets, their editor sessions, and the temporary files they needed. I'd handle everything specific to the Screen Painter and Menu Builder.

Which would be more than enough.

• • •

As our Comdex deadline approached, Sally, Jadzia—who was making changes to the generator in step with us—and I were getting real close to having snippets working as Dave demanded. But at least a couple times a week, he'd heap on a new requirement.

"We need to store the snippet editing window's status with the screen file somehow," Dave said. "If my snippet window was open and minimized when I saved my screen file, the window should be opened and minimized when I open the screen again."

A few days later: "We need an option to open all the snippets with any code in them. Yes, maybe an 'Open all Snippets' item on the menu somewhere."

I could see where that was leading. "Do you want a 'Close All Snippets' item too?" I asked.

Dave thought for a moment, and then nodded. "That's a good idea…yes, open all snippets and close all snippets…"

• • •

Shortly after that meeting, Marty looked into my office and opened the door. "What're you working on?" he asked.

I glanced up from my screen briefly. "Open All Snippets.

Dave wants it in before Comdex." I motioned him closer and gave him a quick demo. His eyes got wide as snippet windows exploded onto the screen.

"Open all snippets," Marty said slowly. He shook his head. Drifted toward the wall with a whiteboard. "Snippets provide no new functionality, you know. None. You can get everything you want the old way."

"Yeah…" I tried to talk Dave out of them. Both subtly and blatantly. Schemed, whined and complained. All to no avail. The snippet implementation code still didn't fit into the product very well, but it worked. I lost the will to fight any further.

"It is just flashier this way," Marty continued. "Flashier to see hundreds of windows pop up on the screen rather than open up one solitary code window and put your procedure in there."

"I know," I said, glancing between Marty and my screen. "It's what Dave wants."

"And by Comdex," Marty continued. "What's that?" He pointed at me, but I think he was *really* pointing at the man in the corner office. "It's never enough to show the cool stuff that's already done. We have to have something 'for the show.' Have to show what's being done *right this second.*" Marty smiled and swatted the air. "Bah." He moved back to the door.

"We're doomed!" I said as he left.

He chuckled. "We're doomed!"

• • •

Some time later Janet stopped by my office with a bag of candy in her hand. "Look, Kerry!" she said. "Snippets!" She took a couple pieces from the bag and handed them to me.

The candy looked like a Tootsie Roll, but emblazoned

across the wax-paper wrapper was the word "Snippits." The spelling was close enough. I gave a half-hearted grin and sniffed. "Thanks."

Janet beamed. "Snippets, Kerry. Snippets!" She left, undoubtedly heading to Sally's office next door.

I pulled the candy from the wrapper and put it in my mouth. It *tasted* like a Tootsie Roll too. I glanced at my monitor. On top was a small metal man my little brother (fourteen years my junior) gave me. It held a racket in its hand and bounced on a spring.

I pulled open my desk drawer and found a little metal twistee. Using it, I bound the candy wrapper to the metal man's neck.

Snippet-man was born.

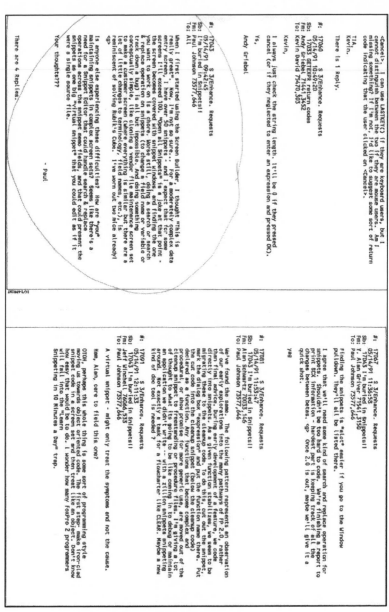

<Cancel>. I can use LASTKEY() if they are keyboard users, but I
cannot distinguish between the two if they are mouse users. Am I
missing something? If I'm not, I'd like to suggest some sort of return
code indicating that the user clicked on <Cancel>.

TIA,
Kevin.

There is 1 Reply.

#: 17060   S 3/Enhance. Requests
05/14/91 10:49:20
Sb: 17033 GETEXPR return codes
Fm: Andy Griebel 74140,3452
To: Kevin David 73470,305

Kevin,

I always just check the string length; it'll be 0 if they pressed
cancel (or if they neglected to enter an expression and pressed OK).

Ys,

Andy Griebel

#: 17043   S 3/Enhance. Requests
         I'm buried in Snippets!!
Sb:
Fm: Paul Johnson 73577,646
To: All

When I first started using the Screen Builder, I thought "this is
really great. Now I don't have to..." For moderately complex data
entry screen, I have over 50 snippets; and I expect that for some
screens I'll exceed 100. "Open all Snippets" is a joke at that point -
the screen becomes covered with snippet windows, and finding the one
you want to work on is a chore. Worse still, doing a search or search
& replace operation on snippets is impossible (or very visible or
conceptually simple, like cloning a vendor file maintenance screen set
to make a customer screen (where everything is similar but there are a
lot of little changes to terminology, field names, etc.), is
reminiscent of solving Rubik's Cube. I've worn out two mice already!
<g>

Is anyone else experiencing these difficulties? How are "your"
maintaining snippets in complex screen sets? Seems like there's a
need for a Snippet Editor that could handle search & replace
operations across the snippet sense fields, and that could present the
snippets as one big virtual snippet that you could edit as if it
were a single source file.

Your thoughts????

                                                    - Paul

There are 4 Replies.

#: 17067   S 3/Enhance. Requests
05/14/91 11:36:55
Sb: 17043 I'm buried in Snippets!!
Fm: Y. Alan Griver 73574,3550
To: Paul Johnson 73577,646

Finding the snippets is "alot" easier if you go to the Window
pulldown. They'll all be listed there.

yag

I agree that we'll need some kind of search and replace operation for
snippets. Shouldn't be too hard to code. We're finishing up a report to
print SCX information - hardest part is keeping track of all the
changes between betas. <g> Once 2.0 is out, maybe we'll give it a
quick shot.

#: 17081   S 3/Enhance. Requests
05/14/91 11:55:47
Sb: 17043 I'm buried in Snippets!!
Fm: Alan Schwartz 70033,145
To: Paul Johnson 73577,646

We've found the same. The following pattern represents an observation
of our early explorations into the many pathways of FP 2.0 rather
than final advice. During early development of a feature, we code
directly into the snippet. As a given function stabilizes, we seem to be
migrating these to the expression. To do this, cut out the snippet,
mark the code into the expression and put the function name-there. Put
declared as a function. Any functions that become complex and
procedural, or show promise for more generic use, are moved out of the
cleanup snippet to freestanding or procedure files. I'm giving a lot
of thought to what its going to be like, coming in to debug or maintain
an application... with a zillion snippets anywhere. Not exactly a task for a flowcharter like CLEAR. Maybe a new
kind of doc tool is needed ?

#: 17091   S 3/Enhance. Requests
05/14/91 12:33:08
Sb: 17043 I'm buried in Snippets!!
Fm: Jeff Winchell 76066,533
To: Paul Johnson 73577,646

A virtual snippet - might only treat the symptoms and not the cause.

Hmm, Alan, care to field this one?

OTOH, perhaps this whole thing is some sort of programming style
moving us towards object oriented code. The first step: make iron-clad
snippet code in a screen set and then treat it as an object. Don't know
how easy that would be to do. I wonder how many foxpro C programmers
will fall into the "Learn Snippeting in 10 Minutes a Day" trap.

CompuServe traffic on the pitfalls of snippets

Chapter 17
Holiday Happenings

By the time Fall Comdex arrived we already had another deadline. The deadline *this* time was the start of our Beta test cycle for FoxPro 2.0, near the end of December. And since Dave didn't want development distracted from its work toward that deadline, none of us were allowed to go to Comdex. We were all still curious, though.

Near the end of Comdex week, the lunch crew gathered at Casa Barron's—another of the restaurants downtown. Barron's was a dimly-lit Mexican place known for its free supply of chips and salsa and the paintings of half-naked women on the walls. Eric promised to fill us in on the latest news.

Heindel was first at the salsa, and the questions. "So, what's the word from Janet?" he asked, bringing a chip to his mouth. "Do the people like our stuff?"

Eric fetched a chip of his own and waved it slightly as he spoke. "Oh yeah, she says they're crazy about it. The booth is always packed." He munched for a while, and then got a sly look. "Even Ed Esber stopped by."

"Was he handing out resumes?" Heindel asked, chuckling. Ed Esber left his job at Ashton-Tate a few months prior. He was now the *former* CEO of Ashton-Tate.

Eric smiled. "You're bad." He took a sip of water. "I guess he just stopped by to tell us how much he liked our product. He told Janet that it was *never* his intention for Ashton-Tate to sue us."

Bill stroked his facial hair. "Really?"

There was a glint of playfulness in Heindel's eye. "I can see how that could happen," he said. "The lawyers probably just misunderstood. Ed probably said he wanted to *see* FoxPro and they thought he said *sue*." Heindel tipped his head. "It could happen."

Those three laughed. I just smiled and found a chip.

"So did Janet say anything else?" Heindel asked, still smiling.

The food was brought to the table. It was a "twofer" day: two tacos, two burritos, or two enchiladas for one low price. I was partial to the enchiladas.

"Oh yeah," Eric said, rolling his eyes. "Chris is at it again."

We exchanged looks. We all knew what that meant.

"So, what's he taking credit for now?" Bill asked.

Eric flipped his hands up. "Oh, the booth, the enhancements to the product. You name it."

I shook my head. From childhood I was taught not to "toot my own horn" so it was hard for me to understand someone who not only tooted his horn, but frequently took credit for the rest of the band's performance as well. I didn't know if Chris saw his "all you see here" trait as a problem or not. I wondered if it would ever get him into trouble, or if it bothered anyone else.

Chris's ego was never far from the surface.

• • •

Soon thereafter we heard the news that Chris would be rejoining us in development. On his first day back, he went to lunch with the 11:30 crew. Afterward, I stopped in to see Sally.

"Sally," I said. "You're a prophet!"

Sally giggled. "Are you talking about Chris?"

"Yeah—how did you know he'd be back?"

Sally turned her seat in a back-and-forth swinging motion. "Things are always greener on the other side for Chris," she said, smiling. "He's just like that." She paused, raised a shoulder. "I knew he'd be back."

I slid over to take a seat on Sally's spare office chair. "Well, he told us at lunch he had a hard time accomplishing anything because the executive committee wouldn't give him enough money to work with."

The executive committee was the ruling body at Fox. It was mostly composed of LaValley and Fulton family members. Given our locked first aid supplies and utilitarian surroundings, one could safely say they were conservative with company funds.

Chris was a bit of a spendthrift, though. He was the only person I knew who had a big screen TV, an in-ground pool, and a second mortgage. A few clashes between the committee and him wouldn't surprise me.

But Sally did. "That's what he told you, huh?" she said.

"Why…" I squinted. "What did you hear?"

Her seat started swinging again. "I heard Dave say Chris couldn't cut it in Marketing. It was either come back to development or he was gone."

I inhaled, breathing through my teeth. "Whoa…" I paused, shook my head. I didn't think Chris would have *that* much difficulty. Faults aside, Chris was a really hard worker in dev. And he didn't even hint about a problem during lunch. "Dang!" I said finally.

Sally shrugged. "That's what I heard."

"I thought maybe he just ran out of stuff to take credit for."

Sally laughed again and I got up to leave.

Regardless of the reason, I was glad Chris was one of us again. He was a solid coder, an amiable guy, and—if nothing else—an interesting character. I missed him.

Soon after his return to the top floor (the Marketing

offices were now situated on the bottom floor, literally beneath our feet), he began work on something called the Project Manager. The purpose of the tool was to allow users to more easily manage the elements of their FoxPro application (code, screen, reports, and the like) by maintaining it in a project form.

It was a feature long overdue, and the perfect thing for Chris to redeem himself with.

• • •

Meanwhile, a company named LoadStone was making noise about suing us.

Apparently, sometime during the period when *Rushmore* was in development, the people from LoadStone sent us a copy of their product to evaluate. They were hoping we would buy the source code and integrate it into FoxPro. The principle functionality of their product was adding information to the end of our index files that allowed some index-based operations to execute faster.

The fact their product modified the index files made it undesirable for us. Our index file format hadn't changed since the early days of FoxBASE+ and now there were literally millions of index files in existence. Any change to the format of that file would break nearly every application ever written for our product.

We couldn't do that.

One thing the LoadStone product did *was* significant, though. The information they attached to the end of the index files was a "bitmap"—a component integral to *Rushmore*, as well. Both products constructed a bitmap based on an index expression, and made use of it to quickly retrieve samples of the data in a database (or databases). The principal advantage of *Rushmore*, however, was it built its bitmap "on the fly," and then disposed of it when it was through. The index file remained unchanged.

Not being directly involved, I never knew whether the LoadStone product was the catalyst for Eric and McClanahan thinking about index optimization, or if it was a mere coincidence that we received it around the same time *Rushmore* was under development.

If I were to bet on it though, I'd bet on the latter. Eric was *always* looking for ways to improve the product's performance, and usually he found them. It wasn't hard to imagine him dreaming up something like *Rushmore* while he was brushing his teeth in the morning. He was just that good.

Yet LoadStone alleged we reverse-engineered their code and even had one prominent computer magazine articulate that theory. Later patent searches would prove they didn't own the rights to anything close to *Rushmore* technology.

Now all that remained was that little disagreement with Ashton-Tate.

One lawsuit down, one to go.

• • •

On the tenth and eleventh of December I had a role in a Christmas play at my church. My part was trivial, but my attendance was key. Of the forty thespians, I was the only adult. Children were depending on me. I needed to set a good example.

I had no worries about the first performance. The tenth was a Sunday and though there was some weekend work at Fox, nobody was going in on Sunday yet. The Beta deadline was still a few weeks off.

It was the second performance that concerned me. It was in the evening on a Monday so I'd have to leave for the play immediately after work. If something major came up during the day...well, I already knew what Dave thought about activities after work.

As I drove in that morning, I knew there were no guarantees I'd successfully make it out that night. Virtually anything could happen. There were things I could do, though, to increase my chances. There were *rules* I could follow.

The rules were undocumented, but by now I had a good idea what they were. They were the things I had to do to avoid getting stuck; the things that avoided confrontation. The four from the top of the list were:

1. The network is sacred. Never check in anything you don't want Dave to play with, and *never* check in something that doesn't build completely.

2. If your check-in will result in a long (greater than twenty minute) build, let everyone know. Saving it until the end of the day is best.

3. Never use the phrase "it works on my machine" to defend a bug. Dave's response to that will be, "Then I guess we'll ship *your machine.*"

4. Don't check anything into the network after about two in the afternoon if you want to avoid being dragged back in the evening and yelled at. Even the safest code could have problems—and Dave stays late.

If I adhered to the rules completely, I might have a shot. But no guarantees.

By the middle of the morning, I was certain I was home free. Dave was out most of the day, and I spent my time tweaking details in the information stored in the Screen Painter's file. In general, this was a low risk change. It was the least amount of work I could do and still be doing something productive.

After my change was made and tested, I checked in the

code. It was just before two in the afternoon. I moved on to other projects I had on my list. Projects I wouldn't finish until the next day.

A little before five, I left for home. *Home* was now in Perrysburg, because over the summer I purchased a small house on the outskirts of town. My commute was less than seven minutes. Upon arriving, I hurriedly ate and jumped in the shower. The play was at seven, and it would take me almost half an hour to get to the church. Time would be tight.

After my shower, I went into my room and located my lone dark suit. It was the only bit of polyester apparel I'd owned for the last two years, and that was fine. Holding the waist up, I slid a leg in.

I heard the phone ring. I pushed my other foot through and went for the phone. This can't be...

It was. Janet's voice was in my ear. "There's a bug in the Screen Painter," she said. In the background I could hear Dave fuming. "It's all f***ed up!" he said loud enough for me to understand.

I glanced at the clock. It read six o'clock sharp. I don't have time, I thought, I have to appeal to reason.

"I have a Christmas play tonight," I said. "I *have* to be there. Can't I deal with this in the morning?" Nothing important was happening the next day, and I usually got in two hours before Dave did. There probably *was* a problem in the Screen Painter, but I could fix it before he got in. No big deal.

"Well..." Janet hesitated, *wanting* to be reasonable.

"It's his responsibility!" Dave yelled. "Get him in here!"

So much for reason. "Never mind," I said. "I'll be in as soon as I can." I pulled on the rest of my suit and headed for the office.

When I arrived, Dave was waiting at the front door. He was already wearing his coat and hat, though. Hey...he's going home!

"Ah, there you are," he said, but I rushed right past him. "Get that Screen Painter fixed!"

I clamped my mouth shut. Now I was *certain* I could've fixed the bug in the morning. Dave came in long enough to find a problem, had Janet call me in, and was now leaving without knowing if I fixed it or not. I could just go upstairs and out the back door. I bounded four steps at a time, reached the top floor, and threw open the door. My instincts have been wrong before, though.

Thankfully, I found the problem almost immediately. It was the "trivial" changes I made that day. I quickly backed them out, and then sprinted from the building.

I arrived at church just in time to go onstage. "Where were you?!" the kids said in unison. There was no easy way to explain it to them. They were twelve-year-olds.

The following morning Dave chewed me out for not testing my work better. Once again, I kept my mouth shut and let him rave at me for a while. Once again, I returned to my office and contemplated being a lifeguard.

I didn't have to convince myself to stay this time, though. Apparently realizing he was a little hard on me; Dave returned to my office later and apologized. The experience did give me another item for my list, though:

5. Always test your work thoroughly. Just running through the scenario you're working on is not enough. A problem that arises due to faulty testing will elicit a "Don't you test this sh**?" from Dave.

• • •

The January issue of the magazine *DataBased Advisor* arrived at the office a few days later. Dave was one of the first to read it, and the following sentence from a letter to the editor caught his attention:

"I never realized all the neat and wonderful things one can do with Chris Williams's Amazing Browse command."

Now, a portion of that statement was true. The current incarnation of BROWSE *was* an amazing piece of work. It allowed FoxPro users to view the data in their database tables in a plethora of different ways. In its simplest form it listed the table's field names across the top of the screen and the individual table records down the screen, providing a snapshot of the data in the table—but it was immensely configurable. It was arguably one of the most powerful commands in the language.

Chris didn't write it, though. He hardly even touched it. That work was done exclusively by Eric Christensen and Brian Tallman.

After Chris went home that night, Dave made multiple copies of the spurious declaration. On each copy he increased the font size from the previous copy until finally the phrase **"Chris Williams' Amazing Browse Command"** screamed out in epic proportions. He posted these ascending copies on Chris's office window for all to see.

When Chris arrived the next morning, I walked over to see how he was doing.

"That guy is a freaking idiot," Chris said as I entered his office. I assumed he was talking about the misinformed magazine subscriber, and not our boss.

I tried not to smirk, but it was hopeless. "Well, why does he think you wrote BROWSE?" I asked. Come on, Chris, fess up…

"I don't know," he said. "I didn't tell him that." He directed his attention to his computer screen and began typing hurriedly. "He's a freaking idiot."

I watched him for a moment. Whatever he was doing, he was really into it. "What're you doing?" I asked finally.

His eyes stayed fixed on the screen. "I'm writing a retraction letter." There was clearly no laughing this one off.

"Oh…" I watched him for a few moments longer, and then, smiling larger, left him to his writing.

Chris's letter was never sent, though. Dave nixed that plan when he arrived a short time later. "You'll not put our underwear out for the world to see!" he said.

So, left with no other option, Chris spent the rest of the day in his office alone.

Sulking.

• • •

Otherwise work on the product was intense, mostly because *Dave* was intense. He became so aggressive, in fact, most of us refused to fight with him over anything anymore. Our "agreeing not to disagree" gave rise to a new slogan: "LTWW."

LTWW stood for "Let The Wookiee Win" and any fan of the classic Star Wars trilogy is familiar with the reference. It comes from a scene where the robot (aka "droid"), R2D2, is playing a game of chess with an eight-foot-tall hairy beast known as a Wookiee. In the middle of the game, the Wookiee gets upset over a move R2D2 made.

Another droid, C3PO, steps in to mediate. "He made a fair move," he says. "Screaming about it won't help you."

A knowledgeable spectator named Han Solo interrupts. "Let him have it," he says. "It's not wise to upset a Wookiee."

"But sir," C3PO says, "nobody worries about upsetting a

droid."

"That's 'cause droids don't pull people's arms out of their socket when they lose," Han explains. "Wookies are known to do that."

"I see your point, sir," the now-sapient C3PO says. He leans close to his robot companion. "I suggest a new strategy, R2," he whispers. "Let the Wookiee Win."

To us, the similarities between Dave and the Wookiee increased as the days of development on FoxPro 2.0 went by. His temperament reached the point where it was just better to let him have his way. "L...T...W...W" was muttered more than once under someone's breath after Dave vehemently ordered a product change. Better to do the work than have your arms ripped off, after all.

To more solidify the analogy, one winter day Dave began sporting a full-length fur coat, along with a matching fur cap.

If he only knew.

• • •

Furry aliens aside, something happened on December 11th, 1990 that would make even a Wookiee cheer.

With little fanfare, Dave called the development team and the various department heads to the upstairs conference room. He then informed us the Ashton-Tate lawsuit was virtually over.

In their original complaint, Ashton-Tate claimed the "organization, structure, and sequence" of their dBase products reflected ideas completely their own. They alleged we illegally copied the "look and feel" of their programs, which included their menus, any text that appeared in their product, and their commands (i.e. the dBase language, which incidentally, was now being called "the xBASE language" by many of the gurus).

Ironically, though, the judge in the case issued an order *invalidating* Ashton-Tate's copyrights for the whole line of dBase products. He found they lied to the US Copyright Office on their original copy registration (many, many years prior) by claiming the dBase language was a language wholly their own. But it wasn't. It was derived from another language program developed by Jet Propulsion Laboratory. The name of *that* program was JPLDIS, and JPLDIS was in the public domain.

In other words, no one owned the dBase language, and no one could. Ashton-Tate's whole case was thrown out on a technicality.

We realized, of course, Ashton-Tate would probably appeal the decision and force us to go to trial again. Nevertheless, the ruling was a big win for us. It may not solve anything from a legal precedents perspective, but it was like seeing the sun after a long, grey winter.

Until told otherwise, we were free to do what we wanted to do all along—create the best database program ever. A fitting finale to our year of hard labor.

Chapter 18
Small Rebellions

Another lunch, another discussion about our fearless leader.

We were at another local place called Charley's. It featured Greek cuisine and walls painted—quite convincingly—to look like marble.

I admired the walls. I found it fascinating that something that looked so real, so much like something carved from the earth, was really the product of an artist's imagination. The painter's work really isn't that much different from coding. A computer program, like FoxPro, is essentially just a mirage.

"Boy Dave's sure...um...*intense* lately," Heindel said, giving a little uncomfortable laugh.

"No kidding!" Bill took a bite of his gyro, beginning the war between gyro sauce and facial hair. Sauce took an early lead.

Eric rolled his eyes and simultaneously dipped a fry in ketchup. "Oh yeah, he's really got a bug up the butt." He pushed his head forward emphatically. "And I *don't* know *why*. There's nothing different this week than last week."

"I think he's just worked up about the bugs," Heindel said, "and the beta..."

Eric shook his head. "There will *always* be bugs," he said, staring Heindel hard in the face. "There'll *always* be betas." He shook his head again. "Getting upset doesn't solve anything. He needs to just lighten up." Eric looked up, studied the walls. "Maybe Amy's been holding out on him," he said finally.

I smiled and Heindel and Bill chuckled. It was nice to see I wasn't the only one feeling the heat.

Finally, they're beginning to understand.

• • •

Since my office was near the end of the row, the job of collecting people for lunch unofficially fell to me. A few days after the trip to Charley's, I was in the process of fulfilling that duty again. I gathered Crites, Heindel, and Bill. Tallman and Sally never went. McClanahan was entrenched in his work and waved me off. Marty was "watching his figure." Chris didn't want to go.

Next up was Eric.

I entered his office. It was undoubtedly the sparsest of the lot. Aside from a small CD-player, and a few family photos, it had little aside from his white desk, black chair, and bookshelves. Plus, well over a year after the move, his boxes *still* weren't unpacked.

Eric sat with his legs crossed and his fist pressed firmly against his lips.

"Lunch?" I said.

He turned toward me. He looked a little distant, a little mentally involved. "Just a second…" He strode past me and turned in the direction of Dave's office.

I tagged along.

Dave was up and mobile. Circling like a shark in a pool.

"I'm going to lunch now," Eric said.

"Well, don't go until you have those bugs fixed." Dave was clearly agitated. I decided not to venture any further. Just waited at the door.

"Dave, there will *always* be bugs," Eric said.

Uh, oh. The phrase was familiar, but I couldn't believe I was hearing it now. Eric was normally the compliant one. Just shut up and do the work, remember?

Dave's began to vibrate as he paced. "We're going to

release a new beta, Eric."

Eric shook his head. "There'll *always* be betas...."

Dave swore repeatedly. "This is important, Eric! It's crucial. We have to get this stuff out...."

Don't make me angry. You won't like me when I'm angry.

Eric dropped his head slightly and walked past me again. "I won't be going," he breathed.

• • •

January and February remained tense. As far as Dave was concerned the product could ship at any moment. Yet, in direct opposition to that goal we continued to add features—features that came directly from the new bane of our existence—the CompuServe traffic.

Since the start of our Beta program, near the beginning of '91, our Beta-testers were able to log onto a forum, via CompuServe, where they reported any bugs they found. These external bug reports were typically quite helpful because the product was now so complicated our burgeoning testing team couldn't test it fully.

The reporting process was the problem. In addition to the useful bug reports, the Beta-testers often sent along their favorite enhancement requests.

Now, in theory, that shouldn't be so bad. A simple request from a single user was never enough to get the proposed feature added to the product. Unfortunately, the area where the reports were filed was a *community* forum, which meant the other Beta-testers could easily read each other's reports and append comments of their own. That's where the trouble began.

It usually happened this way. A Beta-tester would find something in the product they wished acted differently and would casually mention it on the forum. Other testers would read that comment and start a discussion about a possible enhancement. In forum lingo this discussion was called a "thread." The thread would eventually escalate into a thunderous rallying-cry. The Beta-testers simply "had to have this enhancement or the product will be completely unusable!"

Then Dave, who read the traffic every morning, would get caught up in the hullabaloo. He'd call a meeting to see what could be done to address the issue. By meeting's end we would have another feature that someone would have to add. The next thread would start the process all over again.

This continual "feature creep" and Dave's growing intensity level started to impact the development staff.

Morale was at an all-time low.

• • •

Since his hiring, McClanahan furiously toiled away on his SQL implementation, completely on his own and with little supervision. He virtually barricaded himself in his office, coding tirelessly—yet his work remained a mystery.

His whiteboard was filled with scores of formulas. "All necessary for my work," he assured us. We had to believe him, because none of us understood what his cryptic gobbledygook meant. Some SQL queries were working in time for the last DevCon, so we knew he was making progress. But no one was sure what he was working on exactly, or how close he was to being finished.

Plus, McClanahan tended to be reclusive. He worked in his office alone and rarely asked anyone anything. That could mean one of two things. Either he was so ahead of the game he didn't need anyone's help, or he was hopelessly lost and afraid to admit it.

Dave decided to end the mystery. He assigned Eric to "take a look around" and help out, if need be.

Eric's investigation returned mixed results. McClanahan *did* have a good share of work done. However, Eric also found that McClanahan duplicated in his own work code written elsewhere in the product. Code readily available for him to use. All he would have had to do was ask. Furthermore, there was still *plenty* of SQL work left to be done.

Dave wasn't amused. He turned up the heat on McClanahan, hoping the added pressure would motivate the diminutive vegetarian.

What it did instead, was make McClanahan *more* frustrated. "This is ridiculous," he'd say when I stopped in to greet him. "Ridiculous!" And he'd shake his head furiously.

Dave's spotlight was unlike anything McClanahan experienced before. He was even forced to postpone a family vacation until after his work was complete. A goal that grew increasingly further and further out.

He was stressed, frustrated, and had few places to turn.

• • •

The rest of us shared McClanahan's feelings, of course, we just dealt with them differently.

For instance, a regular morning gripe session developed in Sally's office. These meetings started out innocently enough. Sally and I both got in early, our offices were adjacent, so I often dropped in to say hello and shoot the bull about whatever was on our minds.

As the days progressed and the pressure grew, our morning get-togethers turned into a forum for all the latest news and complaints—many of which centered on Dave and whatever unreasonable thing he'd done lately. Over time, the membership of our gripe session started to grow.

The newest member was Marty Sedluk, and he had *plenty* to complain about. His job, since the summer of 1989 when FoxBASE+/Mac version 2.01 shipped, was to work on the Macintosh version of FoxPro, FoxPro/Mac. So, for all that time—nearly eighteen months—he was dutifully moving code from the FoxPro/DOS code base to the FoxPro/Mac code base, making whatever changes he deemed necessary to make it work properly on the Mac. Nobody asked how he was doing. Dave never bothered him. Essentially, no one cared.

"I could sit and code buck-naked," Marty joked, "and nobody would ever notice."

On the rare occasion Dave *did* give Marty attention, it was usually to harass him. I saw this firsthand while in a meeting with Dave and Janet.

We were discussing the way certain windows behaved in our product. Dave felt if a user clicked a window in the background (behind another window) it should not only come forward, but whatever was within that window—in the area where the user clicked—should also be selected. Our text editor behaved that way. It would bring the window forward and select the word under the mouse cursor. Every other tool—Screen Painter, Menu Builder, Label Writer, etc.—just brought the window forward. It took another click to select something within.

"The tools are behaving like the Mac," I said. "The editor isn't." The Macintosh computer was our erstwhile guide for FoxPro's interface, so it seemed like a reasonable argument.

Dave scowled. "The Mac! I don't care about the Mac! Apple never did anything for us!" He picked up his phone and started dialing.

I heard Marty's polite "Hello?" through the receiver.

"Marty?" Dave asked.

"Yes?" Still polite, compliant.

"Marty!" Dave continued, now more animated. "Apple never did anything for us!" Ker-slam! Dave hung up the phone.

A few minutes later Marty walked in with the Macintosh rulebook in hand. Having been briefed by me about the possible meeting topic, he had the book opened to the appropriate page. He quietly pointed at it.

Dave just fanned the air. "I don't care what *Inside Mac* says. Apple never did anything for us."

Marty appraised Dave with wide eyes, nodded slowly.

"Take that away! Apple never did anything for us..."

Marty was a worthy addition to our early morning group.

• • •

Frustration was apparent in others as well. In a separate meeting with Dave—this time with Heindel, Chris, and Jadzia in attendance—I got to see it in Heindel.

The issue this time was "scrollable lists." While playing with the product the night before, Dave noticed these interface elements looked *slightly* different in the Screen Painter than they did in READ.

He pointed at his screen where the two depictions were apparent. "Look at this!" he said. "The lists look like this in the Screen Painter and like this in READ. READ is wrong!" He began punctuating each sentence with a firm slap on the desk. "It's ugly! It's a wart! It's a melanoma! It's like a pimple on the product! It's obvious it doesn't work! It never worked! No one ever tested it!"

As always, everyone sat in stunned silence. Waiting for the storm to pass.

Except Heindel. "Listen Dave," he said. "It *does* work. I *did* test it. It worked when I put it out!"

Now Chris, Jadzia, and I were stunned and staring at Heindel.

Dave opened his mouth to speak again, but wasn't quick enough.

"You're getting all excited about a few little bugs." Heindel cupped his hands and started slapping them together as he talked. "When *you* get excited, *I* get excited, and then I can't think. It's *just* a *bug!*" He chanced a look at Dave. "Now we know about it and we'll fix it. You don't need to yell."

Dave joined the rest of us, speechless. An uncommon occurrence.

My respect for Heindel reached a new level that day. Heindel back talked Dave—and lived through it!

It inspired me to try a little revolt of my own. I could *never* be as overt as Heindel, but I had an idea.

• • •

One of the things Dave was famous for was his use of large, obscure words. In the course of normal conversation, he would randomly fling out a word that only a regular reader of the dictionary could understand. If you wanted to know, you'd have to halt the discussion to get the definition. If you *didn't* want to know, you were left trying to figure it out from the context, and that could be difficult.

It wasn't clear why Dave did this. Whether he was trying to expand his own vocabulary, or improve ours. Part of me suspected it was because he liked keeping everyone slightly off balance. Whatever the reason, though, he did so constantly.

My goal was to hit him where he lived. I would find a word—*any* word—that he didn't know and use it seamlessly in conversation. In fact, it became my mission for some time to find the perfect word. I searched word lists and kept my eyes and ears open. My word had to be so close to the periphery of English that some of the smaller dictionaries wouldn't have it. It didn't have to be complicated, or even technical, but it *had* to be right.

Then one day it dropped into my lap. While perusing a trade journal, I saw the word "agnosia." It meant, "lacking the ability to understand."

This is it, I thought. I've never heard it before, it's easy to say, and I can even use it in a conversation.

Now I only had to find the right time to use it.

A few days later, Dave called me to his office to discuss a Screen Painter detail. As often happened, the discussion arrived at the proposal of a new feature.

"I think that would be a good addition," Dave said, nodding his head once.

"Well, Dave," I said, "I don't want to sound like I'm suffering from *agnosia* or something, but..."

Of course, I knew Dave might already know my perfect word, and its definition. But if that's the case, I reasoned, it's no harm done—we're just making conversation. He may even think better of me for using a word on his level.

"Agnosia?" Dave said, sounding mystified. "I don't know that word. Is that a word—agnosia?"

I willed myself to calm. "Agnosia? Yeah, it's a word. It means *lacking the ability to understand.*"

Dave jerked his head back. "Really?" He brought a hand to his chin. "Agnosia, agnosia...that's a word I don't know." A pause. "I'll give you a bonus for knowing a word I don't know."

"It's a word." I rose in my seat slightly. "I can get a dictionary."

Dave pulled off his glasses and rubbed his eyes. "No, no, I believe you," he said. "It makes sense. Agnosia, that's a good one. Okay, where were we…"

I fought off a smile. Trite? Yes. But I now had a great story to share with the rest of the team. I never saw that bonus, but I already had my reward.

• • •

While the Ashton-Tate lawsuit against us was on appeal with the Ninth Circuit court, the original judge (Judge Terry Hatter) received an affidavit from the Register of Copyrights. In that affidavit, the Register—Ralph Oman—claimed Judge Hatter was too harsh when he invalidated Ashton-Tate's copyrights.

"If Ashton-Tate had disclosed in its Original Registration Certificates the information that was later disclosed in its Supplementary Registration Certificates, including the existence of additional preexisting works, the Copyright Office would *still* have processed the applications and issued registration certificates to Ashton-Tate," Oman said. "Where a copyrightable work is merely influenced or inspired by a preexisting work, but there has been no substantial copying of protectable expression from the preexisting work, the Copyright Office does not expect or require that preexisting work to be disclosed on the application for registration."

So, in essence, the Ashton-Tate's copyrights should have just been amended, not invalidated.

Judge Hatter agreed, and in April of 1991 reversed his December decision. Following that, the Ninth Circuit court sent the case back to Hatter for further proceedings.

After a short respite, Fox was officially in a legal war again.

Chapter 19
Attitude

I was passing through the front portion of the building one Saturday afternoon, en route to my office, when I noticed something peculiar. I stopped dead in my tracks.

What happened this time? I stared at the closed door of Dave's office. The door being shut wasn't abnormal. Most of us shut our doors when we left. The peculiar part was the doorknob. It was completely missing. In its place was a half circle of emptiness, the splintered edges a clear indication that something violent had happened.

Oh, there *has* to be a story behind this.

While I stood appraising the destruction, Matt Pohle emerged from a nearby cube. Matt was a stringy fellow, about six feet tall with dark hair and an easy smile. Only a few months earlier he was promoted from Tech Support to Testing. Though I barely knew him, it was clear he liked to have fun. I heard his laugh a lot during the course of a day.

When he saw me, he grinned wide.

"What happened to Dave's door?" I asked.

Matt covered his grin with one hand and bent forward slightly. "Dave kicked it open," he whispered.

I shook my head slowly. "Do I want to know why?"

Matt's grin got larger. "Well, you know his little boy?"

The boy who used to bounce in the seat-spring downstairs? How could I forget?

I nodded. "I know him."

"Well, this morning Dave came in, put his keys in his office, and walked back out here." Matt motioned toward the open area normally occupied by Dave's receptionist. "The little boy followed him out. But on the way, he pulled the door shut—Ker-slam!"

I smiled, shook my head again.

"He locked Dave's keys inside!"

I sniffed. "I bet Dave was happy."

Matt waved his hands over his head. "Oh, he was storming around…there was *lots* of swearing." Matt pointed a thumb at the door. "And then he just kicked it open!"

I looked at the door again. It was a clean break. "Couldn't he have just called a locksmith or something?"

Matt shrugged. "Probably, but he didn't. He turned around and just mule-kicked it open!" Matt's eyes were wide. "Can you believe it?"

I studied Matt a moment. Things were tough in the department he was promoted from. Fox offered free phone support to anyone who used our products, and some users not only took advantage of it, they exploited it. Some called nearly every day.

Plus, the Tech Support people had mandatory overtime. *Mandatory* in that if they left, they didn't need to come back the following day.

Furthermore, the call list for Tech Support was maintained on a huge stack of pink "While You Were Out" notes. It was insane. Apparently, no one thought to use our perfectly good database product for the task, or if they had, they were overridden. Isn't that what a database is for, though?

When Matt was promoted, his colleagues cheered his success. He was finally getting a better life, they thought. Finally being treated like an employee, not a slave.

They had no idea.

I put a hand on Matt's shoulder and gripped it firmly. "Welcome to Fox Software, Matt," I said. "The *real* Fox

Software."

...the place where crazy stuff happens nearly every day. I hope you enjoy your stay, 'cause most of the time, I sort of hate it.

• • •

A few weeks later, Heindel called my name as I walked by his office. "I need to talk to you about something," he said. He looked serious, an uncommon disposition for him.

"Sure..." I walked in, moved slightly to the left.

Heindel stood up over his desk and shut the door. He *was* serious.

Of any, Heindel's office now looked the most lived-in. There were two white shelves, haphazardly filled with books and old software. There was a bulletin board complete with notes, phone numbers, and a low golf score. And there was a brass and white burlap chair Heindel brought in from home. It was the antithesis of Eric Christiansen's office, actually.

"I need to talk to you about your attitude," he said.

Didn't see that coming. "My attitude?"

"Yeah. It sucks."

Wounds from a friend. I couldn't help but feel defensive. He obviously didn't understand all I'd been through. It was now April 1991 and the development cycle for 2.0 had stretched out way too long. I started work on the Screen Painter in the fall of '89 and now—almost a year and a half later—I was *still* working on the Screen Painter.

If my attitude was bad, it seemed justified.

"You fight everything Dave wants. I don't want you to get a bad reputation."

I picked up the stuffed Cleveland Browns football that

Heindel kept on his desk. It was my favorite item to fool with when I visited. It was getting a little ratty looking now, its stitches starting to fray. I gave it a firm squeeze. "I don't think you understand."

I *did* resist change a lot, but I was sort of at the end of my rope. All my collegiate gung-ho-ness had been thoroughly wrung out. Replaced by what? Anxiety. Stress. Fear?

Dave recently told me I "fought too much" but a few days later, when *Janet* persuaded me to make a Screen Painter change, he said I hadn't fought enough. I wasn't sure how to behave anymore.

I thought we were all in the same place, though. We'd been on a death march so long we were beginning to look like zombies.

Heindel was undaunted. "Just my impressions," he said when I finished. "What you do with it is up to you."

"Okay…" I got up to leave.

If Heindel thought I was fighting too much, I would *try* to ease up a little. It would be difficult, though. Work wasn't much fun anymore. All I really wanted was for the product to ship. I needed a break.

• • •

Every morning was the same as the last. Overnight, or over the weekend, Dave would have played with the product. While doing so he would have found problems that fell into one of two categories: 1) bugs to be fixed immediately; 2) things he didn't like about the product (*melanomas* in Dave-speak) that he wanted "fixed" before the end of the day.

These problems were cataloged on a list he made. Beside each item would be the initials of the developer(s) he thought responsible. The culprits were notified of their guilt in a variety of ways.

The most likely method would be via phone from Dave's secretary. Passing by her desk, Dave would say something like "Mel-ooo-dee! Get Kerry, Chris, and Heindel in here!" Melody would call everyone mentioned and say, "Dave wants to see you in his office. Right away!" The summoned would drop what they were doing and trudge to Dave's office, usually with downcast heads, the fear of impending doom evident in their gait.

Sometimes, though, the call would come from Dave himself. When *that* happened he was typically calling from his car phone (he was the only person I knew that had one) on the way in. If he resorted to this tactic, it meant he was demonstrating the product to someone that morning. His problem would need to be fixed ASAP. Preferably before he arrived.

The final method was the most invasive. Dave would arrive at his office, drop whatever he was holding, turn on his computers, and personally set off for the people he wanted. This method came with the early warning boom-steps, reminiscent of a scene from the movie *Jurassic Park*. We all knew Dave was coming, and hoped he *wasn't* coming for us.

When Dave arrived at the unlucky soul's office, instead of just walking in and inviting them to follow, he would peer through the Plexiglas (usually with a stern look on his face), knock on it with a forefinger, and motion for them to come out. It was like being summoned for that last long walk to the electric chair; I expected a member of the clergy to be walking behind me.

The scene that followed was rarely pleasant. Chris called the experience "getting a rebuttal" or "getting a new orifice carved out for oneself." Dave was seldom diplomatic in these meetings. He was normally agitated and unreasonable, and almost always loud.

His list of problems was laid out on his desk and he blasted through them one at a time, always noting how unusable the product was now, and how quickly the change had to be made. "Egregious infelicity!" he would say. "Heal it! Quickly!"

This was not the time for discussion. The naïve developer might try to argue a point, but that was a good way to get your arms ripped off, so to speak. Never argue, and definitely never say something was hard. Dave didn't want to hear it. He didn't care. Morning meetings were for addressing Dave's concerns and the concerns gleaned from the CompuServe traffic. Implementation details were best left for later in the day.

Afternoon meetings came with their own set of difficulties. Dave was more introspective then. He liked to ponder how problems might be solved. Consequently, his mannerisms would be on full display. Rings would be spinning, ears would be flipping, and popcorn would be spilling. We bit our tongues to keep from laughing, but we did what we had to do to get our problems solved.

And the problems just kept coming.

• • •

Into May the CompuServe Traffic continued to feed the feature mill. We never knew what changes would need to be made next. We lived in constant fear of an enhancement that was beyond our abilities to implement. That somewhere, out there, swimming in the CompuServe Sea, was something that would finally cause us to go screaming into the night.

One fateful day, after reading a particularly long and protracted discussion on the forum, Dave realized the way READ was currently working was unacceptable.

READ. The can of wombats. The tower of eggs. The command that energized an interface. The command that was often the pivot an entire dBase application turned around. It was rearing its malformed and unstructured head again.

What the CompuServe traffic hinted at (*screamed*, really) was the fact that there were serious problems with the way READ interacted with other areas of the product—areas a dBase programmer might normally have in an application—like the BROWSE command, or menus, or *any* other non-READ window.

Specifically, the problem was that READ was never designed to work with other windows. In the days of FoxBASE+, there weren't other windows to deal with, so READ filled the entire screen and handled every keystroke.

In the initial version of FoxPro, our principal goal was to have READ function just like the one in dBase IV. DBase IV maintained the same functionality as Ashton-Tate's earlier products—and so did we. There just wasn't enough time or able bodies to do anything more.

In 2.0 we inadvertently pried the lid open, though. Heindel and I massaged the READ code to allow for multiple windows. It was a nice addition, but it gave our users the expectation that those windows were fully able to interact with the rest of the product.

Such was not the case.

READ was still designed to have one of its windows—regardless of how many there were—on top. If one of them wasn't on top, the READ would terminate and the user's program would continue on.

Most of the time.

Sort of.

Or not.

So, when the problems became obvious, Dave called a meeting to address them. The final result was a list of extremely difficult READ enhancements. These enhancements were collectively lumped under one primary feature, called a "Foundation READ."

The purpose of Foundation READ was to handle interactions from any windows involved in the READ, and everything else on the FoxPro desktop at that time. Because of its all-inclusive nature, and the recent ending of the first Gulf War (that Saddam Hussein promised would be the "Mother of All Wars") Foundation READ was also known as the "Mother of All Reads"—or MOAR for short.

• • •

Since my name was on Dave's list for a totally unrelated problem, I was present when the MOAR enhancements were piled on Heindel.

It wasn't pretty. My friend's face was ashen and his responses slow, deflated. I thought we might need a defibrillator.

"Dave," Heindel began, "I don't know about this…" He hesitated, shook his head. "I mean I don't even know where to—"

"We *have* to do this." Dave was serious, but sympathetic. His eyes were fixed on his computer screen, presumably to avoid having to watch Heindel's reaction. On the screen were a READ window and a companion BROWSE window—each behaving badly. "READ is unusable without these changes."

Heindel glanced at the screen, and then shook his head again. "Yeah, I can understand that...but READ...well, every time I go into that code, I break something."

I knew Heindel's pain. Until that instant, I was certain *I* was going to be the one to have something major dumped on them at the last minute. With as many trips as I made to the corner office the chances seemed good.

But it was Heindel. I felt for him, but to be honest, I was also a little relieved.

I tried to communicate my nonverbal empathy, but Heindel's eyes were locked on the floor. I instead looked across the room. Dave recently had a large clock installed that looked like a map. It showed the path of the sun as it moved across the earth. There were still plenty of hours of daylight left.

Dave looked at Heindel. "Yes, yes, READ *is* bad," he said, still sounding sympathetic. His eyes drifted my direction.

Why is he looking at me?

"Kerry will help you," he said.

The world seemed to grow dark. *Me?* How did I get involved?

Dave waved us away to get started.

I followed Heindel to his office. As soon as I was inside, he threw the door shut. "I can't believe this! It's me *again*! Every time we get to the end of a project, *I'm* on the critical path!" He rounded his desk and dropped into his burlap seat, causing it to make a clanking sound. "I thought I was home free this time, but it's me! *Again!*" He looked at me, eyes wide. "I have *no idea* how to make these changes!"

He paused, shook his head. "I can't believe it's me again..."

It was the truth. In every project we worked on since I'd known him, Heindel was over the fire at the end. In

FoxBASE+ 2.10 there was the CodeGen stuff, and then the integration of CodeGen again in FoxBASE+/Mac. On FoxPro 1.0 his printing work went the distance.

And now with 2.0, it was READ. It didn't seem fair.

I wasn't sure how to help, though. I *hated* READ. It was chaotic.

I found myself a seat and just watched as Heindel fumed. Then a few ideas started to formulate. I thought about some of the things Sally and I had to do for snippet windows. We wrote a number of routines to loop through windows looking for the appropriate type. Then I remembered the places I had to change for multi-window READ.

So, what if READ sort of *hibernated* when another window came up…a window that didn't belong to READ?

I felt a burst of confidence. "Wait, Heindel-man," I said. "I think we can do what Dave wants."

He looked at me as if I'd finally lost it. This was *READ* we were talking about. Hadn't it defeated me before? Wasn't that why Heindel was working on it now anyway? Because I couldn't handle it?

I raised a shoulder. "I've got an idea where to start, anyway."

I soon moved a machine into Heindel's office and we were coding in tandem. We worked for days, from early in the morning until late at night…

And good things started to happen.

• • •

Here's an example of the type of behavior we were trying to fix.

A dBase developer has some code he's written that has a READ with two windows involved, a typical multi-window

READ scenario. The users of the application could click on either window, type in any editable areas, perform any normal interface behavior, and READ would work just fine.

However, if the developer's code opened a BROWSE window before the READ, so when the READ executed there were three windows in play—a BROWSE window and the two that belonged to the READ—things got unpredictable. If the users just interacted with the READ windows, everything would be fine. However, if they happened to click in the BROWSE window, the READ itself would terminate. After that, the users could no longer interact with the two READ windows anymore. They were visible, but completely dead. Only the BROWSE window was available.

Now to work around that situation, the dBase developer might put a button on one of his READ windows that brings up a BROWSE. In that case, when the button was pushed, usually a BROWSE window would open and come forward. The READ window that contained the button would still think it was in control, though. It wouldn't realize a window was on top of it. So, it would still be trying to take every keystroke and mouse click for itself. This would leave the BROWSE window in a state where it *looked* like it could be interacted with, but it really couldn't. It was sort of a zombie BROWSE. It appeared alive, but for all practical purposes, it was dead.

The whole thing was confusing for us, and we weren't trying to make our livelihood by using it. Unfortunately, what *really* needed to be done to READ was the same thing that happened to most of the product for the first version of FoxPro. It needed to be turned inside out so it was completely event-driven.

There was no time for that, though, and no way to test it even if there were. So the hope was to move wraith-like through the READ code, being as judicious as possible, yet still make it behave the way it should. It was a tricky maneuver.

That's where *hibernating* the READ came in. The idea was to detect the specific places in the READ code where window-switching could happen, test to see if such switching occurred (like a BROWSE window opening on top), and put the READ to sleep temporarily. Then, when the BROWSE (or whatever other window) went away, we needed to wake the READ back up.

It was tricky, but I knew enough about the event-driven parts of our product, and Heindel knew enough about READ that it actually might be doable.

• • •

"Computers will never work, you know."

I smiled. Less than a week after we started the MOAR changes, they were nearly complete. Heindel's spirits had improved, and surprisingly, so had mine. It's been said that the quickest way to make *yourself* feel better is to help someone else who's in need. I think there's a lot of truth in that. It worked for me.

Ironically, the person I helped was the one person who told me my attitude was poor in the first place.

"Okay," I said, biting on the line Heindel tossed out. "*Why* will computers never work?"

He circled his fingers over his keyboard. "Well, you've got all that electricity flying around through silicone and stuff. It shouldn't work. It can't work. It's just way too complicated."

I chuckled, and then crossed my legs, rested an elbow on a knee, and put my chin in my hand. "Why are we doing this then?"

Heindel checked his screen. "I don't know about you," he said, sounding serious, "but *I'm* just doing it to feed my family." He looked back at me, and started smoothing the hair on the back of his head. "But I'm going to have to do something else before long. Because someday everyone is going to figure it out."

I nodded my head. "Yeah. And then we'll be in trouble."

"That's right!" Heindel said, now starting to laugh. He cupped his hands and slapped them together, emphasizing each word. "Computers, will, *never*, work!"

I laughed and stood up. One of my "non-working" computers needed to go back to my office. "All right, Mr. Heindel. Whatever you say." I unplugged the cables from the back of my machine and wrapped my arms around the monitor. "Let's hope they don't find out too soon."

"Never work," Heindel said as entered the hall. "Never."

• • •

A few days later Melody brought me a memo. It said we would be working every Saturday until the product finally shipped. The actual release date was still unknown, but Dave was confident it would be sometime in June.

Unfortunately, the flow of wishs, gotta-haves, and "this product is unusable without" forum threads was still as steady as ever.

And now we'd be losing our weekends because of it.

1.   [Dave] Drop everything and make .VUE files work correctly and completely NOW. Neither report writer nor label generator nor view window will work properly until you do.

2.   [Kerry] Fields which are NOT 'Stretch vertically' are being handled improperly when mixed with fields that to stretch the band. All such fields should be anchorable to either the top or the bottom of the band. Fields anchored to the bottom of the band float down one line each time ExprSlice inserts an additional line into the band (provided they are below the current line in the band).

What is done at present is to anchor some fields to the top of the band and others to the bottom.

3.   [Kerry] When it's available, we should fix up quick report to use the field picker to permit a subset of fields to be included in the quick report.

4.   [Kerry] The column titles inserted by Quick Report should be Capitalized (sic) ... not all caps.

5.   [Kerry] When dragging to resize a box, you really should be able to force a horizontal scroll by dragging through the right-hand screen boundary.

6.   [Kerry] The problem with two pages displaying in page preview for one click is still there.

7.   [Kerry] When multiple fields are selected and the shift key is down, double clicking should NOT bring up the field dialog.

8.   [Kerry] Let's not forget to tell the documenters about Ctrl-clicking on text objects as a means of entering textedit mode.

9.   [Brian] If a field has been resized to zero width and the BROWSE window is closed and BROWSE LAST is issued, the field reopens at default width, not zero width.

10.   [Amy] It appears that CLOSE ALL isn't wired into the view window properly.

11.   [Amy] Don't forget to remove redundant calls to 'usestatus'.

12.   [Brian] When you're in the last record of a browse window with a memo field open and you press downarrow, it moves to EOF and the memo field contents becomes blank. If you're on the last record, down-arrow should have no effect.

July 15, 1989   - 1 -

One of Dave's bug lists

Chapter 20

Desertion

It was like something from the back of a comic book.

It was my first trip to California, when I was only a college freshman. I traveled with my friend Rusty to visit a couple friends there (one who was the groom in the wedding I attended years later). Rusty and I were sunbathing on Venice beach while our California friend was on the boardwalk buying shirts. Suddenly I felt sand hit me in the face.

"You two were looking at us, weren't ya?"

I turned to my right, in the direction of the voice. Standing over Rusty were two shadows. Shadows, because the sun was almost directly behind them. There was a thick shadow and a thinner shadow. Their hair was straggly and matted. They were unshaven and—on a hot, summer day—wearing flannel and blue jeans.

What brought this on?

I looked at Rusty. My pale-haired and already sunburnt friend was staring forward, doing his best to ignore our nameless tormentors. The thicker shadow pulled back his foot and kicked again. Another wave of sand hit Rusty, and then indirectly hit me.

"Answer me. Were you looking at us or not?"

Rusty continued to stare forward. "No," he said.

"You weren't looking at us?" The foot came back. More sand and then the thin one laughed.

"I think you were looking at us," the thick one said. "I think you *like* looking at us."

Man, I never saw you before two seconds ago. I can barely see you now.

I glanced at Rusty again. He was still staring forward.

How are we going to get out of this? I searched the beach in front of me. Not a lifeguard or policeman anywhere. And even if I were big enough, I wouldn't take these guys on. They could be hiding anything in their clothes.

Another kick. Rusty's right side was now partially buried in sand. I decided to join him in staring straight ahead.

The sand flew a couple more times, and there was some swearing, and finally—after a few more taunts—the shadows just moved away. Undoubtedly to harass someone else.

"What was that about?" I said after they moved out of range.

Rusty still looked a little scared. "I don't know," he said.

"Were you looking at them?"

He shook his head. "I never saw them until they were standing here."

I gazed at the ocean, thinking. "I guess it's time to start pumping some iron," I said.

Rusty frowned, repositioned himself on his beach towel. "I think it's time to buy a gun."

I laughed, but when we returned to Ohio, I *did* start lifting weights. Over my remaining years in college I gained over thirty pounds from what I weighed in high school. It wasn't enough to make me look like "Ah-nold," but it was enough to keep me from being bullied physically again.

There are other ways to be bullied, though.

• • •

The Friday before Memorial Day 1991, Dave called a development meeting. The purpose of the meeting boiled down to two sentences: "There's a three day weekend coming up. I expect everyone to work two."

That's good, I thought. My life was way too relaxed.

We were past the breaking point already. The enhancements were still coming, the code had to be kept in perfect shape, and we already lost months of Saturdays to work. Even our time away from the office didn't seem like time away anymore.

• • •

Sally again had a pre-chewed pen near her mouth and a leg crossed beneath her. "I'm afraid of the phone," she said one morning in her office.

"Why's that?" I asked. It seemed like a strange admission.

"I'm afraid it will be Dave trying to call me in. Every time I hear the phone ring I tense up."

I didn't realize Sally was called in that much. I remembered a time when Janet had her come in because a single pixel was the wrong color on a dialog. I didn't think *Dave* ever called her in, though.

Still, people don't have to actually fall out of planes to be afraid of the experience. Sally may have accrued some anxiety from listening to me. I worked on the visual tools—the things Dave liked to play with. Consequently, I was called in more than most. At least, so it seemed.

I wasn't afraid of the phone ringing, though.

Since moving to Perrysburg, I got lots of calls at home after work. Nearly everyone I knew was now twenty minutes away. The sound of the phone ringing usually meant a friendly voice on the other end.

I couldn't imagine that changing.

• • •

Because of the routine I started in college, at least three evenings a week I tried to make it to the gym. This brought me no small amount of grief from my fitness-challenged workmates, but I didn't care. Besides keeping me in shape, it gave me a positive way to work out my frustrations. My attitude improved following the MOAR solution, but it was still a struggle to maintain. Especially now that I was working weekends and Dave cancelled Memorial Day.

My current workout place was located in Perrysburg. It was called Holiday Fitness and Fox employees were given the option to join, a fairly recent addition to our "benefit package." It wasn't a free membership, mind you. We just got a slightly reduced rate.

The gym was located on the east side of town, on a street called Holiday Lane. It was right next door to an earlier Fox home, a small white office building that served the company in the years before I joined it. I never saw the inside of that building, but I always wondered what it was like. The only story I ever heard from Heindel was about how his partitioned office space steadily shrunk as the building's occupancy grew.

The fitness center itself was rarely crowded. In fact, it was better than most gyms I frequented. It had an indoor track, a pool, and a good selection of free weights and aerobic machines. It was airy and open and manned by young people (mostly women) in athletic uniforms. What's not to like?

Shortly after the infamous Memorial Day meeting, I stopped by the gym after work.

Since the California incident, my preference was always weightlifting. So, as I did every visit, I changed into my gym clothes and went about my normal routine, working my way slowly through their assortment of equipment.

At about the halfway point of the workout—just as I grabbed a set of dumbbells—I heard someone call my name. I looked up to see one of the gym attendants clutching the wall phone's receiver. A tall guy in a green athletic suit.

"Are you Kerry?" he asked.

"Yeah…"

He held out the receiver. "This is for you."

"Who would call me at the gym?" I wondered aloud. "*I* don't even know the number." I shook my head and returned the weights to the rack. "Who would call me here?" I crossed the running track to where the attendant stood and took the phone.

"Hello?"

"Yeah, hi Kerry! It's Melody."

Dave's secretary; the tulip that grew outside the lion's den.

"Hi Melody," I said, feeling my stomach muscles tense. "What's up?"

"Well Dave has this problem…" She paused and I heard activity in the background. "Just a minute."

I expected to hear Dave's voice next. I braced myself.

Bill Ferguson's low rumble filled my ear. "Never mind," he said. "We figured it out. It was something Chris did."

"What?" I was still hearing a lot of commotion. Like there was a wrestling match going on.

Another slight pause, "Never mind," Bill repeated.

Melody was back. "Hi, Melody again. Dave had a problem and he wanted me to call you in. I tried your home, but you weren't there, so I figured you were at the gym." She was talking rapidly but it sounded like she was smiling. "Anyway, Bill figured it out. It was something Chris did. So, never mind. Bye!" Then she was gone.

I held the receiver in my hand, dumbfounded. I was almost called in *from the gym*! I replaced the receiver and brought my hands to my sides. Was I now on call no matter where I went? At a moment's notice? At Dave's every whim?

I had plenty of energy for the rest of my workout.

I couldn't escape the feeling, though, that I was becoming a slave. Little of my time was my own anymore, and the time that was *supposed* to be mine, was slowly being encroached upon.

The product needed to ship, but there was no real end in sight.

• • •

Dave McClanahan still wasn't enjoying the Fox Software experience. He was struggling to get all the bugs out of his SQL implementation and there were still whole parts of it that weren't finished. Even with Eric's help.

When I asked McClanahan what was left to do, I'd get one of two responses. Either he would smile and point to the infinity sign I placed—months earlier—in the middle of his whiteboard's display of symbols, or he would start talking about mysterious things called "join conditions" and "tuples" until my eyes glazed over. Whatever remained to be done, only he, and maybe Eric, really knew.

It must have been a concern, though, because one day McClanahan walked into Dave's office to level with him. He gave Dave a status report, told him how stressed he was, and said he needed at least two more weeks to complete his work.

Dave wasn't very sympathetic. He demanded the SQL code be finished on time and McClanahan do "whatever it takes" to make it happen.

• • •

On June 28th—a Friday afternoon—Dave called the developers to his office. It had been at least a week since our last "ship this sucker" speech, so I assumed we were due.

I noticed Dave's demeanor as I entered the room. In motivational meetings he was usually quite animated, eating popcorn or juggling something in the air. But this time he just slumped in his chair. His movements were slow, nearly despondent.

Something major was up.

Dave wasted little time. "I called you all here to tell you McClanahan resigned today, taking his wife with him…"

What? McClanahan quit? No developer had *ever* quit. It was a fact Dave took pride in. He mentioned it frequently in interviews.

We *did* lose Carol, of course, but I don't think she counted toward the record.

And McClanahan's wife quit too? She was in Marketing. She was a sweet lady who laughed when we called her husband a "picky eater."

Dave looked at Eric. "Unfortunately, this means the product will be delayed for a week or so. In order to give Eric enough time to complete the remaining SQL work."

The office grew very still. Aside from the shock of the McClanahans' departure, none of us wanted the release to drag out any longer. It was more opportunity for features to be added. Which meant more bugs. Which meant more time…

Equally unsettling was Dave's emotion over the whole thing. It wasn't easy for him to *lose* a developer.

Then he perked up a little. "Listen, McClanahan's health wasn't very good," he said. "He had problems…"

That justification wasn't very good. We weren't in boot camp, after all.

Dave looked at Eric again. "…and there is some indication that the Emperor had no clothes. Some of the things McClanahan was doing…duplicating code… Well, he just wasn't much of a coder."

I didn't know whether that was true or not. I heard about the duplicating code issue, but that was ancient history. Dave was sort of hurling stones at the guy's back after he left. McClanahan deserved better than that, especially given the conditions we all toiled under. Apparently, he was now the black sheep of the family.

His departure *did* leave us one developer short with a product left to finish, though. Two more weeks meant at least twelve days of CompuServe traffic.

A dozen more days of torture.

• • •

"We're going to lose another summer," Sally said, shaking her head. "Three years! I can't believe we're going to lose another summer." She hunched down, turning her office chair slightly. "I hate this place."

I sighed and dropped my head. I shared her frustration.

We were now into July. Unless Eric finished SQL soon, we had only the winter to look forward to. Ohio has strongly marked seasons. The spring and fall months are usually pleasant with an occasional thunderstorm or tornado thrown in. The summers are nice and warm—sometimes too warm, but in general, they are perfect weather for doing anything outside, especially any kind of water sport.

The winters, on the other hand, are about as close to Hell as anyone would like to come. The months of December through February are filled with near continual snow, wind, and ice—not great conditions for a day at the lake. Or anything else for that matter.

Thanks to a roughly one-year product cycle, Fox was in the habit of shipping a product in the fall. Shipping a product in the fall meant the bulk of the work was done in the spring and summer. This meant we essentially missed the best months of the year for close to three years.

That can really get on your nerves. Any joy you get from releasing a product quickly dissipates when you step into a pile of ice cold slush.

Now, all that stood between us and another lost summer was Eric's efforts with the SQL code. Time to start praying...

• • •

Two weeks later, Dave called another meeting. This time he was gleeful.

"Dave," Janet said as we began to filter in, "Pat Adams called and she has a problem she wants to talk to you about." Pat was one of the dBase gurus. A frequent contributor to the forum, she'd been suggested changes steadily since the Fox Reunion, now almost a year ago.

Dave rested both arms on his desk, and then rested his chin in one hand. "Pat called, did she?" He thought for moment. "Pat called...Pat..." He hopped forward in his seat, grabbing a pack of sen-sens as he did so. "Well, so *what*!" He laughed and straightened himself. "I wish they'd all shut the f*** up and give us their money!" He chortled louder and some of us joined him.

When silence returned, he got more serious. "As you may or may not know, Eric finished SQL, which means we can finally ship this sucker." He looked at Eric, and then played the crowd. "Eric has done an amazing thing. He's done what nobody else could do."

Dave scratched the side of his face. "What McClanahan had was not good, my friends. The Emperor just had no clothes." He panned the room again slowly, making eye contact with everyone. "Eric essentially rewrote SQL in two weeks. Nobody else could've done that," he said. "Nobody."

Nobody? I started to feel ambivalent. I wanted to be glad our misery was finally over. But I couldn't help but feel a little hurt by the way Dave kept repeating that Eric did something "nobody else could do." I didn't see a lot of joy on the faces of the other developers either.

Hadn't McClanahan asked for two weeks originally, anyway?

Most thought Eric was the brightest among us. It was impossible to take away from the work he did over the years or some of the miracles he pulled off. He sped up the product in numerous different ways. He wrote substantial portions of our text editor and BROWSE. He did tricks with code swapping so our bulky product could run in an extremely small memory space. He came up with Rushmore—or, as he called it, "the amazing bit-stacking algorithm." All of it amazing, amazing stuff.

There were many talented people in the room, though. We all worked extremely hard for Dave. Everyone pulled off a miracle or two.

Yet, when you got right down to it, we were *all* expendable. We knew that Eric was the only developer Dave wouldn't fire, aside from Amy. It was a fact we understood, and learned to accept.

This felt like Dave trying to rub it in, though.

To Eric's credit, he never held his "most favored" status over us. From comments he made to me earlier, I knew he appreciated the work the rest of us did, even when Dave didn't.

"I promise to put blinders on long enough for us to ship," Dave said.

The official release date would be July 12th, early enough for us to enjoy part of the summer. After nearly two years of coding, we would soon be free.

• • •

Of course, there is always one final trial.

On release day I stood in the central cubical division talking with Amy and Janet. Everyone was starting to relax a little. The final build was made and the testing department was making one last verification pass through it. Just one final sanity check, and then it would be out the door.

Amy mentioned how much hair she lost during the development cycle.

I squinted. "It doesn't look that much different to me," I said, smiling.

"Well, no," she said. "But I can tell. More hair falls out in the shower."

Janet nodded. "Stress can do that."

I'm surprised I have any left then, I thought.

John Beaver, one of our younger testers, walked up and stood just behind me. He was one of the two college grads recently made testers—the other being Matt Pohle. Both were Computer Science students. Testing was the new training ground for potential developers.

Personality-wise, the two were about as different as could be. Matt was an extravert and a frantic hockey player. John Beaver was quiet, polite, and probably enjoyed a good book even more than I did.

He waited patiently for us to notice him.

"Yeah, John," Janet said finally. "What's up?"

John straightened his glasses, and then pushed his bangs back. "Uh, yeah, I got a crash in one of my verification suites." The testers were pushing to automate some of their testing and the suites were part of that effort. Essentially, they were programs written to severely exercise various product features. An example might be a program that created, opened, moved, and then destroyed a thousand windows using the appropriate FoxPro commands to do so. The suites were still an unproven science though.

"Really?" Janet crossed her arms and started to rock side to side. "What in?"

I took a few steps back. Janet and John had work issues to discuss. The last thing I wanted to think about now was more debugging.

"Um...the Report Writer."

Time stopped for a moment and everyone turned to look at me. I felt my life begin to drain out through my shoes. I looked down to watch it go.

This can't be happening. Just when I thought it was over, a bug springs out to get me. This product will *never* ship.

I couldn't take it anymore. I wanted to run...or strike out at something. I looked at John. You, tester, you... I pulled my eyes over to look at Janet.

She looked skeptical. "The Report Writer?" she said. "That's been stable for months."

"I know," I said softly. My chest tightened so much I could hardly speak. "I haven't changed *anything*."

Janet continued to rock. She looked at John. "Show us."

We followed John to his cubicle where he quickly reproduced the problem. It occurred only under extremely low memory conditions.

"I don't think we'll hold the build for this," Janet said.

I felt my life start to return.

"Just try to reproduce it," she said to me. "See what you find."

"Okay..." I still didn't really want to deal with it. I dreamed of being able to grip them both Vulcan-style and say

"Forget…" and then pinch myself.

John gave me the necessary files to reproduce his "low memory" problem. I crept back to my office to take a look. Feeling shamed. Seriously unsettled.

For FoxPro 2.0 we were actually shipping two separate products in the same box. There was "the standard product," the one that started if a user typed "FOXPRO" at the DOS prompt. This one was built (compiled and linked) in a manner similar to version 1.0 of FoxPro. The advantage of this version was that it ran on essentially every computer the first version of FoxPro ran on.

The disadvantage was that it was confined to using roughly 640K of memory. (Possibly a couple hundred more depending on how the machine was configured.) Consequently, there was a limit to the complexity of the applications that could run on it.

The other version of the product was our extended version. ("FOXPROX" from the DOS prompt). It was geared toward higher end—more expensive—machines, but its principal advantage was that it could make use of "extended" memory. Extended memory could be configured as high as 8000K, so it allowed a lot more wiggle room for the applications our users wrote.

It had another advantage for us Fox developers, though. We could debug on it using "source level debugging." This meant we could use another program—a debugger—to see the human readable code we wrote and step through it line at a time to find a problem.

That wasn't the case with the standard product, though. Because of the 640K memory limit, any debugger we used with it couldn't use much memory (i.e. it had to be what was called a "light" debugger). That meant no source code. All we'd be able to see was the machine-readable form of our code—strings of letters and numbers that most people would think of as gobbledygook. We didn't much like the look of it either. Most of us *hated* having to debug the standard version.

So, my initial hope was that the problem was reproducible in the extended version. I also had another complication. Because John's bug only happened under low-memory situations, I had to run another program—a memory eating program—to swallow up just enough extended memory so I could reproduce the problem, yet not so much that I could no longer make use of my source code debugger. It was a balancing act. One that I succeeded in performing, but with disappointing results. After getting the memory set the way I needed it, bringing up the product, and starting John's program, I couldn't reproduce his problem at all. The Report Writer worked fine for hundreds of iterations of his code.

That left me with only one other option. I'd have to try it in the standard product.

So, after restarting my machine (to remove the memory eating program I loaded) I fired up my light debugger, the product, and ran John's program. All I had to do was wait for the product to "crash" (i.e. to come to a stop, which was the behavior John reported). When a crash occurred, the debugger would pop up and show me where the problem happened.

Of course, all I'd see was machine code, but I would have a few human readable clues to go by. Just enough to tell me which subroutine (a small part of the product's code) the problem was in out of the *thousands* of subroutines that composed the product. Then I could eyeball the source code for that subroutine and see if I could figure out the problem. It was like being a detective at a crime scene. You have clues. Now, what happened?

After John's program ran for only a short time, the product crashed and I saw where the problem was. It wasn't in the Report Writer code, per se. It was in another part of the product the Report Writer made use of. I brought up a code editor to examine the source code for that routine.

And I saw the problem. It was an unlocked handle over a subroutine call.

A "handle" was what we used to reference chunks of the computer's memory. We had a rule about handles. If your subroutine calls another subroutine, you need to make sure that the handles you are using get "locked." This keeps the memory you are accessing from moving around on you because of something the called subroutine does. (And in fact, sometimes the act of calling the routine *itself* could move your memory on you). Having your memory move on you when you weren't expecting it was like coming home from work and finding your house replaced by someone else's. Not good.

The fix was simple, though. I just added a call to lock the handle down. I then compiled the change. Tested it. Found that it worked. I then went to tell Janet.

"So…" she said when she saw me. She looked a little apprehensive.

"Found it," I said. "Fixed it. What do you want me to do with it?" I gave a brief description of my detective work.

"Save it," she said finally. "We'll probably have a maintenance release later anyway."

"Okay."

I returned to my office and stared out the window. The summer sun was still shining bright and boxed copies of FoxPro would soon go out to meet it. One last scare, but it was finally over.

MEMO

On Tuesday, February 14th, Dave is going to be interviewed on camera for a Public TV program (Bowling Green's station). The crew will be arriving at 9:30 a.m. and the interview will take place in Dave's office. They may be filming throughout the building.

Because we all may be on camera, I am requesting that each person clean up his or her area or office (or *hallway area*, as the case may be) before Monday evening. I know that we are very crowded right now, but if you can make your area look as presentable as possible it would really help.

Everyone's cooperation is gratefully appreciated.

Thank you.

Norm

Norm Chapman

Norm's "clean up your space" memo

Chapter 21
Spit and Polish

At the height of development of 2.0, Dave gave me a jazz CD entitled "Walking on the Moon." I wasn't much of a fan of jazz. I was more of a Classical or Pop person, at least for music to listen to while I coded. I took the CD anyway. It wasn't the music style that made it interesting, it was the performer. A musician named Phillip Kahn.

Phillip was a saxophone player, but that wasn't why he was known in the software industry. A French native, Mr. Kahn started his own American software company in a garage the year before I graduated high school (1983). The company's name was Borland and its first products were programming language packages, the most popular being a Pascal program named "Turbo Pascal."

Led by this self-proclaimed "barbarian," Borland grew to be a recognizable force in the software industry. By 1991 their popular spreadsheet program, Quattro Pro, wrestled away substantial market share from the once-dominate Lotus, and their non-dBase-compatible database program, Paradox, cut a significant slice from the database pie. Ashton-Tate accounted for 39% percent of database sales, Borland's Paradox was at 35% and the remainder was divided among other database companies.

Fox Software was a part of that remainder, and at the time of 2.0's release we were still a niche player. We had a great product, and it was out there, but there were many unknowns. The lawsuit against us was just reinstated; so our legal challenges continued. We were a small company, and our fight was now primarily against large opponents. Our marketing team was still floundering.

Yet for a few months in the summer and fall of '91, I kind of liked jazz.

• • •

Following the shipment of 2.0, our next official work item was to create a version of FoxPro for Microsoft's new operating system, Windows.

During my first few years as a developer, Windows got little respect in the industry. Originally released in '85, it attempted to splice a graphical interface, similar to the one found on the Macintosh computer, on top of the prevailing—but aging—DOS operating system.

The first two versions of Windows were novelty items really. Their usefulness was limited by the fact they had to share the 640K of memory most machines came with, with whatever application was being run. With both Windows and a word processor running, little memory was left for actually creating a document. Few software companies beyond Microsoft produced *anything* that ran on either Windows 1.0 or 2.0.

The third version, released in '90, removed the memory limitation, improved the interface, and was actually somewhat useful. More independent software products were developed for it, and eventually more than 10 million copies of Windows 3.0 were sold.

It wasn't until the next version though, version 3.1, that things got really interesting. Scheduled for release in '92, it was hailed by trade journals as the "next big thing," so every company was scrambling to make their software work on it.

Dave decided we'd be one of them.

Because Windows ran on DOS and was functionally similar to the Macintosh, it seemed a natural progression to take with FoxPro. The general consensus was that we could create a 2.0-equivalent Windows version with a minimal amount of time and effort.

There wasn't a strong immediate push to get started on it, though. "Doing a Windows product is about as interesting as a bucket of spit," Dave said during an interview. And he meant it. He felt the upcoming version of the pseudo-operating system would "do about as well in the market as the previous version" and that just wasn't enough to excite him. Privately, he told development that we were doing a Windows product solely for its token value. "It's a checkbox item for magazine reviews," he said, "no more and no less."

Still, after working on the DOS product for nearly two years, most of us were looking forward to a change. Windows would bring us that.

We had our own reason for not wanting to get started right away, though. None of us had a vacation in well over a year, so there was a lot to catch up on. Chris—who already missed one week of his annual family reunion—left immediately after 2.0 was shipped. And, knowing the best time to take off was just after a product shipped, the rest of us escaped in turn, hoping to enjoy as much of the summer as was left.

While the weather was fair, Windows could wait.

• • •

Meanwhile, in a move that was no surprise for many industry pundits, Borland International bought our longtime rival, Ashton-Tate. The purchase was made through a stock swap of nearly $439 million in Borland stock—a pricy investment at the time.

The sale highlighted just how far Ashton-Tate had fallen.

In 1989 they were the top producer of database software for the PC. They had 60% of the market share and over 300 million dollars in sales. (Our sales were probably a twentieth of that.) They were one of a trinity of dominating PC software companies, along with Microsoft and Lotus.

But due to the release of a bug ridden product (dBase IV), better than adequate competition (FoxPro 1.0, and others), and the bad PR from suing us, Ashton-Tate went into a tailspin they couldn't pull out of before someone bought the whole plane.

The buyout, which was finalized in September, also had a pleasant side effect for us. Concerned that the resulting Borland, which would now own *two* popular database products, might stifle competition, the U.S. Department of Justice required that the case against Fox be dropped as a condition of the takeover bid.

So, after living under the shadow of the lawsuit for nearly three years, we were free to innovate again, unhindered by any legal entanglements.

• • •

One day, while waiting for my machine to compile, I studied a photocopy I was given. Any time Fox was mentioned in a magazine article I'd find a Xeroxed copy of that article on my desk. Early on I wondered what to do with these things after reading them and Heindel told me he kept a file in his desk. So I did the same thing. Three years later, my "photocopy file" was over two hundred pages thick.

This newest item for my collection was interesting. It was an article from our local newspaper, the Toledo Blade, and it discussed the ending of the lawsuit. Following the specifics of the case and the Borland buyout, one of the article's sources began to speculate about the eventual fate of our company.

"It increases the pressure on Dave Fulton and Fox to be able to compete," the source said. "He makes great products, but he just doesn't have a big enough company behind him."

The article went on to outline two possible scenarios. The first was that we'd "stay private" and "gamble" that we could stay ahead of our larger competition. The other was we'd be purchased by one of the two remaining software powerhouses, Microsoft or Lotus.

I wasn't sure what to think about the article's conclusions. I couldn't imagine Dave selling something he obviously felt so strongly about.

The other option seemed to suggest stagnancy, though. "Staying private" sounded like something hermits do. We were a fast, highly-driven software house. It didn't make sense that we'd stay stuck in the mud when the rest of the industry was moving ahead.

Hinted at in that article was actually a third option, though, one that wasn't nearly so static. It was called "going public" and I knew the term simply because I heard it around the office. It had something to do with the stock market, but that was all a mystery to me. The closest I ever came to "the market" was helping my father take corn to the local grain elevator.

I needed information. I needed to understand.

I checked my monitor. The machine was still compiling. Alright... I pushed away from the desk. Time to get some answers.

I left my office and walked the thirty-something feet to Heindel's. After the normal greetings, I got right to it. "Did you read that article about our future?"

Heindel was facing his machine, but at the question, he turned to look at me. Socializing came easy now that the product shipped. "You mean the one in the Blade?" He paused to straighten his hair with his hand. "Yep. I read it."

"So what do you think? Do you think Dave would sell the company?"

He turned over his hands. "Dunno. But I doubt it."

That's what I thought. "One thing's for sure," I said, "Dave doesn't need the money." I reached out to grab the stuffed Cleveland ball. Started spinning it in the air.

Heindel watched the ball. "Nope."

Our boss was one of the first people to buy a ZR-1 Corvette—a car where the initials alone cost $27,000 over the price of a regular Corvette—only to have the engine give out in the first month. Dave's toys were a constant source of discussion. His purchases included luxury cars, telescopes, and things made by Stradivarius.

Heindel turned his seat toward me, anticipating my next move. "And any company we were sold to would want us to move somewhere," he said. "Nobody would go."

I thought that too. Part of Dave's plan from the beginning was to hire people with strong ties to the area. Most of us had something in Ohio other than work. We were living in the Midwest because we wanted to.

"So you think *nobody* would move?" I threw the ball hard at Heindel's chest.

He caught it, returned it. "My kids' school is here. My family…we're really involved in our church. I can't leave." Heindel thought for a moment. "I don't think Eric would leave either. For the same reasons."

I nodded. There was another reason I couldn't see Dave selling, though.

I threw the ball back hard again and chuckled as Heindel gritted his teeth. "Dave couldn't take orders from someone else," I said. It just wouldn't happen. Not in my wildest dreams. Never.

"True enough." Heindel returned the ball. "It's funny," he said, "Eric and I were talking about this the other day on the way into work." He and Eric both lived in Bowling Green and carpooled whenever Heindel's car was wrecked. Which was actually quite often. "Eric said the only way he could see Dave selling was if he got bored."

We saw no sign of that, though. Frequently I *wished* the good doctor was a little more bored. "What about this 'going public' thing?" I tossed the ball back. "What's that all about?"

Heindel shrugged and started juggling the ball between his hands. "Well, it means there would be a Fox stock, I know that. It would have a ticker symbol like IBM and Microsoft do..." The ball came my way again. "Actually, ask Chris. He knows all about it."

The passing went on a little longer, and then I left Heindel to his work.

I checked my build again. Still going strong.

Next up, Chris's.

Chris was one of the few people who actually had artwork hung in his office. Marty was the other. Marty's paintings I understood. Boats sailing on a pond. The focal point of Chris's pictures—both of them—was a large red dot.

"Hey Chris," I said as I entered. "Heindel says you can tell me about a company going public. So, what's it mean?"

Chris leaned back in his chair. He recently taught a course at one of the local colleges and obviously still liked the position of instructor. With an elbow on his desk, he grabbed the air as he spoke. "Well, it means there would be a public offering of stock in Fox. Most companies use it for an influx of capital."

I knew the definition of "capital." It meant money. But our company really didn't need any. Sales had been good for quite some time. Dave's toys proved it. Plus we still had little overhead, beyond salary. We were sitting on chairs like rocks, after all. The medicine cabinet was still locked.

"Why would we do that?" I asked. "Dave doesn't need the money."

Chris shook his head a few times quickly. "No, but the company needs the clout. When I was in marketing, I ran into that a lot. Some companies won't buy from us just because we're privately owned."

Why would someone care about the company they bought software from? You buy it, you use it. As long as someone answers the phone when you call... "Really?"

Chris widened his eyes and jiggled his head. "Oh yeah. Some of them have policies against it. They're afraid the company will fold when the owner dies, or something."

That seemed silly. Especially when mismanaged publicly-owned companies could be just as instable. Hadn't we just witnessed Ashton-Tate's meltdown?

"Okay," I said. "It seems dumb, but okay." I took a few steps toward the door, contemplated checking my build again.

Chris's eyes tracked my movement. He fluttered an eyebrow. "If I were you, I'd *hope* we go public, though."

"Why?" The *influx of capital* wouldn't be coming to me, after all.

Chris's voice sped up, indicating his interest. "Well, in other companies, like Microsoft, the key developers have gone from being poor smucks like us to millionaires overnight."

I took a step closer. "How?"

"Because commonly the developers are given low-priced shares at the initial offering. The price shoots up..." He threw his arms up. "Woohoo!"

I frowned. "Okay, give me that again."

Chris slowed himself a little. "Okay, say you are given ten thousand shares of the Fox stock at its IPO price—say a buck."

"I-P-O?" I asked.

"Initial Public Offering. The first day the Fox stock appears on the market."

I nodded. "Got it."

"Anyway, so you have ten thousand shares at a dollar a share, which is ten thousand dollars. But, what *usually* happens the first day or two is the stock shoots up as people invest. So, if the stock goes up to twenty dollars a share, your value goes up twenty dollars for each share you own. So now you're looking at two hundred thousand dollars." Chris's hands went up again. "Woohoo!"

I was starting to feel a little interested. "Wow," I said. "That really happens?"

Chris nodded his head quickly. "Oh yeah."

"Wow…" I left Chris and made the return trip to my office. I tried not to let this new insight distract me, but it was difficult. Chris just explained how someone could make better than six times my annual salary in only two days.

The phrase "going public" took on a whole new meaning.

• • •

Soon we had another reason to delay the Windows work.

While we were all vacationing and daydreaming, a crop of bugs were found in 2.0. In fact, shortly after its release, reports of problems began to trickle onto CompuServe and as time went on, we started to get them from Tech Support calls as well. Most were isolated issues or had easy workarounds. But, the company policy of immediately addressing external bugs was still in effect. If we heard about a bug, we had to fix it. Even after two years of development time, our product still needed more polishing.

The most remarkable thing, given the chaotic way in which our products were delivered, was how few heinous bugs were actually found. The public perception of Fox products was always one of speed and stability, and that was fortunate. We saw the effect the opposite perception could have.

Usually it went like this. A reporter from one of the trade magazines would find a bug in a product while writing a review of it. As part of the review he would mention the bug he found, no matter how innocuous. This declaration served as a bit of blood in the water. What followed was a feeding frenzy. From then on, every review written would mention the bugs encountered and how unusable the product was. The product would get labeled as "buggy." Soon after, sales would begin to slip.

That never happened to us, though. Reviews of FoxPro 2.0 would tout the amazing speed of Rushmore, the wonderful design tools, and would make no mention of any bugs found. We were still perceived as an underdog.

And even journalists like to root for underdogs.

• • •

Outside of Sylvester Stallone's Rocky movies, it's difficult to stay the underdog forever, though.

At the start of the nineties, the days of a small company surviving on the revenues of a single product were rapidly coming to a close. Companies were merging or being sold all the time. It wasn't hard to imagine a time when only companies like Microsoft and Lotus had the resources necessary to compete.

None of that escaped Dave's attention. Fox Software had the potential to grow into other markets, but we had few resources to foster that growth. We hoped to release a Windows product, a Mac product, and a UNIX product, and still make updates to the DOS product, yet we had only a handful of developers.

We could hire more, of course, but recent history proved that throwing more programmers at a problem wasn't necessarily the best solution. Ashton-Tate's team of seventy hadn't produced a product any quicker than our seven, nor had the final result been any better. In fact, it was much worse.

What we needed was a way to reach our goals using the limited resources we had.

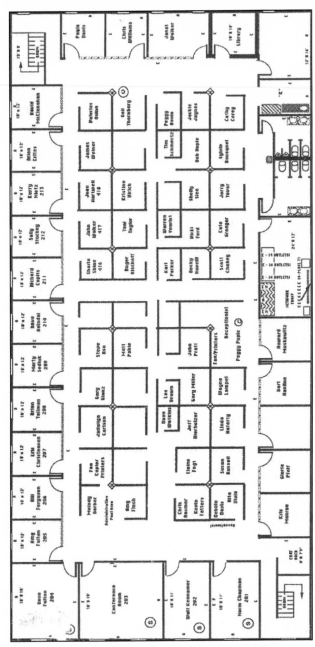

Map of the upstairs

284

Chapter 22

Unification

DBMS: In addition to keeping your programmers for a long time, you've kept your team small. Why does it always seem that a small team of programmers will turn out a better product than a large team?

FULTON: It's simple. If you put dots on a piece of paper, the number of lines it takes to connect those dots increases by roughly the square of the number of dots. So, if I double the number of dots, it takes four times as many lines to connect them. Now, if you think of the lines as interpersonal communications, you'll begin to understand why large groups fall apart. They spend most of their time communicating rather than getting the job done...

(From "An Interview with Dave Fulton," DBMS magazine, October 1989)

• • •

Since the spring of 1988, Fox Software had the only family of database products that ran on more than one operating system and worked seamlessly together. Using FoxBASE+/DOS (and later FoxPro/DOS) and FoxBASE+/Mac, each running on their respective operating systems, advanced users of our products could create applications that simultaneously shared the same data over a network. This allowed for systems where the data entry personnel entered customer orders on a Macintosh while those in the shipping department viewed those same orders on a PC-compatible computer. None of our competitors had that level of interoperability. We were the only true cross-platform story in the software industry. Period.

The story wasn't nearly as good as we would have liked, though. Our cross-platform strategy was difficult to maintain, and even more difficult to broaden to include additional operating systems. (Like Windows.) The difficulties arose from the fact that nearly all of development worked on the product on one platform until it shipped, and then switched to the other platform to work on the product *there* until it shipped. So, we'd spend a huge amount of time getting the DOS product finished, and then jump over to work on the Mac product until it was finished, and then move back to the DOS product again.

At least, that's how the process was intended to work.

Unfortunately, because the demand for the DOS product was greater, and the amount of time spent on it tended to be longer, this "platform-hopping" resulted in a Macintosh product that consistently lagged the DOS product by close to a year. So there were huge spans of time where our users lacked consistent products on both platforms. And the problem amplified as years went by. Because of the extended development time taken for FoxPro 2.0, by August of 1991, FoxPro 1.0 for the Mac still hadn't shipped. It was lagging the DOS product by nearly two years.

Of course, measures were taken to *try* to bring the Mac product to market sooner. Marty was never brought in to work on the DOS product so he could move (and adapt) the code we were creating to the Mac code base. He was diligent and made some progress, but with eight of us creating code for FoxPro/DOS (thousands of new lines by the product's end) it was a huge job for just one person to replicate that work for the Mac. It was like feeding a funnel from a fire hose.

So, to help with that effort, Brian Crites joined the Mac "team" a year later. Ultimately *he* wasn't enough, though, so two additional Mac developers, Henry Seurer and Brad Serbus, were hired to shuffle over code as well. Yet FoxPro/Mac *still* never shipped. It was real close a few times, but for various reasons, it never actually went out the door.

Now, with the pending full-scale development of FoxPro for Windows, the problem was about to be compounded. We were either going to have to hire a lot more developers and risk the cohesiveness of our smallish team, or deal with continued lengthy lags between product releases. Neither of these solutions was well liked, but we'd soon be forced to make a decision.

• • •

During the month of September I heard rumors that *someone* in the senior end of the row had proposed a solution to our connect-the-dots problem. Curious, I went looking for facts. I sought out Brian Tallman first. If there was a good idea floating around, he was certain to know about it. He was probably even part of it.

I already knew the name of the proposed solution. That in itself was intriguing.

"What's the Grand Unification Scheme?" I asked Brian, now seated in his office. I knew what the "Grand Unification *Theory*" was. Astronomy was a favorite subject in college. The Theory is an attempt by physicists to explain all physical phenomena with a single underlying unity. It postulates that all forces—gravity, electromagnetism, and two others—are the same at some level. And at the instant of creation, they were indistinguishable.

"Well…" Brian said, crossing his arms. "The Scheme grew from the fact that we have our own Fox API…"

I nodded. The API (Application Programming Interface) originated with the first version of FoxPro and proved amazingly flexible throughout the development of the second.

"...and at a certain level we have most of the functionality that would be provided by an operating system. Our own routines to create windows, to draw menus, to handle text..."

All the routines necessary to write an event-driven application. Of that, I was well aware. The tools I wrote made extensive use of them.

Brian nodded at his computer screen. "Like, I started playing with getting the windowing in the Windows product to work, and it seemed like the best way to get it up and running was to stick to our current architecture. Just keep our current windowing routines the way they were, and put the operating system specific stuff at a lower level somewhere." He moved closer to his desk and clicked a few keys. A couple windows opened to reveal listings of C source code. Brian pointed at one. "I used conditional compile flags to ensure the right code gets compiled for the right product."

I leaned in to study what he'd done. It didn't take long to see the beauty of the Scheme. It was real cool. Take the hypothetical scenario where both the Windows and Mac operating systems had routines to draw an imaginary thing called a "widget" and I wanted to allow users of our Screen Painter to draw a widget as well.

The low-level Fox API subroutine might look like this:

```
void FoxDrawWidget(int x1, int y1, int x2, int y2)
#ifdef MAC
{
    Point a, b;
    a.x = x1; a.y = y1;
    b.x = x2; b.y = y2;
    DrawWidget(a, b)
}
#elseif WINDOWS
```

```
{
    WidgetDraw (x1, y1, x2, y2);
}
#endif
```

Yet from the Screen Painter code, all I would have to do is make this call:

```
FoxDrawWidget(5, 5, 10, 10);
```

And a widget would be drawn along a line from point 5, 5 to point 10, 10.

I wouldn't have to worry about what operating system I was drawing the widget on, because the lower level FoxDrawWidget() routine would take care of that for me. So, even if the specific Mac and Windows calls were radically different—DrawWidget() in the case of the Mac, and WidgetDraw() in Windows—from my perspective it would look exactly the same.

The conditional compile flags (the "#ifdef MAC" and "#elseif WINDOWS" statements) were where the magic happened. They made sure that the right version of FoxDrawWidget() was built for the appropriate product.

"So I told Dave about what I'd been doing," Brian continued, "and he got excited. In fact, everyone I've talked to so far has liked it."

"Me too," I said. If implemented, The Grand Unification Scheme would allow most of our work to be done at a level where the operating system was irrelevant. It seemed like the sort of thing we needed; the right idea at the right time. We could keep our smallish team and still make huge amounts of progress on any number of products. "What downside is there?"

Brian flipped his arms out, palms up. "Well, there's the Mac code..."

"The Mac?" I then realized what he meant. In order to fit in with the Scheme's "cross-platform" code base, the Mac code would have to be completely re-implemented. All the code-shuffling work Marty and his gang had done over the past several years would have been for nothing. I shook my head slowly. "Yeah, that's a problem." No one likes to see their work thrown away.

Brian shrugged. "Well, maybe," he said. "But maybe not. In the long run it might be better for the Mac product. It would be integrated. Everyone would be working on it, to some respect."

I glanced at the code samples again. It seemed like such an eloquent solution. "What do the Mac Dweebs think about it?"

"Well, I don't know. Marty seemed okay with it."

I recalled Marty's complaints about coding *buck naked*. "I'll bet." We'd already ignored the Mac product for close to two years. Any additional delay in its shipment should be offset by the advantages of having its code integrated with the code of the other products. Subsequent product shipments could, in theory, almost occur simultaneously across all platforms. Instead of working on a secondary product, the Mac Dweebs would essentially be working on the same product. The Fox product.

"Is that the only thing?" I asked. "The Mac product?"

Brian caught his pants at the knees and scooted back in his chair. "Well, no one knows just how long The Scheme will take. Whether it would be quicker this way to produce four working products (DOS, Windows, Mac and UNIX), or to keep going the way we've been going. In the long run, the Grand Unification Scheme seems like a better solution, but for the short run..." Brian raised his shoulders. "Who knows?"

Brian brought an elbow to his armrest and caught his chin in that hand. "So, we're planning a meeting to discuss the whole thing. Get everyone in a room together and see what's what."

I nodded. "When?"

"Tomorrow or the next day."

"Sounds good," I said, drifting toward the door. "We'll see..."

Brian smiled. "That we will."

• • •

A few days later, all fourteen of us gathered in the main conference room to chart the course of the product's future. Sitting around the large oval table was Amy Fulton, Bill Ferguson, Eric Christensen, Brian Tallman, Dave Heindel, Chris Williams, Sally Stuckey, and I having just finished work on FoxPro for DOS. We were joined by the Mac team made up of Marty, Brian Crites, Brad Serbus, and Henry Seurer and the newly formed UNIX team of Jim Simpkins and Steve Shue. Dave, who rarely got involved in implementation details anymore, wasn't invited.

The meeting was essentially a free-for-all for Unification issues with no specific leader. The better part of a day went by as we discussed the feasibility of the proposal and the intricacies of pulling it off. In a meeting that size, and with so much at stake, there was a tendency to get distracted by the details.

"How are we going to do child windows on the Mac?" someone asked. It was an interesting question, because our DOS product and the Windows operating system allowed for child windows—windows that lived within other windows— and the Mac OS most certainly did not.

"What about source control?!" Another good question. Previously the Mac sources were maintained using the source control system that was a part of the C language program the product was designed and built on. If the source code was shared between four different operating systems, how would the checking in and out of source files be handled? And where?

"What will push buttons look like?" Every platform's push buttons were visually unique. The DOS product buttons were delineated by the characters "<" and ">". The Mac product used the standard graphically drawn black and white buttons. Windows push buttons were colored grey and had a raised 3D effect to them.

"What about color schemes? Do we have to support *those* everywhere?" The definition of color on FoxPro for DOS had grown so exhaustive; it was almost too cumbersome for users to deal with anymore. Nearly to the state menus were prior to the Menu Builder.

In addition, Windows had its own, more global, way for users to specify the colors of different parts of the interface, like windows and menus. Mac systems used colors sparingly. And UNIX…well…most UNIX users were happy with two colors: black and green. Sometimes black and amber.

It was Eric who tried to keep us on track. "We have to bind the strong man," he said.

Initially, his comment was ignored. The conversation meandered off onto another design issue. Many minutes passed.

"We have to bind the strong man," Eric repeated.

Quiet returned. "Okay," Chris Williams said, "what's the strong man?"

"Pixels or characters."

Chris's eyebrows lowered. "Pixels or characters?"

"Yes," Eric said. "Pixels or characters. We have to decide

what the native units for our routines will be."

Everyone was silent.

Eric wrenched his head forward, as if trying to pull-start the discussion. "We have to decide whether, if I'm calling a routine to create a window, the position and size information I send in is in pixels or characters. Or if I'm trying to draw a rectangle, do I send the rectangle information in as characters or pixels?"

Then we started to see it, and discussion ensued. Our DOS product, the only *shipping* FoxPro product, lived in a character-based environment. Because of this, everything about it—from the way windows were created, to the commands in the language—was geared toward characters.

A character is actually a big thing, though. It is many pixels long and high. Forcing users on the Mac or Windows environments to deal with a measurement that imprecise would be like trying to force them to turn a screw with a shovel. Ultimately, the answer we arrived at, the right answer, was that pixels should be used internally for the graphical products (Windows and Mac) and characters for DOS and UNIX.

"What about the language, then?" Eric asked.

That was another problem. Using pixels for measurements on the graphical platforms would mean that xBASE code written on the character platforms wouldn't run unchanged on the graphical platforms. And we didn't want that. We addressed that issue with our FoxBASE+ and FoxBASE+/Mac products earlier, but nobody really liked the solution we used then. The end result was that any code written on the DOS platform would run on the Mac platform, but the inverse wasn't true. It was a kink in our cross-platform strategy. We wanted no restrictions on the code our users could write. Code written on any and every platform should run on every other platform without change. We needed a different solution.

One interesting idea, that of allowing fractional characters (jokingly referred to as "foxels"), was proposed, but we realized it was pointless to discuss this aspect of Unification any further. Specific changes to the language *always* had to go through Dave.

And we didn't want to involve him yet.

We were still left with one burning question, though: How long would the Grand Unification Scheme take us?

Again we weighed, deliberated, and discussed. And just when I thought we could discuss no further, we finally reached a consensus. We estimated it would take somewhere between a year and eighteen months to pull the whole thing off. That meant we felt we could produce three new Fox products: FoxPro 2.0 for Windows, FoxPro 2.0 for Mac and FoxPro 2.0 for UNIX from the same cross-platform code. All the while maintaining the viability of the existing FoxPro 2.0 for DOS product. It was an ambitious estimate, but we were fairly confident we could do it.

Then an even greater question arose: How were we going to tell Dave? How could we tell him that we intended to sit and code for a year and a half before we had a single working product? That the Mac product was going to be delayed at least another year? That Fox Software wasn't going to be able to release *any* products in all that time?

We would need to be diplomatic. I glanced at Simpkins. Maybe we needed to write another script?

We started to formulate a plan, and then Dave walked in. "Why are you all here?" he asked, eyes panning the room. "This decision doesn't take *all* of you! Why are you all here?" He paced the space near the door anxiously. "This meeting is costing me a year's salary!"

In an instant, our spirited sense of optimism was replaced by a quiet sense of nervousness. Fourteen pairs of eyes stared across the table at each other, begging *someone* to speak first.

The room was silent for some time.

"Well, Dave," Jim Simpkins said, still as bold as ever, "we're meeting to discuss the Grand Unification Scheme and since it affects everyone, we thought it'd be best to have everyone here."

Dave dug his hands into his pockets and turned to look at Jim. "What's the consensus?"

"Well, we think it's a good idea." Jim brought a hand up to support the side of his face. "We think we should do it." He tipped his head. "We were just trying to come up with a time estimate for the deliverables."

Dave jingled change nervously. "So, what have you come up with?" he asked. "How long will it take?"

Jim hesitated. "Well Dave…" He glanced around the table. "We think it will take around a year and a half…maybe a year."

Dave stopped moving. "What?" he exclaimed. "It can't take that long!" He bowed his head and started pacing again, more animated this time. "A year? Well, it can't take that long!" He looked around the room, frowned. "Listen! I want to discuss this some more. We don't need everyone here, though."

The meeting spontaneous dissolved. Aside from the senior members, we all suddenly had somewhere else to be.

The end result of our meeting? We would pursue the Grand Unification Scheme. It just couldn't take as long as a year.

And how would we do that? The conventional wisdom was clear. When confronted by one of Dave's impossible deadlines, just work on your project a day at a time. In the end, the deadline will change, and you'll likely have more time than you need.

So, we proceeded to do just that.

MEMO

To: All Fox Employees

From: Dave Fulton

Date: October 28, 1991

Re: Fall 1991 Comdex -- Awards

It was a very good Comdex for Fox this Fall!

FoxPro 2.0 and Fox Software received no less than 12 different industry awards. This is probably unprecedented and signals the fact that Fox has truly broken out of the pack and into national prominence.

> PC Magazine — King of the Awards! Won in competition with Lotus, Microsoft, Borland, and Aldus.

> - PC Magazine's Technical Excellence Award in the Applications Software Category

> PC Computing Magazine — Queen of the Awards!

> - PC Computing's Most Valuable Product Award

> Data Based Advisor Magazine — 8 Awards:

> - Best Database Management System
> - Best New Database Product
> - Most Improved Database Product
> - Best Advertisement Seen In DBA
> - Best Documentation
> - Best Technical Support
> - Best Database Development Language
> - Best Macintosh Database Management System

> DBMS Magazine — 2 Awards:

> - Best Xbase Language
> - Best Macintosh DBMS

You all shared in these remarkable achievements and should all take great pride in them.

Congratulations, thanks for a job well done, and let's keep up the great work!

Memo about Comdex '91

Chapter 23
Works of Art

One autumn day I was sitting in my office with the window slightly open. On my screen was a picture of our trademark fox head. The head itself was placed on a white square that appeared to have grown from a crossword puzzle-like background. I wasn't certain of the meaning of the design, but I knew Dave liked it. I had the picture, also called a "bitmap," opened in the painting program that came with Windows and had it zoomed in so I could see the individual pixels—the colored dots that compose the picture—as large, easily-changeable squares.

Using my mouse, I changed the color of one pixel, and then zoomed out to look at it. It looked a little better. I zoomed in again and searched for another pixel to change.

I heard boom-steps walking in the direction of my office. The pattern of the footfalls was uneven. There were at least two people.

I squinted at the screen, and tried to ignore the clamor. I altered another pixel. Checked it.

I heard the steps pause outside my door. The door handle squeaked as it turned, and then I felt a rush of air hit my face.

"Kerry," a familiar voice said, "Could you show Richard the bitmaps you're working on?"

I looked up and smiled. "Sure, Dave. Bring him in."

• • •

With the end of summer came a diversion from my usual set of tasks. Somehow, Dave learned that I took a course in

Computer Art while in college and that I still enjoyed drawing on the computer on occasion.

I'm not certain *where* Dave got that information, but if I were to guess I'd say it was Heindel. Heindel didn't think I got the credit I deserved, so he frequently did things to help me out. Sometimes he helped. Other times he ended up getting me more work to do, as was the case in this instance.

Development was in the process of creating two graphical products, FoxPro for Windows and FoxPro for Macintosh, so Dave decided we needed new background images designed for them. Making use of the knowledge that *someone* gave him, he thought I might be the person to create them. Surprisingly, when approached with the idea, I said "Sure!"

These background images were one of the most immediately noticeable features of the product. They resided on the background (desktop) window and featured an approximation of the artwork that appeared on the product's box, along with some script that identified the product version. They were visible the entire time a user was in the product—at least, until they did something to remove or obscure them.

And because they were such a highly visible part of the product, they were something Dave greatly cared about. So, by accepting this new assignment, I was in danger of being on the hot seat again.

That would be a shame, because otherwise things were laid back in Fox-land. Even though the third DevCon was approaching, the stress on the development team was minimal because most of the products we were working on weren't complete enough to show. The UNIX product was the only product nearing any form of "demo readiness," and that affected only two of our number, Jim and Steve.

This left the rest of us in the easygoing stage of early product development, a place where there are few distractions and a lot of work gets done. It was a spot securely out of the limelight. A place I *liked* to be in. Even though I readily accepted the "using the computer as a brush" work, inside I was a little worried I opened up a whole new can of wombats.

As the work progressed, though, my fears diminished. The image project was enjoyable, a welcome break from coding. Dave's expectations were also lower. He wasn't nearly as critical of my artistic endeavors as he was of my code. I was able to work for days without a confrontation. And most of the time, Dave was downright encouraging.

Of course, there was still the occasional impromptu showing for whomever Dave deemed worthy. Those showings didn't bother me nearly as much as they used to, though. They showed Dave was interested in what I was working on, which wasn't all bad.

At least he knew I was busy.

• • •

Then came the week of DevCon.

It was a normal Tuesday night, at around eight in the evening, and I was at home. A commercial break had just come on, so I made my way to the kitchen for a snack. As I stood with my head in the refrigerator, contemplating the few options I had, the phone rang.

My nerves were immediately on edge. Even though the atmosphere at work was more relaxed since 2.0 shipped, my fear of the phone hadn't subsided. Call it a learned behavior. There were too many prior incidents to reinforce the fear.

This couldn't be Dave, I assured myself. It's much too late. I crossed the room to the phone. Every time he'd called before it had been right after work. It must be my parents or something. It *can't* be Dave.

I was wrong.

"Yeah, Kerry," Dave said, his voice slightly distorted. The car phone again.

"Yeah...?"

"Yeah, Tallman got the Windows product working today."

I knew that. I saw what Brian had done that afternoon. He got the product to a *limping along* state of functionality. This meant you could start the product, be presented with a Command window, and type in a few commands. Things generally worked, and it didn't crash *too* often.

If you did the right subset of things.

In the right order.

Most of the time.

It didn't look much like a Windows application, though. It looked mostly like a DOS application running in Windows. All of the interface elements, aside from the menus, looked wrong. It was partly functional, but not very pretty.

Put simply, it was butt-ugly.

Dave was excited, though. "I'd like you to go in and help Brian get the bitmap into the product."

I couldn't help but ask, "Why?"

"Because," Dave explained. "I'm showing the Windows product as part of my closing session tomorrow."

Unbelievable. The product's barely working today and we're going to show it tomorrow? I know Dave likes to keep the customers informed, but this is going a little far. Even for him.

Still, Dave's exuberance was infectious. "Okay, I'll go," I said and hung up the phone. I ran to the garage and jumped in my car. My first public art show since high school!

That night Brian and I worked until after midnight to try to get the bitmap into the Frankenstein-like Windows product. After I left, Brian toiled away another six hours on his creation, hoping to ensure that—unlike the fictional monster—it would prove to be a positive reflection on its creator.

· · ·

The next day found all of development dressed and present at the closing session. Unlike prior DevCons, this year we chose seats near the front, well within throwing range of the stage. We were a larger and more relaxed group. Few of us had anything on the line. The only ones showing any nerves at all were Jim, Steve, Brian, and I. Those whose children were about to take the stage.

When the time of the session arrived, the back doors swung open to admit a surge of attendees. Unlike the ho-hum year before, many of the attendees ran—and I mean *ran*—to find a seat near the front. Apparently, the word was out that something exciting was going to be shown.

Janet Walker ran the demonstration this time. Seated at an onstage computer, the first thing she did was bring up, by all appearances, FoxPro for DOS. On the room's large screen, the familiar oversized "FoxPro" letters blazed out atop a blue background. Janet entered a few commands, yielding typical results, and went on to run a small application—again providing the results one would expect from our DOS product.

The audience response was a collective "So what?"

Janet then exited the application to the operating system. "I want to list out my files here," she said. She typed "DIR", the command that, in DOS, would produce a list of the files on her hard disk.

That brought an error message.

"That's odd," she said, looking confused. "Let me try again."

She did, producing the same error message.

There was a nervous silence while Janet sat staring at the screen. Then a wave of "oohs" and "ahhs" rippled through the exhibition hall. Janet's DIR command didn't work because it didn't exist in the operating system. She wasn't running the DOS version of FoxPro, at all. It was the UNIX version. Janet typed "ls"—the UNIX equivalent of DIR—and everyone understood. The room erupted in applause.

From there, Janet continued her naïve wandering act, eventually winding her way first into Windows and finally into our product. Brian's work flashed to life, adorned with the bitmap I created. On the big screen, the bitmap *did* sort of help. The product looked a *little* more like a Window's application.

The attendees were beside themselves. Janet ran the same dBase application she ran on the UNIX product, producing similar, but more graphical, results.

Of course, a trained eye would notice that the results were a little strange. The graphical elements didn't appear quite like they should, and some of the items were a little misplaced.

The attendees didn't care, though. They roared their approval.

Following Janet's presentation, Dave took the stage and talked about the future of Fox. He waxed poetic about our plans for the following year. He outlined the Grand Unification Scheme, detailed our road ahead. All in the "lovable professor" style he exhibited at shows.

The crowd ate it up, cheering and applauding throughout. When the clapping subsided, Dave turned our direction.

"And there are some people sitting in the front here who I'd like to recognize…" He indicated us with a hand. "The Fox developers. They deserve a lot of credit for all the hard work and virtuoso stunts they've performed over the years."

The crowd applauded emphatically, ending in a standing ovation.

To the reserved members of the team, this last bit was embarrassing. We took turns staring at the floor, or each other, smiling and shaking our heads slowly.

Heindel was a row ahead of me. He turned, looked at me, and smiled. "It's just a computer program!" he said, mimicking a Saturday Night Live skit that featured William Shatner at a *Star Trek* convention. In it, he is asked one asinine Trek question too many and explodes. "It's just a TV show," he tells a room of socially challenged trekkers. "Get a life!"

Our users weren't *quite* that zealous, but at times they were close.

As the crowd started to quiet, Chris stood up.

What is he doing? I glanced at Sally, who just rolled her eyes and shook her head.

"And we owe it all to this man!" Chris said, pointing toward center stage. "To Dave!"

While the crowd politely applauded, the rest of us shared a groan and more than a few stifled laughs.

Some things never change.

• • •

We had a meeting to discuss the event the following day. Dave was relaxed at his desk and noticeably happy. The rest of us were strewn haphazardly around his office.

"The demo was the highlight of the conference for me, boys and girls," Dave said. "It was truly a virtuoso stunt." He placed his Diet Vernor's can on the desk and tapped it softly. "Sure the controls looked a little funny, and some of the positions of things were off. But those people didn't know." He looked at his can, pulled it closer. "Having something new to show, finished or not, well…it's important." He glanced at Brian. "Thanks again to Brian." He flipped a hand my direction. "And to Kerry, as well, for the last minute Windows product work."

I felt a little embarrassed. My work on the bitmap was in no way as crucial as Brian's work. The virtuoso stunt was all him really. My *next* assignment was to get the graphical Screen Painter working on both Windows and the Mac. It would be a proving ground for the Grand Unification Scheme—an idea I thought really cool—so I couldn't wait to get started. My art venture was officially over.

Still, accolades from Dave came rarely. "Thanks, Dave," I said softly, and Brian echoed.

That was my highlight of the conference.

Chapter 24
Hints

Following DevCon, developer life returned to normal. Each of us toiled away at our respective Grand Unification task, pushing toward our indeterminate deadline, nearly oblivious to all that was going on around us

Meanwhile, our company was entering prosperous times. Early reviews of FoxPro 2.0 began to appear and they were extremely positive. Most focused on FoxPro's improved speed and data handling, made possible by the product's new *patent pending* Rushmore technology. Reviewers also noted the product's language and interface enhancements, while giving kudos to its new user-friendly tools.

Over time, the positive press started to have an impact on the bottom line. Sales of the product through the fall and winter of '91 consistently exceeded expectations. This left our production department, whose slogan was now "FoxPro, don't drop it on your foot," hard pressed to keep up with demand.

It also created a need for more people to test, sell, and support the product. Our nascent Human Relations department moved quickly to address that need. By the start of 1992 the number of employees had grown to well over two hundred worldwide.

Space in our two-year-old building became a premium. The tech support area evolved into a maze of confining passages surrounded by gray cubicle walls. Two of the building's three conference rooms were converted into offices. We even had one poor soul with an office in a closet. It was a situation that couldn't continue.

To help alleviate some of the pressure, Fox acquired

additional parts of the Country Charm shopping center. Our initial move displaced only a radio station and a fitness shop, but now we were moving out a hardware store and a drug store as well.

But the space shortage continued. It reached the point where even the developers were beginning to notice; it's hard *not* to notice when someone's desk gets moved into your office.

The first to double up was Sally. Jadzia Carlson, who was promoted from testing to development shortly after 2.0 shipped, became her officemate. Soon after, Henry and Brad doubled up in McClanahan's old office.

Rumors began to fly about who might be next.

The trend bothered me. I calculated that there were maybe one or two junior developers left to go before, I too, had a second desk in my office. I loved having my own space, the solitude it allowed. I didn't want to lose it.

• • •

On Friday of Comdex week, 1991, Dave summoned development to the one remaining conference room for an update. Until then, we'd heard little news from Comdex. Similar to the year before, Dave wanted none of us distracted from our Grand Unification tasks. So, only he and Amy attended the Vegas event. The meeting was his way of filling us in.

Dave was serious, but happy serious. I could tell he had good news.

"I just wanted you all to know," he said, scanning our faces, "and this should come as a pat on the back to everyone in the room…" He reached out to grasp the table's edge. "…that FoxPro has won PC Magazine's Award for Technical Excellence this year."

Another award is good, I guess. We received a number of accolades over the years. Every magazine had an award. It was hard to keep them all straight, really.

Dave leaned back, and placing his arm on the armrest, shifted over to rest the back of his head in his hand. "This is a great honor, my friends. It's really the closest thing our industry has to an Oscar. You should all be very proud." He smiled pleasantly and looked around the table again.

Eric and Bill were smiling and nodding. The rest of us were still clueless.

"FoxPro beat out some serious competition," Dave said. "Some of the most recognizable and widely used products out there. Excel, for instance."

That brought out the smiles, and a "Wow!" from Henry. Excel was a new spreadsheet product from Microsoft. It was quickly becoming the darling of the industry, putting serious pressure on the other longstanding spreadsheet, Lotus 1-2-3.

Amy smiled impishly. "You should have seen it. Bill Gates was there. He pouted when they announced the award."

Dave wiped the top of his head. "Yes, Bill did look a little distressed." He cackled softly. "Unfortunately, there's only one plaque. We'll display it somewhere here. We have t-shirts for you all, though."

Amy looked at Dave and frowned.

"They're quite garish, actually," Dave said.

The t-shirts were handed out. They were black with a bright orange and pink logo on the front. They weren't from PC Magazine, though, they were from PC Computing. Apparently, we'd won one of their awards as well.

Um…thanks, PC Computing.

Still, the Technical Excellence award was cool. Our David-sized product had not only beaten down the Goliath of Ashton-Tate, it was going after his brothers, as well.

Dave next told us that we had more in common with Operation Desert Storm than the MOAR nickname we gave 2.0's READ command. Dave had met someone named Brian Jones, a contractor for the armed services, who wrote a FoxPro application used for all the logistics for the desert war. Essentially, all the decisions on moving men, supplies, and armaments were relying on our product to do its job. And do it well.

The room grew serious. There was stunned silence, followed by expressions of disbelief.

I couldn't help but think of the bugs that I knew still existed in the product. FoxPro was a critical part of a major war. An uninitialized variable in the wrong section of code could have caused troop deployment from Iraq to Guam by mistake.

Dave had no such fears, though. He was cheery, talkative. He mentioned the possibility of our company going public. He told us lawyers had been pursuing that goal for some time and a decision would be reached shortly.

Since most of us saw dollars signs whenever the subject was discussed, we were instantly in a good mood again. A mood that continued through the rest of the meeting, the rest of the month, and on into the holiday season.

• • •

The holidays at Fox were marked by an event called, appropriately enough, the Fox Holiday Party. My experiences with previous holiday parties weren't altogether positive.

The first one I attended was the worst. The day prior I asked Heindel how I should dress.

"Ah, it's no big deal," he said. "I'll probably just wear a sweater."

So I'd worn a sweater, only to find that I was one of only two sweaters in the room, the other being Heindel, of course. Every other man was wearing either a suit or a tux. Worse still, I was the *only* man in the room not wearing a date.

To compound my discomfort, a bully from my high school showed up as the date of one of our receptionists. It made for a memorable evening, but those aren't the sort of memories I usually seek out.

The following year was even more unremarkable. Since the previous year's event was a decidedly couples-only affair, I tried desperately to find a date. But, as frequently happened, I was unsuccessful. So, I decided to skip.

The 1991 party was different, though. I found someone to go with me—an ex-Fox employee who left for reasons I had nothing to do with—and had a really good time. The food was good, the company was pleasant, and the entertainment was…unique. The highlights were Jim Simpkins's *full motion* karaoke of "Walk All Over You" and Norm Chapman's *soulful* rendition of "Down on the Bayou."

Another thing that stuck out at me, though, was the two ownership tables.

One table was clearly all Fultons. Dave and Amy were seated there, along with Amy's father Norm Chapman (our Vice President of Administration) and his wife. Also at that table was Dave's daughter from his first marriage. I knew her from the summers she spent working for Fox.

The LaValley's table was equally stocked with Fox employees. Joining Dick and his wife were two of their daughters, Diane and Elaine. Diane was our Controller—the lady that handed out the checks—and Elaine was an Administrative Programmer. Also at that table was "Marketing" Richard, still clearly a family friend.

The two tables were essentially islands unto themselves.

Though side-by-side, there was little interaction between the two groups. Their conversations remained trapped within the bounds of their table. They hardly even looked at each other.

That seemed weird to me. Although I'd seen hints of a rivalry before, Dave and Dick always appeared cordial around the office. They were partners in a successful software company, right? One that beat the odds on numerous occasions. I thought that, despite any personality differences, the two families would be close. Usually surviving against long odds does that to people, brings them together. Like disaster survivors, or soldiers at war.

I began to suspect it wasn't just Dave versus "Marketing" Richard or Dave versus Diane. It might just be Dave versus Dick and anyone associated with him. I wondered whether that would affect the company over time...

I didn't think on it long, though. On that night, I had a date, and I was enjoying myself.

Everything was fine.

• • •

On the fourteenth of January 1992, much of northwest Ohio awoke to the effects of a blizzard. Over the course of the night prior, and continuing on into the morning, ten inches of snow fell, covering Perrysburg and its environs in a blanket of white fluff.

It wasn't going to be a normal day.

Following breakfast, I got dressed and went out to clear the driveway. The snow was thick and heavy. A half hour passed as I moved huge pillow-like clumps out of the way. Then, when I finally reached the road, I discovered it was still in the state the storm had left it. I looked to the south, the route I usually took to work. There were a number of cars

310

already stuck or pulled to one side. The way was completely blocked.

I'll head out sometime after the snowplow shows up, I thought, and turned back for the house. Once inside, I pulled off my boots and tossed them aside. What now?

I glanced down the hall, toward the center of my home. Why not?

I walked to the small bedroom that served as my den.

In college I learned that video games are a great stress reliever. The University's Union housed one of the computer labs where I spent much of my time. There I would submit my programs and wait fifteen minutes to an hour for a printout to come back from the mainframe. The printout was the only way to know if my program worked or not. A bulldog of a man guarded the printer and distributed the printouts. He strongly discouraged student loitering. So, I typically spent my waiting time next door, at the Union's video arcade.

But now the Nintendo game system was my thing. I was well on my way to becoming an expert tester.

I switched on the machine. Come on, Mario. Let's see what you can do…

At nine-thirty the phone rang. I paused the game and picked up the phone. One of Fox's receptionists was on the line. "Do you want a ride to work?" she asked, sounding way too chipper.

How do I answer that? In actuality, I was happy with what I was doing. "Huh?"

Her voice was still smiling. "Dave bought a new 4x4 last night," she said. "He'll come and get you…if you want."

I frowned. I heard rumors about the four-wheeler Dave had ordered. He bought it to haul around his telescope. His wife already christened it the "Star Truck."

It was supposed to be waiting for a hydraulic lift to be

installed, though.

He must have gotten it early.

I glanced at the TV screen. Mario was stuck in mid-jump. I shook my head. Clearly, there was only one right answer. "Tell him to come get me." I switched off the game. "I'll be ready."

Fifteen minutes later, a white GMC sport utility rolled into my driveway. I was already bundled up, waiting. I trudged out through the still-falling snow. Brian Crites was in the front passenger seat, so I opened the vehicle's back door.

In the driver's seat was someone I'd never met before. It looked like Dave, and sounded like Dave, but this person was *definitely* someone else. There was a wide grin on his face. "Get in! Get in!" he said excitedly.

Crites turned to look at me. "We've had an interesting trip." He then gave a little uneasy smile.

Dave just chortled his agreement.

"I can bet." If it were possible for a 4x4 to make a person intoxicated, Dave was soused. Is this a good idea? I reluctantly got it.

Dave giggled again as I closed the door. We were then on our way.

I was told that Jadzia, who lived just to the east of me, was our next pickup. As we passed the trapped (and unoccupied) cars down my road, Dave waved and said "Ta-ta." He and Crites then shared a laugh.

I secured my seatbelt. Who is this man?

The trip to Jadzia's home was relatively uneventful. She came out bundled like an Eskimo. There was a wide-eyed smile on her face as she got into the vehicle—a foreign-born appreciation for her employer's latest purchase. She had no idea what was in store.

A few miles later we took a turn down one of Perrysburg's side streets. For safe travel to work, it wouldn't have been my first choice. There were wider streets available. And this one looked particularly impassable.

The snow that fell now was powdery, almost fog-like. "Where's the deepest part?" Dave asked, squinting.

Crites's head shifted back and forth. "On the left, I think."

"Left it is," Dave said, cackling again.

I glanced at Jadzia. Her eyes were wide and she had a reserved, Mona Lisa-like smile on her face.

We eased toward the left side of the road. There was an extensive snow bank there. I felt the engine bog down as soon as we reached it. Snow flew up from the tires, and Dave laughed maniacally.

He's crazy!

The rest of the trip was more of the same. A proving ground for Dave's new conveyance. The sight of a drift in our path brought gleeful laughter. Power on all four tires was his new opiate. The Star Truck, his tank.

We somehow made it to the office, though. When we arrived, many of the others had already managed to make it in. The few exceptions that lived within range of Dave's new shuttle service were Marty Sedluk and Bill Ferguson. Calls were made to both of them. Marty, along with his wife Eleanor, unknowingly agreed to be picked up.

Bill categorically declined. "I have things to deal with here at home," he said.

I suspect he was just being wise.

Dave dressed and went looking for someone to ride along. Crites apparently had his fill of the snow adventure. "I've got to get some work done here," he told Dave.

So Dave appeared at my door. "Do you want to go out again?" he asked.

It already felt like I'd been hauled into school on a snow day. I could barely concentrate. And the trip to Marty's would doubtless prove more entertaining than anything that would happen at work. "Let me get my coat," I said.

This new side of Dave was intriguing. It was a little dangerous, but also a little fun. I had little contact with Dave beyond the office setting. All I *really* knew of him was the enigmatic stuff I saw at work. If I could understand more of "peripheral" Dave, it might help with the rest. Maybe this trip will be my chance? I had some form of friendship with everyone else on the team. Why not Dave?

But any hope I had for building camaraderie was dashed about as completely as the drifts we plowed through. Between Dave's animated outbursts and my unfamiliarity with talking to him about *anything* other than work, it was a lost cause. The only coherent conversation happened as we passed Bill Ferguson's neighborhood.

"So that's where Bill lives, eh?" Dave nodded in the direction of Bill's home.

I hadn't actually been to Bill's place, but I knew approximately where it was. It was in one of the more exclusive neighborhoods just west of Fort Meigs. "I think so," I said.

Dave snorted. "That Bill doesn't want a ride into work today. Says he's got too much to do." He frowned and looked at me. "You know what I think?"

I had no idea. "No," I said. "What?"

Dave glanced back at Bill's neighborhood and gripped the steering wheel tightly. "I think he's just lazy!"

I smiled and watched the road ahead. Bill was frequently called "Eeyore" at the office because of his pessimism. I never heard anyone call him *lazy*, though. He wrote some important parts of the product. Many of them extremely complicated. As part of the original four, I thought Dave held him in high esteem.

I'm glad I let him pick *me* up.

Dave spotted another drift and the conversation ended. Shortly thereafter we picked up the Sedluk's and shuttled them to work. We survivors then went off to our offices.

Less than twenty minutes later, though, I was standing next door talking to Jadzia. (Sally never made it in.)

"...and then he said that Bill was *lazy*," I said, smiling. "The lesson for the day? If your boss offers you a ride to work, take it!"

We shared a laugh. I glanced down the hall toward Dave's office. He had his jacket on and his laptop case in one hand.

"Hey," I said, squinting. "It looks like Dave is going out again."

Jadzia raised an eyebrow. "Oh, really?" she said. "I wonder who he's getting this time."

I watched as Dave made his way toward the front door. The laptop seemed like an odd thing to have with him. "You know what?" I said. "I think he's going home."

"What!" Jadzia stood in time to see the front door swing shut behind him. "He's going home?"

I looked at Jadzia. "How are *we* getting home?"

"I don't know," she said excitedly.

I turned to look out the window. The snow was still a fog.

Well, that's a good way to make sure work gets done, I thought. Strand your employees.

Five minutes later we heard the voice of Howard, the Technical Support manager, over the company intercom.

"Fox Software is closed for the day," he said. "Everyone please go home. And be careful."

Jadzia and I exchanged looks. "But our ride just left!"

"Any of you who need transportation," Howard continued. "Come see me. Dave told me to find you a ride home."

"I wonder if he mentioned developers," I said, smiling. "I

bet Dave never specifically mentioned taking the developers home."

Jadzia pulled her coat on and went fishing behind the door for her scarf. "I don't know. But, let's go before the four-wheelers get away."

• • •

The next morning, after the storm broke and the roads cleared, we returned to work to discover another calamity.

"Did you hear?" Sally asked.

"Hear what?" What has Dave done now?

She looked somber, pen near her mouth. "Glenn Hart died at MacWorld yesterday."

I didn't know what to say. MacWorld was one of the premier trade shows for the Macintosh computer. It was held in San Francisco that week. Glenn was a marketing advisor for us in years past, but I didn't know he was still involved. "What happened?" I asked.

Sally shrugged. "I guess he was having dinner with Janet and some of the other presenters and he had a heart attack. Just slumped down at dinner."

Wow. Even though I was corrupted to think of Glenn as "the Emphysema Poster Child," he was a real gentleman every time I met him. None of us wished him ill. He'd given FoxPro its name. For that alone, we owed him gratitude.

From awards and parties to snowstorms and death. You never knew with Fox Software. What would happen next?

Chapter 25
Shock and Awe

It was another Kwong's day. The group this time was Heindel, Bill, Marty, and I. Our food had already been delivered, and in between light conversation, everyone was busy shoveling it in. I was having moo goo gai pan, one of my perennial favorites.

"Someone is smoking in that restroom again," Marty said, scowling.

"That's gotta be against company rules." Heindel glanced at Bill. "Is our policy on smoking in the handbook?"

Bill sniffed. "It has to be. It should be standard for every company in the industry."

"Yeah?" I said, raising an eyebrow.

Bill skewered a piece of chicken with his fork and nodded. "Oh yeah, software and smoking is right out."

Heindel chewed hard. "Smoke particles are bad for the disks," he said, looking at me. "You know how they wear those white particle-free suits when they make silicon chips?"

I nodded. Most people had seen images of the particle-free environments used in hardware companies like Texas Instruments and Intel. In fact, I had people ask me if *we* wore those white suits at work.

That would be a little worse than wearing a polyester suit all day. But just barely.

It was hard to believe someone was actually smoking in our building, though. "Who is it?" I asked. "Do you know him?"

"He works in Tech Support," Marty said. "I think his name is Bill something."

Bill frowned. "That's unfortunate."

I grinned at Bill, then pushed aside a mushroom to spear my own piece of chicken.

"They've got that d*** smoker's stairway," Marty said. "I don't know why they can't keep it in there."

Heindel shrugged. "I imagine it's a little cold back there these days." Since it was the middle of winter and the stairwell *wasn't* heated, that was a safe bet.

"Tough," Bill said. He and Marty shared a laugh.

The conversation stalled as everyone returned to their meals. Then Heindel pointed his fork Marty's direction. "You know what would be funny?"

Marty took a sip of tea and focused on Heindel. "What's that?"

"To play with that guy a little."

Marty bobbed his head slowly. "How?"

Heindel smiled. "Well, say you and I were in the restroom when that guy was there."

"Yeah?"

"Yeah, and say I said something like 'Smells like someone has been smoking in here again.'"

Marty hiccupped a laugh. "Oh, okay. Then I could say something like 'Boy, I sure hope Dave doesn't find out.'"

Heindel laughed hard enough to bring his hands to his face. "I got it…" His laughter then stole his ability to speak.

Where is this going?

Heindel calmed himself finally. "I could say 'Yeah, that *last* guy got fired!'"

Marty made an erasing motion with his hand. "No, no…" He began to laugh deeply himself. Tears formed in his eyes. "It would be better if you said 'Yeah, like he did with that last guy.'" Marty pointed to himself. "Then I could say 'He would have been *better off* fired'."

Those two fell into a sea of shared laughter. Bill and I just watched them drown.

"That was a good one," Marty said finally. The conversation then drifted another direction.

Following lunch we returned to the office. Like I usually did, I went to my desk and fished out my toothpaste and brush. I then went to the men's room. As I entered, I noticed a hint of smoke in the air.

Maybe Marty's right, I thought. Maybe someone *is* smoking in here. I crossed to the sink. I glanced down and noticed a pair of feet in one of the stalls. The perpetrator? I removed the cap from my toothpaste; put a line on my brush.

Marty walked in, followed closely by Heindel. Marty had a toothbrush in his hand too. He tipped his chin up and sniffed the air. He then grinned at me before turning to look at Heindel.

Oh, no…

"Smells like someone has been smoking in here again, Marty," Heindel said.

Marty shook his head. Paused a moment. "Boy…I sure hope that Dave Fulton doesn't find out."

Heindel nodded. "Yeah, like he did with that last guy," he said.

Marty smiled broadly. "He would have been better off fired."

There was motion from the occupied stall and the sound of paper being crumpled. I saw the profile of one of our newer support technicians above the stall's wall. He was a tall guy, but I didn't know his name. He looked worried.

I felt the urge to laugh, so I quickly walked toward the door. As I pushed the door open, I heard a loud flush. I glanced back to see Marty and Heindel following closely behind.

"Awesome," I said when we were safely outside. "You two

were awesome."

Only laughter replied.

• • •

For me the rest of the winter months at Fox Software were great. There were few times when I felt better about my job.

To start with, I was more than happy with my progress on the graphical Screen Painter. Using the code for our Mac Screen Painter as a starting point, I removed each line that called directly to the Macintosh operating system and replaced it with a call into our FoxPro API instead.

The process was slow at first, because there were a *large* number of holes in the Fox API. I'd attempt to convert a bit of code and find there was no Fox equivalent for the routine I needed. Then, because the rest of team was up to its neck in conversion work as well, either Marty or I would fabricate the missing API routine and test it on both the Macintosh and Windows. When we were confident it worked, we'd check it in, and I'd go back and make use of it.

The forward momentum was steady though, and by March, some semblance of the Screen Painter was working on both platforms—proving that the whole Grand Unification thing would work.

It was really cool to see the same code running in two places. Why hadn't we tried this before? It was like helping the Wright brothers build their first airplane.

In addition, my working relationship with Dave had, for the first time in nearly four years of employment, grown almost comfortable. It was easier to talk with him at a professional, non-reactionary level.

I started to see a change in Dave too.

• • •

I was in Brian Tallman's office one morning discussing a bug. Like so many times before, Dave barged in and directed me to his office with a hand wave.

As I followed, I fought with responding the way I always had. I couldn't think of a reason *why* I'd be in trouble, but that was usually what The Walk meant.

It's going to be okay though, I reminded myself. Even if I did something wrong, it's okay. I've survived this many times before....

When we reached Dave's door, I forced a look of professional interest and gave my usual, "What's up?"

"Have a seat," he said, and then nodded at his computer screen. "Which of these do you like better?"

I looked at the screen. I saw three small icons, each with our trademark fox head as part of their design. They looked like potential icons for our Windows product.

Wait a minute... I glanced at Dave and then back at the screen. I think he's asking for my opinion. My brain froze for a moment. I wasn't sure how to deal with it.

I focused on the designs. They all were nice, but one clearly stood out to me. It just felt right. "I like that one," I said, pointing.

"That one...?" Dave squinted at the screen, cradled his chin. Mused a moment. "Yes. That's my favorite too." He gave me a short nod. "Thank you."

I kept myself from grinning, but I wanted to.

Wow. He actually cares what *I* think. I could get used to this.

• • •

Near the end of March of 1992, Dave called the developers to the conference room.

It was a Friday afternoon and I suspected it was going to be another "body parts" talk. Whenever we had a long, relaxed lull and Dave wanted to re-motivate us, he'd give a speech with the phrase "a**holes and elbows" in it. The phrase apparently came from the motivational repertoire of a drill sergeant Dave once knew. When ordering his subordinates to scrub a floor he would remind them that "All I want to see are a**holes and elbows until it's done!"

FoxPro was the developers' floor and Dave was our sergeant. We'd been comfortable for close to nine months and that seemed past due for change. There *must* be a reason the products needed to ship *right away*, a reason we needed to work harder.

As I entered the conference room and found a seat, I sensed something different. The people who were present were an unusual assortment for the typical "body parts" talk. Everyone in development was present, of course, but also the test manager and the two youngest testers, Matt and John.

Why not the whole test team? If we are gearing up again, they should be here.

Janet Walker was present too. Not unusual. But a couple of the writers were there as well: Crites's wife being one and Janet's husband the other.

The writers worked like slaves already. Could they possibly need more motivation?

It just didn't make sense.

There was also a feeling in the air; something not quite right. I couldn't put my finger on it exactly. Apprehension? Unease? *Something.*

In truth, the entire month was strange. Dave's new approachability was a welcome change, but there were other things that bothered me. Office gatherings that broke up when I drew near. Conversations in low tones. Shared looks of concern.

Every meeting with Dave had its own character, though. Strange feelings and behaviors were not uncommon. Fox was the definition of a software thriller. You never knew what would happen next.

Dave took a seat near the head of the table. "Alright, is everyone here?" He glanced around the room, clearly checking faces. "Okay...okay...good!" He rested a hand on the table. "The reason you all are here is to inform you that a letter of intent has been signed between Fox and Microsoft to begin proceeding toward a merger of the two companies..."

A letter of intent? Merger! *Microsoft?* I hadn't even heard rumors of such a thing.

That would mean Dave was going to give up control of his company though, right? It just didn't make sense. Especially after all we'd been through.

This *has* to be a joke.

Dave's face looked really serious, as did the faces of the senior developers.

Still, it might not be *all* bad. Microsoft was nearly a hundred times our size. Working for them might bring more stability to our schedule.

I knew we'd stay in Perrysburg, though. Heindel and I talked about this. There were people in the group who'd *never* move. We had strong ties to the area, right? It was part of the reason Dave hired us; he wanted developers who weren't going to run away.

So of course we'd be able to stay. Now what was Dave saying...?

"There was a time earlier when Microsoft talked about buying us, but they wanted us to relocate, and no one wanted to do that. So, the whole thing sort of fell through." Dave paused and the room caught its breath. "Well, this time it was one of Bill's first conditions that the development team move to Redmond. They've promised it would be like a helicopter just picked us up and moved us..."

My heart dropped. Move? A helicopter! I didn't like what I was hearing.

I'm not gonna move! I grew up in Ohio. My parents are here. My best friends are here. My church is here. My college is here. My high school is here. All the girls I'd ever dated are *here.*

Then there was the large purchase I'd made two years earlier. I have a *house* now! No way was I going to be able to unload that at the drop of a hat. So take that ya merging so and so...

"For those of you who have houses, Microsoft has arranged for them to be bought by a relocation company so you don't have to worry about them. See, it will be just like I said. Like a giant helicopter."

Dave went on to say that some of the more senior team members were aware of the negotiations for weeks. Which explained all those meetings that ended when the participants saw me.

Dave turned to look behind him, where the testers stood blocking the windows. "And for our young testers..." He smiled slightly. "You may consider this your *apotheosis.*"

Matt and John exchanged confused looks. They'd seen Dave in action. They probably thought they were about to be castrated.

"Apotheosis roughly means 'ascension to godhood'," Dave explained. "When the merger is finalized, you two will become developers."

"Oh," Matt said, giving a sheepish little grin. He stepped back and his face got serious again.

John smiled broadly. "That's fine with me," he said. "I have a brother in Seattle…" His head bobbed a little. "This is all fine with me." He was alone in his joy.

Dave asked if there were any questions.

Only silence answered. I felt like sobbing—or punching the wall. I was conflicted; laid waste inside. The rest of the team just stared absently at the floor or at each other. This new reality was hard to face.

"Also," Dave said, "since this information isn't general knowledge yet, you aren't permitted to tell anyone until it is released to the public. We'll have an announcement to the rest of the company early next week."

Oh, that's just great. The biggest news of my life, and I can't tell anyone either.

The meeting ended and Dave abruptly left the room. Everyone else slowly coalesced into small discussion groups. Heindel and Tallman were in one corner of the room, so I walked over to join them. They had a couple more weeks to think it through. Surely they had a better grasp on it all. Could give me some guidance.

"What do you guys think?" I asked.

Brian smiled a little. "It's a big change," he said.

"Yeah, a *big* change," Heindel echoed.

I knew that. Come on, guys, help me out.

"So what do you think about moving?"

Brian shrugged. "We'll see. I've read things about the area. Well…it's *real* expensive."

Heindel looked at the floor. "Yeah, I don't know…" He looked back at me. "I wanted to tell you earlier." He frowned. "We don't have it worked out either, really. We only heard last week." He shook his head slowly. "It's going to be a big deal. I just don't know yet. I wanted to tell you."

Apparently, the additional lead time hadn't helped much.

But how could it?

I stepped away, and then aimlessly left the room. What a shock! From there I slunk into Sally's office and sat down.

Sally was clutching her hands together in her lap. Jadzia was present, but absent.

"Did you know?" Sally asked

I shook my head. "No. No idea."

"Wow...I watched you. And the way you sat there, I thought you knew."

She never saw me in shock before. "I didn't know." I joined Sally and Jadzia as they stared at the grey carpeted floor. A dozen seconds went by.

"What do you think?" I asked finally.

Sally shook her head slowly. "Dave's screwing us again. Move or resign. It's just like him."

It was a detail I missed in Dave's speech. The developers had *two* options following the merger: either we moved, or we resigned. I didn't know what other alternative there might be, though. "Yeah...but what else could he do?"

Sally sniffed. "Usually in a buyout like this the employees would be offered severance. Some money, maybe a half-year's salary. Enough to get by until you find another job." She shook her head again. "But we aren't getting any. Just move, or resign."

"Yeah, that's sorta weird," I said. It seemed almost cruel to do such a thing to people who worked so hard for you. "I wonder why Dave's doing that?"

Sally raised her hands. "Because *we're* part of the deal! Microsoft doesn't just want the code. It isn't nearly as valuable without us. They want us!"

That made sense. No one knew a child better than its parents. Of course they'd want the developers. At last *someone* wants us.

I stared at Sally quietly for a few moments.

"What are you going to do?" she asked then.

I glanced out the window at the adjoining building's tarpaper roof. Black crows played in a puddle there. "I don't know," I said, standing. "But right now I think I'm going home."

. . .

There was no easy way to get my arms around the enormity of what had happened. As I left the office, all I felt like doing was going home, sitting on the floor, and petting the dog.

So that's what I did.

As it turns out, dogs take devastating news about the same way they take everything—friendly consolation, with little actual advice. That's not what I needed, though. I needed someone to share the pain.

I heard Dave's voice: "You aren't permitted to tell anyone..."

Screw it. If the other guys can tell their wives, then I can tell my folks.

I phoned my parents, but they were about as much help as the dog. Though equally shocked by the news, their guidance was completely divergent.

"You could find a job around here, couldn't you?" Dad said. "You could at least look around."

"It'll be alright, dear," Mom said. "Maybe you should try it out there. You can always come back if you don't like it."

Together they encouraged me to do what I felt best.

The only thing I felt "best" was to sit on the floor and pet the dog.

. . .

A few days later the entire company gathered in one of the special event rooms of a nearby hotel. It was another strange experience. Similar to the developer meeting, the tension in the room was palpable. It was the first whole company assembly since the lawsuit meeting four years earlier. That alone was enough to make people edgy.

Dave began the session with a little speech detailing the history of Fox Software. He segued into what he saw happening in the software industry in the future. "The computer market will tend to condense into larger and larger companies," he said, "and smaller companies will be forced to sell out or fade away."

He talked about finding the right company to merge with and theorized about who the eventual winners would be. He outlined the planned merger with Microsoft and introduced the Microsoft people who were hovering near the back of the room.

Six or seven Microsoft employees marched down the center aisle to join Dave. As they did so, the temperature in the room dropped ten degrees and the Imperial March from *Star Wars* started playing in my head. It was weird. Like the Empire had finally discovered our rebel base.

Dave surrendered the podium to Mike Maples, a Microsoft VP. The large, sandy-haired man then gave what would normally have been a good speech. He talked about "amazing changes" and "bright futures," about "Fox's success" and our "wonderful products."

In the context, it was too much like one of the pep rallies I was forced to go to in high school. Except there were no skirts and no cheering. The employees just had their world destroyed. You can't comfort them by telling them "we're headed for a wonderful tomorrow."

Nothing Maples could have said would have sounded better though. Anything aside from "I'm sorry" was too much.

Following his speech, there was a short question and answer session. Most of the answers were things I already knew, but there was some new information. Outside of development, employees would get no help in relocating. Unlike development, though, employees who for whatever reason couldn't join Microsoft, would be offered a generous severance package. Up to a year and a half's salary.

Then the meeting adjourned. As the crowd cleared out, Dave beckoned the developers to the front, where the Microsofties still lingered. He introduced each of us, first to Mike Maples, and then to a handful of other people, all who seemed to have the first name "Mike," as well.

One of the Mikes was Mike Murray, Microsoft's Director of Human Resources. He was short with brown, feathered hair—reminding me of the actor Dudley Moore. Following the initial round of introductions, he threw out a typical HR question.

"What do you think of when you hear the name *Microsoft?*"

I turned to look at the others. The only 2.0 developer not present was Sally. I expected either Bill or Eric to answer.

"I think we'd all say *Quality Products!*" Chris gushed.

I swallowed a groan. I checked the faces of the other developers. Tallman had a small little smile on his face. Everyone else was just watching. Waiting for the balloon to inflate.

"Do you all work on the Macintosh product?" Mike Maples asked.

"I'd say we all swing both ways!" Chris again.

I pinched my leg through my pants pocket. I really wished he would stop speaking for us. Chris never even compiled the Macintosh product. And even though I had, I wouldn't have described it as *swinging both ways.*

I shook my head and looked toward the back of the room. It was getting pretty empty. No sense staying any longer.

I excused myself and made my way to the door.

• • •

The remainder of the week was horrible, the atmosphere heavy with emotion. The usual morning meetings in Sally's office were both poignant and exciting at the same time. We now had something to discuss that overshadowed anything we ever talked about before, yet it affected us so profoundly we almost didn't know where to begin.

The normal participants' feelings were decidedly mixed.

Sally was pretty negative. She hated the thought of relocating, but mostly she was upset with the way the merger was handled. The "move or resign" ultimatum bothered her the most. "It's as if their saying: 'Thanks for the hard work and have a nice life!'" she said. Plus, the fact that the rest of the company was getting a severance package only rubbed more salt in the wound. "Dave screwed us," Sally repeated.

Another thing she took issue with was the "signing bonus" we had waved in our faces. Microsoft was desperate to know how many developers would be going, so they offered a monetary bonus to anyone who signed before a certain date, which was less than a month away.

It served only to divide and confuse our team more. Ten thousand dollars would be given to any "senior" member that signed, five thousand to the rest. But the definition of "senior" was arbitrary. It had nothing to do with time served or products shipped. Senior apparently meant anyone in the pecking order higher than Sally and I. "They can take that money and stuff it," Sally said.

She had a point.

Thankfully, Sally had more potential employment options in the Toledo area than most of us. She retained a number of connections from her time at Chris's company and would have no problem using them. I figured Sally as a "no go."

Jadzia didn't like the way things were handled either, but that wasn't her main concern. She *wanted* to be a coder, and if that's what you wanted, Microsoft was a great place to be. In her heart, she *really* wanted to sign up.

She had other difficulties, though. Her husband was a professor and had *just* achieved tenure at the University of Toledo. He understandably didn't want to give that up.

Their situation was further complicated by the fact that their first child was on its way. The due date was in late June, just a short time after the merger was to take place. Jadzia wasn't keen on making a Madonna-like trek across country while pregnant. I figured her a "no go" as well.

Marty was standing on the opposite side of the fence entirely. He was the most pro-merger person on the team. Part of his excitement came from the area of the country we'd be moving to. He loved biking and hiking—anything to do with the outdoors actually. With its moderate weather and beautiful scenery, the Pacific Northwest offered many new possibilities to him.

Marty also liked the variety of employment opportunities Microsoft offered. After coding "buck-naked" in his office for years, the thought of having other outlets for his skills intrigued him. We were required to stay with the Fox group at Microsoft *only* until the Windows product shipped. Marty liked that option. He *needed* a change. He was a "go-go" for sure.

I barely knew what to think yet, much less what to do.

MEMO

To: Distribution

cc: Supervisors, Managers & Directors

From: Kris Munroe

Date: 7/1/92

Re: Checklist for the Last Act

There have been a lot of questions about what employees need to do on their last day at Microsoft/Fox. We will have a check-out team meet with you on that day. One of the team members will be from MIS and he/she will go over your hardware/software inventories. The other team member will be from Human Resources and she will collect the following items from you:

> Fox Picture ID Badge
> Office Key
> Desk Key(s)
> File Key(s)
> Fox Visa Card(s)
> Fox Phone Card
> Expense Reports
> Last Time Sheet

If you owe the company any money, you will need to contact Dianne Tankoos prior to your last day and make payment arrangements with her.

As always, let me know if you have any questions.

HR memo for our "last day"

Chapter 26
Valediction

From a fifty thousand foot view of the software world, the merger made good sense. It was a "pooling of interests" that appeared to have nothing but benefits for both companies.

The benefits for Microsoft were obvious. They had no real presence in the database market, and at close to a billion dollars, it was a market too large to ignore. They struggled for years trying to produce their own database product. But in the spring of 1992, that product (codenamed *Cirrus*) was still at least half a year away.

An additional six months forfeited to the competition could be disastrous, because the competition was already well ahead. The purchase of Ashton-Tate positioned Borland to dominate the database market. They now owned two of the most popular products for the PC—dBase IV, and Borland's own Paradox.

Joining with Fox would not only get Microsoft into the game, it would get them a marquee player in FoxPro.

The merger would also give them the means to ensure their future database products were successful. "The merger…will provide Microsoft with great development talent," Bill Gates said in the initial (March 24th) press release, "as well as leading-edge database technology." In a later missive, he said the Microsoft plan was "to integrate the individual strengths of the Microsoft and Fox development teams."

The Fox developers *were* a crucial part of the transaction. Aside from continuing to produce quality Fox products, we'd bring along knowledge that could be integrated into future

Microsoft products.

There were many benefits for Fox as well. First off, it would solve the problem of not being a publicly traded company. As soon as FoxPro was a Microsoft product, we could begin to sell it to all those companies who'd been hesitant because of our "privately owned" status.

The merger would also give the Fox team access to more resources than our company could otherwise support. Microsoft's productive sales and marketing force would now be available to us. We'd be able to use their recruiting to find new developers, testers, and writers. Many of the day-to-day hassles of running a software company would become infinitely easier. Dave hyped this benefit the most. "I am thrilled to have the vast resources of Microsoft at my fingertips," he said in a press release. "I feel like a kid with the biggest train set in the world."

On a more personal level, it gave Dave a way to sever his ties with the LaValley family. As many episodes during my employment suggested, the relationship between the two families was no longer amiable, nor had it been for some time. Dave's preferred method of resolving personal difficulties was evident. He terminated them. The partnership with LaValley was a divorce waiting to happen. Microsoft would play the part of the rich paramour, allowing for a clean break.

• • •

Though the merger was a match made in heaven for the companies, for the developers it seemed like a small taste of hell. We had our own version of Dave's train quote: "I feel like I've been *run over* by the biggest train set in the world."

Shortly after the merger was announced, all development work came to a halt. It was *impossible* to do anything but discuss the coming change. There was constantly new information to absorb. Crites and Heindel traveled to the Pacific Northwest and reported on all they saw. Everyone was making phone calls out there, or making trips to the library. The thirst for knowledge was paramount. Impromptu meetings were held in every office. The pros and cons constantly weighed.

There seemed to be many positives. The Microsoft campus was an ideal working environment. We would be trading views of rooftops and dumpsters for those of mountains and fountains. Instead of a lunch outing to Burger King or Pizza Hut, we would be able to dine at one of the company-subsidized cafeterias. Instead of an occasional snowball fight in the parking lot, we could play basketball, volleyball, or soccer on one of Microsoft's sport courts.

Additionally, the Greater Seattle area offered a plethora of new activities. There were professional sports teams for the sport lovers, trails for the Marty-types, and skiing, diving, boating, and beautiful scenery for everyone else. It was a welcome change for our farm country eyes.

Yet there were many negatives, and the negatives were what fueled our discussions.

• • •

A few weeks after the announcement, Dave sent Amy and a *pseudo* employee named Sue Miller to "do some leg work for us."

Pseudo comes from the fact that Sue was better described as a friend of Fulton family who occasionally did work for us. She didn't have an office at Fox, or a title. She just randomly made visits and sometimes helped. Her largest contribution was probably helping with the manuals for FoxPro 2.0. Her work there earned her the nickname "Eureka woman" from the other technical writers. "Eureka" seemed to be her favorite word to transcribe.

To me, Sue's role seemed more like that of Salacious Crumb in the movie *Return of the Jedi*. Whenever she was in the building, she could be heard laughing uproariously at something Dave said. She was one of his staunchest supporters. She once chastised Heindel for complaining when Dave took Heindel's candy bar from his desk and ate it. "You owe him that for all he's done for you," she said.

The stated goal of Sue and Amy's trip was to research the cost of living differences. When their information was actually presented, though, I suspected the trip was more about shopping. They giggled as they told us things we didn't want to hear.

The essential fact was that nearly *everything* costs more in Seattle: water, gas, sewer, property tax, household goods, insurance...all of it, more expensive there. The only utility that *wasn't* twice as expensive was electricity, and that was because the electric company they used for comparison, Toledo Edison, has some of the highest rates in Ohio. (Toledo Edison has a nuclear power plant. They use it to generate power from uranium and money from consumers.)

The most alarming difference for us, though, was the cost of housing. Nearly every developer owned a home, and though a relocation company was hired to buy them, it wasn't clear we could buy replacements on the other side. Brian Tallman's wife called the Redmond city offices (where Microsoft is located) to ask what sort of place she could get for a hundred and twenty thousand dollars. The snickering answer was "a shack."

In contrast, the house I purchased just two years prior cost me $73,000. Granted, it was a starter home of only 1200 square feet, but it was all brick and on nearly an acre of land. It was also in a pleasant neighborhood on the edge of town.

If I were to buy a house, I would need every bit of the

signing bonus I was offered.

• • •

Another source of concern was the rumored number of hours Microsoft employees worked. We heard a typical workweek at Microsoft was on the order of sixty to eighty hours. During the busiest weeks of a shipping cycle, our team might have touched those hours, but it wasn't the norm. Most of us had some semblance of a normal—though highly interruptible—life outside of work. Many of us had families. None of us wanted to live at work.

But, we couldn't get a definitive answer. The Microsofties usually waffled, saying things like "in development it's expected you'll work some extra hours" or "we do what we have to do." Not very reassuring.

So I decided to ask Dave.

I reached his office to find him seated at his circular table. Marble tile samples were laid out in front of him. Potential patterns for the floor of his Washington home.

Dave held a tile up to appraise it. "So, Kerry," he said, "do you have any questions left about the big move?" He squinted at the tile. It was white with black specks. Like gnats on soured milk.

I frowned. "Well, I do wonder about Microsoft some," I said. "I heard they work a lot of hours."

Dave put the tile down, grabbed another. "You'll be working for me," he said, "just like here!" He shifted a little and I saw a glint of light on the tile's surface. "We'll be working just like here…"

That wasn't much comfort either. I paused, unsure of what to say next.

Dave paused, looked at me intensely. "Look Kerry, life's a

banquet."

I wrinkled my forehead. Life's a *what?*

"Life's a banquet," he repeated. "You've got to *sample* it." He returned to his samples, picking up a shadowy pattern and studying it closely.

I waited for a few moments, wondering if he'd say anything more. There were no further reassurances, though. Just more tile study.

I shook my head and left for my office. I understood the concept of "nothing ventured, nothing gained," but some of us were clearly taking a larger risk than others.

Marty's hope to work on another product was starting to seem wise.

• • •

In an effort to focus our exceedingly divided attentions, Dave dropped development on every product *except* Windows and made *Chris* our lead (and unofficial whipping boy). For one last time Dave tried to rally the troops, scraping for a reason *why* we needed to ship right away. We'd seen the song and dance many times before.

FoxBASE+ *had to ship* because the company needed the money. FoxBASE+/Mac *had to ship* because we lacked a cross-platform story. FoxPro 1.0 *had to ship* because it was our "response to the lawsuit." FoxPro 2.0 *had to ship* because we were in danger of losing market share to Borland. Now FoxPro for Windows *had to ship* because it would be our "calling card to Microsoft."

Come on, guys! We need to make a good impression!

We couldn't push any more, though. We had no emotional energies left. Those of us who'd been through shipping cycles before, simply ignored Dave's gyrations. We worked, but we spent just as much time discussing aspects of the merger.

That left Dave with a lot of energy to burn. He spent it on the easy targets.

"Shamu!" he yelled as Chris walked by his office. "Get your mighty flukes in here!"

Chris hustled into Dave's office, a harried look on his face. "Yes, Dave?"

"I want the person responsible for the Index dialog and the Modify Structure dialog in here, right now!"

Chris rushed to the far end of the building, to where Brad and Henry shared an office.

Following the merger announcement, there was a push to make the dialogs in our product look *precisely* like those in other Microsoft products like Word and Excel. As part of that effort, Janet studied those products in excruciating detail. She came up with a multi-page description of what she *perceived* Microsoft's standards for dialog design to be. It bore images of dialogs and instructions like "if configured horizontally, the OK button is 6 pixels from the bottom of a dialog and the Cancel button is 6 pixels from the right..."

Brad and Henry's job was to make every dialog in our product fit those exacting standards. The rest of us called their task "asinine dialog scootching."

"Dave wants you guys in his office," Chris told the two youngsters. "Right away."

They followed Chris back. After they seated themselves, Dave flew into a rage.

"MODI STRU is all f***ed up!" He moved closer to the room's circular table and kicked one of its chairs Bobby Knight style. "Do you two even know what you're doing?!" He stormed around the room. "Don't you test this sh**?" The tirade continued many minutes.

Brad and Henry left looking like they'd been hit.

As soon as they were beyond audible range, Dave looked
at a wide-eyed Chris and smiled. "That was a good one, wasn't
it?"

Dave's heart wasn't really in it either. At least, not the way
it used to be. Now *he* was the one doing the acting.

• • •

My biggest concern was whether there was any real gain for me
in joining Microsoft. I'd be employed, of course. But aside
from the potential signing bonus, which made me feel no more
wanted than the guys who'd just been "apotheosized," there
seemed to be few monetary advantages.

Dave gave us each a spreadsheet that showed what our
salaries would be and the stock options we'd be eligible for the
day we walked into Microsoft.

My salary didn't look that great. The prior summer I was
given a raise that put me just over thirty thousand a year—
respectable pay for northwest Ohio. But a bonus program
based on sales was started soon after 2.0's release. Because of
that, my salary nearly doubled in '91. Sales were good.

My "spreadsheet" salary was only a thousand dollars more
than my current salary, excluding the 2.0 bonus. I quizzed some
of the Microsofties about my pay. Again, they waffled. When I
finally pressed, they revealed a little more.

"Listen, Dave set the salaries," they said. "Ask him."

I saw no reason to ask Dave, though. His mind was on his
own move, his *own* home. I hadn't seen anything to show that he
valued me as a developer. I didn't get the early "heads up" on
the merger. I wasn't offered the larger signing bonus. Now it
appeared he gave me a salary that I could barely live on.

What was the use?

There was another portion of the spreadsheet though. The

stock options portion. Aside from the mini-lecture Chris gave me months earlier, I still knew little about the market.

But I was becoming an expert on stock options.

An "option" was the right to buy a certain number of shares at a low price, usually the price for the stock at the time the option was offered. These stock options could be "exercised" (i.e. the stock could be purchased at that lower price) at some later date. In *my* case that later date was roughly four years from the day of the merger.

Those four years of waiting are called the option's "vesting period" and the reason a vesting period is typically attached to options is to encourage the employee's commitment. When that vesting period has passed, the employee is free to exercise (or not) the options. Once exercised, the purchased shares of stock can remain in the employee's possession—giving him a sizable investment in the company—*or* he can turn around, sell the shares, and pocket the profits. The profit results from the difference in the share price at the day of exercise versus the day the options were received. It cost companies little to offer options to employees, so an average option offering may be thousands of shares. Sometimes even tens of thousands.

My spreadsheet specified the amount of options I would be eligible for. Dave also entered possible growth rates to illustrate what the options might be worth...someday. His estimates assumed the stock would go *up* during all those vesting years, though. There was obviously no guarantee of that. The stock might just as easily go down.

· · ·

One day, as I scowled and closed the spreadsheet, Marty walked in.

"What are you looking at there?" he asked.

"My spreadsheet."

He smiled. "Well, don't be plugging in any Chris Williams-type numbers. Microsoft's stock won't do that."

I returned his smile. Dave's default numbers were projecting the kind of growth that Microsoft had over the last few years—nearly doubling every year. In Chris's world, the stock would be doing four times better.

"Don't worry," I said. "I won't." I shifted my chair his direction. "In fact, I'm wondering if I can survive."

Marty crossed his arms. "Oh, you'll survive. Just don't count on those options. They'll go up. But not like that Chris Williams thinks."

"But what if they don't?" I said. "How can you be so up on moving?"

Marty raised his shoulders. "I've done research. Microsoft's a good place to be. And if Fox doesn't work out, I can go somewhere else. To another product."

I couldn't understand someone who was such an Apple-fanatic, now being so pro-Microsoft. The two companies had been locked in a lawsuit of their own for years.

And I never thought about working on another product. I had a lot of time and energy invested in Fox. I didn't want to change that too.

Marty raised a hand in a calming motion. "It won't be like here, where Dave can fire you if he wants. It takes a *lot* longer to get rid of someone." He lowered the hand and shrugged. "And if not, there are other companies out there too. Just having Fox and Microsoft on your resume is enough."

He then echoed my mom. "And if all else fails, you can always come back."

• • •

As the "signing bonus" deadline approached, I had a pretty good feel for what my teammates were doing.

Eric and Bill were essentially signed on since the beginning. I assumed they were consulted even before the deal was announced.

Chris had the development lead position now, so he was apparently onboard.

Marty was a sure thing.

Heindel was surprised to find his wife was okay with whatever he decided. He was one of the first to fly out to look around and he came back pretty convinced. He saw a few houses, talked to a pastor or two, and toured a school for his kids. "I think we could be blessed in this," he said.

Sally stuck to her word on the signing bonus. She was going to make her decision at the last possible moment, in late May. She was still really fearful. "Sheep!" she said. "Everyone here is acting like sheep." She scowled and shook her head. "Dave hired sheep."

• • •

Tallman was the one senior developer I wasn't sure about. He stayed in his office, beyond the whirlpool of conversation. I decided to take the whirlpool to him.

I found him contemplating his computer screen. "So, are you going?" I asked, getting right to the point.

He swiveled his chair toward me, crossed his arms, and gave a little smile. "Oh, I reckon so."

"Really?" Brian probably relocated more than any of us. He moved from Florida to work for Fox, and before that from Ohio to Florida. So *that* aspect probably didn't bother him much.

He seemed really concerned about finding a home, though.

"Even with the cost of everything?" I asked.

He frowned. "Yeah, it may be a little tight for a while. But we'll survive."

I recounted my conversation with Dave about work hours.

He shrugged. "Hard to know until you're there, I imagine. But it's just like that Psalm."

I noticed the Bible on Brian's desk. "What one is that?"

Brian shifted in his seat, straightened his shirt. "Thirty-seven, twenty-five," he said. "It says something like 'I've never seen the righteous forsaken, or their children begging for bread'."

I nodded. I probably read that at some point in my life, but it wasn't hardwired. Leave it to Brian to boil things down to their essence. "True enough," I said. "Things will be all right."

"Yep," he said, nodding. He was floating on a raft in the eye of a storm.

I returned to my office. It seemed nearly everyone had made their decision.

Now I had to make mine.

• • •

I took my first trip to the Seattle area with my dad a short time before, and we enjoyed the experience. We got a tour of Microsoft and saw some of the sights. We even checked out a few houses.

I figured with the equity in my Perrysburg home and money I saved, I should be able to swing the down payment on a similarly sized home there (on land the size of a postage stamp). In the meantime, Chris found a bank officer that would take our stock options into account when offering us a loan. That would help.

Things would still be tight. My salary was low, and there

was really no one I could talk to about it. If I went to Microsoft, I'd just have to live simply for a while.

There were *many* unknowns.

As there were when I started working for Fox. I took that earlier opportunity as a blessing, as God working in the circumstances, and much had happened. True, much of it was difficult. I nearly quit a few times. But, I was shaped in the process. I was more confident, knowledgeable—an asset whether Dave realized it or not.

And it had been *extremely* interesting.

I had a decision to make, but ultimately it was one between fear and faith.

A sheep I might be, but Dave wasn't my shepherd...

I knew what I was going to do.

• • •

Through April and May the number of developers taking trips to Washington continued. Most of us took two trips. One to "sell" us on the area, and another for us to "buy" a new house. As the list of those taking "buy" trips got longer, it became clear that most of us would be joining Microsoft.

That meant we had a lot of planning to do and plenty of "good byes" to say.

My personal goodbyes were tough. I was leaving my family and the friends I knew my whole life. In some ways it was fortunate I still (due to what my friends and I were now calling "the Curse") had no significant other. One less emotional trauma to deal with.

I was hopeful on that score, though. Having exhausted the possibilities in my section of Ohio, I now had a whole state *full* of women who had never met me.

In the end, there was only one Fox developer to say

goodbye to. Out of all of us, only Jadzia stayed behind. No comparable job could be found for her husband, and with a child on the way, the security of his tenure was important.

The rest of us were on our way to Redmond. Plenty of familiar faces would be joining us. Over a hundred Fox Software employees found work at Microsoft somewhere, some in Washington, some in the Carolinas, and some in Texas.

The swift and wily Fox would become a part of Microsoft. It was inevitable. The development group moved in waves throughout July. The eager (Chris and Marty) left immediately, the bulk of the team moved during the middle of the month, and the willing-but-wary (Brian, Sally, and I) left just as July was coming to a close.

One by one, we packed up. One by one, we moved on. One by one, we let go.

• • •

On June 26, 1992 I had two mementos that the merger was a reality.

The first was a small square of Lucite I got the night before. The Lucite bore the Microsoft and Fox logos along with a small script that read:

Microsoft Corporation has
acquired all of the common stock of
the Fox Corporation in exchange for 2,033,850 shares of
Microsoft common
stock in a transaction accounted for
as a pooling of interests
June 1992

Those Microsoft shares would be divided equally between the two owners. After a recent stock split, it equaled about ninety million dollars apiece. No problem buying a house there.

The second memento was an interoffice memo that all Fox Software employees were given. It was written by Dave Fulton and the subject line said "The Merger's Complete!" The text read as follows:

> I am very pleased to report that the Fox / Microsoft merger was completed yesterday. Fox and Microsoft are now one and the same.
>
> The Fox Story is surely one of the most remarkable success stories in the software business. Who'd have thought that we could start out humbly as one of many dBASE work-alikes, then survive Ashton-Tate itself to become the acknowledged leader in database technology? Now we are a significant part of Microsoft, the one true "class act" in this business.
>
> You've all been part of this story. For your loyalty, your support, and your hard work please accept my profound thanks.
>
> Many of us will continue as part of Microsoft. This means we'll have the opportunity to do what we do best—building, selling and supporting world-class software—on an unprecedented scale. The challenge is exciting, and more than a little intimidating. Nevertheless, I'm certain we will succeed.
>
> For those who won't be joining Microsoft, this may be a melancholy time…good-byes are never fun. I hope you will look back on your

time with Fox as a period of personal growth, learning and perhaps even some fun. I think your experiences at Fox may serve you well in your future careers.

My personal best wishes to each one of you as you enter upon a new career at Microsoft or pursue other opportunities. Thanks again for your efforts!

And so ended the story of Fox Software. If I had written the story myself I would've written a different ending. I would have Fox grow to ten times the size, our product catalog increase, and the developers become wildly rich.

But life wrote a different story. A success story? Sure, but a nebulous and uncertain success story.

In many ways the growth of the company paralleled my own. I went from a kid out of college to being one of Fox's perceived cracker-jack developers. I watched a company of only a handful of people grow to hundreds. I was berated, scolded, applauded, and cheered. I saw the best and worst the software industry had to offer...

The last Friday of the last week of July, I packed my office, turned in my ID badge and walked out of Fox Software for the last time. There was a summer breeze blowing across the Country Charm parking lot, and with it came a strong feeling of melancholy.

Left behind was a wealth of experiences—some good, some bad—but all interesting. What lay ahead, God only knew, but I had a feeling He would be there, working in the circumstances.

And without a doubt, I'd have a tale or two to tell.

There and Back Again

What happened next is full of ironies. The irony for me is that I'm headed back to Ohio again. As I write this, my house in Washington is sold, my stuff is in boxes—and within a few weeks—I'll be back. I guess it's as they say: You can take the boy out of the country, but never the country out of the boy.

Nearly eleven years have passed since the merger. Ashton-Tate is a far distant memory. Borland's market presence is virtually nonexistent. Microsoft, on the other hand, has been wildly successful. There is no part of the software industry where their influence isn't felt. Their "Cirrus" database product is now a part of Office. It's called "Access."

But with all those changes, one thing remains. The product that was the central focus of my existence for eight years, FoxPro, survives. The latest version, Visual FoxPro 8.0, was released this year (2003), and the gurus love it. Few products that started in the eighties are still viable. None of our competition is still around. Not dBase, not Paradox, not Clipper. Yet FoxPro remains.

I am still a relatively young man, but sometimes I think FoxPro will outlive me…

As for the characters in the story, the astounding Fox team, their stories diverged shortly after we relocated. Ironically, many of those stories also passed through the exact same checkpoint a few years later.

One perk of joining Microsoft in the early nineties, though perhaps only Chris saw it, was the company's stock options program. Few would have imagined that the growth of Microsoft's stock would be such that a person given options for only a few thousand shares in '92, would see the value of those options grow to be over a million dollars just six years later.

Because of that unparalleled growth, many of the Fox team found themselves with the ability to pursue other interests when they finally grew tired of programming. Which many did.

Here's what I know, starting from the top.

Dave Fulton created quite a stir at Microsoft. As suspected, he didn't take well to being employed by someone else. He lasted at Bill Gates's company about a year. In that time he managed to oversee the shipment of FoxPro on all four platforms—Windows, DOS, Mac, and UNIX. Dave also tried to fire a handful a people, mouthed off to a couple key executives, and started—what's reported to be—an outstanding collection of rare musical instruments.

The last time I saw him was at the party thrown for his retirement from Microsoft. The highlight of that gathering was a reenactment of "a day in the life of Fox Software" that included many of the scenarios described in this book. Members of the original development team served as actors, and Heindel played the part of Dave, complete with a bald cap and a full length fur coat. Following the presentation, Dave Fulton's comment to the group was: "How did you remember all that stuff?" My unspoken answer was: "Weren't you there? How could we forget?"

Dave's wife, Amy, was present at the performance and smiled from ear to ear. At Microsoft, she worked on FoxPro for Windows until it shipped. She left the same day Dave did.

Eric Christensen began his Microsoft career in an unenviable position. Company rules prevented husbands from directly supervising their wives, so *Eric* was made Amy's direct supervisor. Yet Dave was still his. Rock and a hard place.

Rumor has it the first review period was interesting for all involved.

As development of the Windows product continued, and then the Mac product began, Eric became less and less a Fox commodity and more a division-wide resource. He subsequently left to work on SQL Server, where he still works today. The last time I saw him was in a production of "the Pirates of Pensanze" with two of his children. (Both now *much* older than I remember.) That guy is still a genius.

Brian Tallman stuck with the Fox group for quite a while. At the start of next Windows version, Visual FoxPro 3.0 for Windows, he became the development lead. He was arguably the best supervisor the Fox team ever had. His talent, patience, fairness, and faith were the hallmarks of his leadership. After 3.0 shipped, Brian stepped away from his lead position, and then transferred to the Windows OS team. A short time later, he retired from Microsoft. He now lives the life of a farm boy with his wife and children.

For all the jokes about being Eeyore, Bill Ferguson was a solid developer and an even better architect of software solutions. Good ideas were his forte. After a few years with Fox at Microsoft, he transferred to the C/C++ group. He then left the company to pursue other interests. Last I knew he was heavily involved with his family, his church—and somewhat surprisingly—his music. At Fox it was Eric, not Bill, who was the musical one.

My friend, the Heindel-man, hung with the Fox group through the release of the Mac product and on into the development of the 3.0 Windows product. The idea of finally bringing "Objects" to FoxPro—a principal component of 3.0—really torqued him though. He was convinced the idea was killed years before for the right reasons.

"This is not what our users want," he said, echoing Dave's earlier sentiments.

Still, Heindel begrudgingly did the work of converting READ to use objects. In the process, he cleaned up the mess that was that code.

We have met the enemy, and they are ours.

After that, Heindel moved to a new group at Microsoft, one centered on travel. This group eventually became the online travel site, Expedia. He was there for a few years, then went to a group working on online bill payment and presentment, called TransPoint. Shortly after its technology was proven to work, that group was sold to another company (CheckFree, originally from *Ohio*). Before that transaction took place, though, Heindel left Microsoft. He is now active in various ministries at his church, one of which is a free computer training course for the unemployed and computer illiterate.

Still helping those who are a little misplaced.

Marty's Microsoft career was full of ironies. His area of responsibility on the Windows product was the Report Writer. This brought him the attention he desired, but...well, I think I've illustrated the downsides of that.

Dave threatened to fire Marty. Not surprisingly, that bothered him.

"Move me two thousand miles and then threaten to fire me?" he said one day in my office. "No way." He wagged a finger toward that troubling corner office. "After this product ships, I'm outta here!"

During our first review period in December—which was when transfers were allowed—Marty left the group. He joined the Works team and worked on that product for a number of years. He then worked on mapping tools before ending his Microsoft career as a well-respected lead in the Natural Languages group.

Marty then claimed another first. He was the first to move

back to Ohio. He and his family returned less than two years ago.

Chris grabbed the handrail of the Microsoft *up* escalator. He left the Fox group shortly after the first Windows product shipped, to take a management position with the C group. Shortly thereafter, he procured the enviable title of "Director of Product Development" for all of Microsoft.

Over the course of the next few years Chris moved around a lot, but always in the *up* direction. He finally landed in Microsoft's Human Resources division. While there, he reached the pinnacle of success for the upwardly mobile at Microsoft: Vice President. Apparently, the up escalator works best for those who wear monogrammed shirts. He served only a short time as VP before he too left the company.

Jim Simpkins seemingly found the up escalator as well. After the UNIX product was released, he became a Program Manager for Fox (chiefly a design position), and then hopped over to Microsoft's other database product, Access.

But if Jim found an escalator, it was one that got off at a different floor. He was the first developer to leave Microsoft, after the Fultons. He stopped short of calling it retirement, though.

"I tell people I work for Microsoft," he said when I saw him at the gym. "It's easier to explain."

I smiled. "Okay. So what do you do with your day?"

Jim shrugged. "You know those things in your life you stop doing so you can go to work?"

"Yeah…"

"Well, you just keep doing them."

I always liked Jim.

Brad Serbus and Henry Seurer were given scant attention by this narrative—and in fact, scant attention was what they usually got during their Fox career. They were rarely given significant projects to work on, and so rarely got significant credit. In either case this was unfortunate, because they're both interesting characters. They fit well into the Microsoft experience. The three of us even played together on a Microsoft-sponsored whirlyball league.

Team D forever!

Henry, a South Dakota native, was a big part of both the Mac 2.5 and 3.0 efforts. Following that, and partly due to my brotherly urging, he moved to the mapping group at Microsoft. He eventually wound up as a part of the Expedia spinoff company. I hope he found a place where he enjoyed the work and his efforts were finally appreciated. He deserves that.

Brad, originally from Michigan, also left the Fox group after the 3.0 Mac version released. Last I heard he was in the Windows team. Brad is a fun-loving and personable guy. I have no doubt he eventually found success. And he's a fairly good actor!

Another notable character of the Fox story not only received scant attention by my narrative, he was left out entirely! His name is Walt Kennamer and he joined Fox Software in '90 from the accounting firm of Ernst & Young.

Walt was hired to be Fox's Chief Operating Officer, but before that he was well known in the dBase community. After the merger with Microsoft, he too was apotheosized (if that were possible from the position of COO). As a developer he worked side-by-side with the rest of the Fox team. I even got to teach him a few coding tricks myself. ☺

Walt has a rapier wit hidden within an unassuming facade. He was a welcome addition to our team. He worked with the Fox group for roughly five years, principally on interface components. His hands were in every FoxPro product up to, and including, 5.0. He then left the group to work on a number of Internet projects, the most visible being the Microsoft

Investor site. He then retired from Microsoft.

Brian Crites was the captain of the 2.5 Mac effort. After that, he went to a team that was working on something called "demand video." The system his team developed got limited utilization in an apartment building near Microsoft and was fully implemented somewhere in Japan. He and his wife, now parents, are both still hard-at-work for the company. Joan is the head of Tech Writing for a whole division and Brian is a lead on Windows Media Player.

Matt Pohle, another of the apotheosized, stuck with Fox through the 3.0 Windows effort, working primarily on OLE. OLE knowledge was a hot commodity at the time and Matt used his skills to get a position with the Access group. After that I, beyond hearing about a marriage and a house on the lake, lost touch with him.

John Beaver (primarily known as "Beave") became a good friend, though. I was even one of the best men in his wedding. Career-wise, Beave blossomed at Microsoft. After close to five years at Fox, he moved to the TransPoint effort with Heindel. He later joined a group constructing tools for monitoring web traffic and presenting online advertisements. That group was run by a former Fox guru, George Goley. Beave's still at Microsoft, and surprisingly, still has lots of hair.

In the end, Sally was the biggest Fox diehard of us all. She stayed with the ever-shrinking Fox group until she left Microsoft, less than a year ago. She was responsible for many key components of the product. In my time working with her, her most notable contribution was the Object Manager, a pivotal part of Visual FoxPro 3.0 and its successors. She too is on her way back to Ohio. She'll arrive a couple weeks before me.

As for me, I worked on both the Windows 2.5 and Mac 2.5 products until they shipped. I was then brought over to work on the Windows 3.0 version where I got to write—for the third time—a Screen Painter. This time it was actually called a "Form Tool" and it was much more sophisticated than my earlier efforts. It was doubtless some of the best code I ever wrote. Third time's a charm!

After that, I transitioned to the 3.0 version of the Mac product and became its captain. When the development of that product was winding down, the rumor swept through our division that the Fox group and its products were about to be dropped. With the help of another developer, Greg Smith, I composed a song to commemorate the occasion. The lyrics went like this:

Hi-ho, hi-ho, it's off to Consumer (division) I go,
Our product's dead, that's all they said,
Hi-ho, hi-ho, hi-ho, hi-ho...

The supposed death of the product, and the paltry attention my team and I subsequently got at review time, was enough to motivate a change. I followed Heindel to Expedia and stayed there about a year. Aside from learning the inner workings of the travel industry, that experience wasn't much fun for me. I never felt like I belonged, and I was starting to question whether I wanted to program anymore. So, shortly after Heindel left for TransPoint, so did I.

The TransPoint group was great and I found some enjoyment in programming again. Still, a part of me grew restless. I knew there was something else I needed to do. I couldn't imagine writing C "for loops" for the rest of my life.

Then I wound up sitting next to an elderly man on a plane.

"What do you do?" I asked him. That's the normal way to initiate conversation on a plane, after all.

The man glanced at his wife and smiled. "I'm a writer," he

said, straightening himself in his seat. "And I'm that most uncommon of creatures—I'm a *published* writer."

"Really?" I said. "I've always wanted to write."

The man sniffed. "Well, start early," he said. "You might get published before you die."

I took that as a sign. A little over a year later I left Microsoft, purchased a laptop and started "dinking around" with this text.

Over the course of the next three years, I wrote a couple novels (yet to be published) and gave some time to ministry opportunities myself. In that time I also met someone who liked listening to my stories nearly as much as I liked telling them. To guarantee she'd remain a captive audience, I married her.

Then, on a whim, I searched for my name on the Internet. I found a website that detailed the history of Fox and its products. Many of the contributors were names I recognized from my days in Perrysburg.

Someone might actually care to read my stuff…

I dug out my Fox scribbling. And now, less than a year later, you hold it in your sweaty little hands. It is the first of what I hope to be many published works.

So there you have it. Some tales just deserve to be told.

I hope you enjoyed mine.

Kerry Nietz
October, 2003

Author's Note

For this, what will essentially be, a tenth anniversary edition of *FoxTales*, I thought it appropriate to mention how the legacy of Fox continues to affect my daily life.

Following the publication of *FoxTales*, I assumed the path to becoming a published novelist would be fairly straightforward. I already had a handful of finished manuscripts on my computer. And I'd already proven that I was a writer, right? My name on a cover was evidence of that. I'd shown I could get the job done. All it should take is a well-formed query letter or two...

How naïve I was.

Turns out getting a novel published is about four times as hard as getting a non-fiction book published. (At least, it used to be. Until eBooks and POD technology changed everything. But that's another story.) It took me another six years before one of my stories, *A Star Curiously Singing*, finally found a home.

Two pieces of information were critical to that eventual success, and they were both Fox-related. The first came from an attendee of the conference where *FoxTales* was first revealed. This person, whose name I unfortunately can't recall, raved about the book, but specifically mentioned how much he enjoyed the style of the prologue. As you may have noticed, that chapter is written in first person present tense. It is an unusual—and typically frowned upon—tense and point-of-view. Extremely effective in its immediacy, but difficult for most first-time novelist to pull off.

The second bit of information came from Jim Lawry, another *FoxTales* reader who contacted me via email. He mentioned how much he enjoyed the book, of course, but he also suggested that I try writing science fiction next. What is interesting about that suggestion is that, even though I'd been a fan of science fiction my whole life, none of the manuscripts I'd written until then were in that particular genre.

So after years of writing, revising, and rejection letters from every publisher I submitted to, in 2008 I found myself contemplating abandoning my dream. "I'll write just one more story," I told myself. "Just for me."

The tense I chose? First person present tense. I remembered what that conference attendee had said and always wondered if I could write a whole novel that way.

The genre? Science fiction.

So again, Fox interjected itself into my life in a pivotal way, and this time through the very book I wrote about the subject.

And the rest, as they say, is history...

Other Writings by Kerry Nietz

Mask

The DarkTrench Trilogy

    A Star Curiously Singing

    The Superlative Stream

    Freeheads

"Graxin" (short story) appearing in *Ether Ore*

But Who Would Be ~~Brave~~ Dumb Enough To Even Try It
(contributor)